T0334418

Organisation Development in Healthcare

Organisation Development in Healthcare

in Healthcare

A Critical Appraisal for Practitioners

John Edmonstone

Routledge
Taylor & Francis Group

A PRODUCTIVITY PRESS BOOK

First published 2022
by Routledge
605 Third Avenue, New York, NY 10158

and by Routledge
2 Park Square, Milton Park, Abingdon, Oxon, OX14 4RN

Routledge is an imprint of the Taylor & Francis Group, an informa business

ISBN: 9780367765156 (hbk)
ISBN: 9780367765149 (pbk)
ISBN: 9781003167310 (ebk)

DOI: 10.1201/9781003167310

Typeset in Garamond
by codeMantra

Contents

Acknowledgements

Given the historical emphasis of this book, it is perhaps inevitable that some of the people who influenced it either directly or indirectly are no longer with us. They are, first, Malcolm Robertson, a John the Baptist-type figure who recognised very early on the importance of Organisation Development (OD) in healthcare in the UK and then laid the ground for its creation in the Trent region of the National Health Service (NHS), then my two former colleagues, John Sturt and Tony Collin, with whom I worked collaboratively for nine years, and also Brian Molteno, who had the vision to make what must have seemed at the time a speculative investment in a novel resource.

Still with us, Dr Michael Walton played a seminal role in the flourishing of OD in the NHS and made helpful comments on early drafts of two of the book chapters. Finally, my wife and life partner Carol has endured my writing for many years. I really do promise this is the final book!

Author

John Edmonstone is a leadership, management and Organisation Development (OD) consultant who has worked over many years in the public services in the UK and internationally, with extensive experience in the OD field, having been one of the first internal OD consultants appointed in the UK's National Health Service. He is also Honorary Teaching Fellow at the Centre for Leadership in Health and Social Care, Sheffield Hallam University, and Honorary Research Fellow at the Liverpool Business School, Liverpool John Moores University.

John has over thirty years' experience of consultancy work in the Human Resource and OD field within the UK National Health Service, local government and higher and further education in such fields as leadership and management development, coaching and mentoring, action learning, evaluation research, team development and partnership working.

He is on the editorial boards of the international journals *Leadership in Health Services*, *Action Learning: Research and Practice* and the *International Journal of Healthcare* and is the author of several books including *Systems Leadership in Health and Social Care* and *Action Learning in Health, Social and Community Care,* together with many journal articles on leadership, management and OD themes.

Previously, he was Senior Research Fellow at the Centre for Health Planning and Management at Keele University, where he taught on the MBA (Health Executive) programme, and was also Research Fellow at the Institute for Global Health and Development, Queen Margaret University, Edinburgh, where he contributed to the Master's programme in Human Resources for Health. He has acted as external examiner for Master's level programmes at Alliance Manchester Business School and Brighton and Sussex Medical School, University of Brighton, and is a member of the Advisory Board for the Executive Master's programme in Medical Leadership, Cass Business School, City University of London.

Introduction

One of the earliest progenitors of Organisation Development (OD), Kurt Lewin, once formulated an equation: $B = f(P, E)$, which states that an individual's behaviour (B) is a function (f) of the person (P) in their environment (E). The formula emphasises the importance of the current and previous situation or context in understanding a person's behaviour. Lewin has been called one of the founding fathers of OD, although he died before the concept gradually became mainstream in the 1950s and 1960s.

This book proposes that this equation applies just as equally to organisations as to individuals and that organisational behaviour is a function of the organisation in its current and previous political, social and economic environments. In order to understand the development of OD, it is therefore necessary to understand the evolving context in which it has taken place. This is because:

> The forces which influence the conditions we desire to change often exist at a deeper level than can be dealt with by adhering to the criterion of working within organisational norms and meeting felt needs. [1]

This insistence on a correspondence between the emergence of OD and the social, economic and political changes associated with particular points in time has been reinforced by Brook's [2] examination of an OD/action research/action learning initiative in the learning disabilities field in the UK's National Health Service (NHS). Unfortunately, such examples of historical and contextual analysis have been extremely limited because so much of the material produced from within the OD field appears to have been written in an a-historical and almost unchallengeable manner, for reasons which are outlined below. It has been suggested that "the past is largely forgotten or at best misrepresented in the race towards unknown futures" [3] and it has been proposed that "What we see is partly a function of what we believe we see: our truth is constrained by the times in which we live" [4]. So, in part, this book is concerned with retrospective sense-making [5] as a means of understanding where healthcare OD has come from, where it is now and where it might go in future.

It is important to highlight this major a-historical limitation because so much of the published literature on OD, either as written-up case studies and accounts of practice on the one hand, or more conceptual material on the other, seem to see it as being devoid of any historical context – rather as being obsessed with newness, as something "of the moment" and as reporting only OD success stories. This a-historical and a-contextual orientation in OD was previously noted by Pettigrew [6] in his major study of OD in Imperial Chemical Industries (ICI), and this aspect may possibly be rooted in what has been termed a positive publication bias in the OD literature [7]. The causes of this failure-phobic orientation have also been explored by Edmonstone et al. [8] who examined such relevant aspects vis-à-vis this apparent bias as the overriding importance of such factors as organisational prestige and institutional enhancement; individual career progression; personal and group micro-politics; a fear of loss of control and the public and personal dangers of recording instances of failure and confusion alongside those of successes and useful insights. De Loo [9], adopting the earlier framework of manifest, assumed, extant and requisite organisation [10], suggests that there is an overemphasis in the OD literature on requisite (or prototypical) organisation, where everyone is assumed to be intrinsically motivated to achieve organisational goals – an obsession with the ways that it is projected that an organisation should behave and function, rather than how it does so in practice.

This organisational orientation may, at least in part and especially latterly, reflect the influence on OD thinking and practice of the positive psychology movement which emerged in the USA in the late 1990s and has subsequently spread more widely. Positive psychology has been strongly critiqued as being founded on a whole series of fallacious arguments; as involving circular reasoning and tautology; as embodying a failure to clearly define or properly apply terms; as identifying causal relations where none exist and as featuring unjustified generalisations [11]. Nevertheless, it has permeated much OD theory and practice. The positive psychology viewpoint proposes that, rather than focusing on any deficits evident within both individuals and organisations, we should instead seek to enhance only their positive internal characteristics – a focus on strengths only, ignoring any weaknesses, which have been most often labelled as development needs [12]. As a result, an entire "happiness industry" has emerged in the leadership and management sphere combining aspects of psychology, economics, sociology and philosophy into a popular intellectual project to purportedly make people happier and improve society through supposedly "scientific" understanding and the manipulation of human beings [13]. Such an extension of managerial control seeks to directly influence both what people do in the workplace and how they do it.

This perspective is based upon two major flawed assumptions: first, that the source of personal unhappiness (and hence also of a lack of organisational success) lies solely inside people's heads, that is, in how they see the world; and second, that the solution to such problems lies only in change at the level of the individual, through normative/re-educative interventions, sometimes rather cynically called "training people into submission" [14]. By assuming that all that needs to change is the way that people view themselves, their employing organisation and the world in general, the risk is run of failing to address any of the more fundamental organisational, social and political factors in society [15–19]. A person's ability to make any such changes in their life and work depends not only on that individual's personal motivation but also on their social context or setting – such major factors as whether they have meaningful employment, earn a reasonable income and have a network of supportive family and friendship relationships. Yet there exists a powerful tendency to attribute an individual's behaviour only to purely personal factors, such as their "emotional intelligence" or their "strength of character", rather than to their economic and social context. Such a view also ignores the importance of the legacy of history, as Marx remarked:

> Men make their own history, but they do not make it just as they please; they do not make it under circumstances chosen by themselves, but under circumstances directly found, given and transmitted from the past. [20]

Moreover, it is difficult to simply change one's mind in a positive direction. Human behaviour is often governed less by what we personally think than by what we imagine that others think. If we believe that our attitudes are at odds with a group norm, then we will be far less likely to express them and then to act on them [21]. This may possibly be one explanation for what is known in the education and training field as the learning transfer problem [22] where the learning acquired during a training course fails to be actioned on the return to the workplace. What people do as a consequence of their development is of much higher importance than what they know. Knowledge that cannot be applied will soon be forgotten.

Human beings typically seek confirmatory evidence in order to reaffirm their existing beliefs and correspondingly tend to discard any contrary evidence. Therefore, it is more effective to enable people to change their personal **actions** rather than to change what they think or believe, not least because their individual knowledge, skills and attitudes are most often shaped and reinforced by the recurring patterns of work activity and by interactions between people [23]. This orientation towards action is what Ibarra [24] has called the "outsight principle" (as opposed to insight). Pentland's study [25] has indicated that our rationality is largely determined by the surrounding social fabric. On a whole range of different issues, it was found that the most significant factor driving the adoption of new behaviours was the behaviour of peers. Pentland noted that the effects of this implicit social learning were roughly the same size as the influence of genetic inheritance on behaviour or of IQ on academic performance.

So this book hopefully aims to reflect a form of what has been called vigilant realism [26] or an honest attempt to see things as they are, uncoloured as far as is possible by particular movements or ideologies and recognising both successes and failures, opportunities and dangers, while always accepting that this may not always be possible in practice. The book seeks to combine an attention to both practice and theory and to provide an overview of the evolution of OD in healthcare considered as a field of practice together with a challenge to its future development. It examines some of the underlying assumptions behind OD and tracks its historical growth in healthcare, with special attention devoted to the UK's NHS, including a case study of the seventeen-year existence of an early internal OD Unit.

The unusual nature of healthcare organisations delivering human services through the work of professional clinicians who, in their professional practice, are inevitably engaged in what has been termed emotional labour and are often also involved in addressing many of society's wicked problems, provides a quite unique context. A range of challenges for healthcare OD are identified, including questions of conformist or deviant innovation; hierarchy versus democracy; the importance of power and emotion and the implicit organisational metaphors which underlie both OD theory and practice. Understanding the unfolding of healthcare OD through time helps to identify the current challenges and to lay out potential future ways forward.

Chapter 1 considers previous and current definitions of OD and locates the underlying assumptions behind it. It reviews whether OD can be seen as a profession or a field of practice. Chapter 2 examines the historical development of OD with its roots in the USA and the UK and the way that the various strands combined to reflect current practice. Chapter 3 turns to OD in healthcare, drawing on the experience of the UK's NHS. This leads into Chapter 4, which is a case study of the creation, development and demise of an internal OD Unit. Chapter 5 addresses the current context for OD activity, and Chapter 6 considers the unusual nature of healthcare organisations. Chapter 7 identifies the challenges facing OD in healthcare, and Chapter 8 seeks to explore the potential next stages for the development of healthcare OD.

This book is sub-titled "A Critical Appraisal" – appraisal in the sense of a review or assessment and critical in two senses, one characterised by analysis and the other by the making of judgements. This latter implies undertaking scrutiny at a deeper level, as suggested above by Harrison [1]. As a result, the book will undoubtedly be challenging to many current OD practitioners in healthcare, some of whom might even dismiss the author as a "utopian radical hell-bent upon fanning the flames of revolutionary consciousness" or as a "mindless existentialist who will not or cannot adjust to the world of everyday 'reality' and accept the inevitable march of 'progress'" [27]. The book has been written from my own experience as a "pracademic" – someone who has always sought to link practice and theory. With Lewin, I believe that "there is nothing as practical as a good theory" and that all theory should, in turn, be firmly grounded in informed practice. Writing it has involved returning to my own motivations in making OD such an important part of my career and so, for me, the words of T.S. Eliot [28] in Little Gidding certainly continue to resonate:

> We shall not cease from exploration
> And the end of all our exploring
> Will be to arrive where we started
> And know the place for the first time.

References

1. Harrison, R. (1995) Choosing the Depth of Organisational Intervention, in Harrison, R. (Ed.) *The Collected Papers of Roger Harrison*, New York: McGraw-Hill.
2. Brook, C. (2020) An Instrument of Social Action: Revans' Learning Disabilities Project (1969–1972) in a Politico-Historical Context, *Action Learning: Research and Practice*, 17 (3): 292–304.
3. Burnes, B. and Cooke, B. (2012) The Past, Present and Future of Organisation Development: Taking the Long View, *Human Relations*, 65 (11): 1395–1429.
4. Fortey, R. (2005) *The Earth: An Intimate History*, London: Harper Perennial.
5. Weick, K. (2001) *Making Sense of the Organisation*, London: Blackwell Publishing.
6. Pettigrew, A. (1985) *The Awakening Giant: Continuity and Change in Imperial Chemical Industries*, Oxford: Blackwell.
7. Kahnweiler, W. (2010) Organisation Development Success and Failure: A Case Analysis, *Organisation Development Journal*, 28 (2): 19.
8. Edmonstone, J., Lawless, A. and Pedler, M. (2019) Leadership Development, Wicked Problems and Action Learning: Provocations To A Debate, *Action Learning: Research and Practice*, 16 (1): 37–51.
9. De Loo, I. (2002) The Troublesome Relationship Between Action Learning and Organisational Growth, *Journal of Workplace Learning*, 14 (6): 245–255.
10. Brown, W. (1960) *Exploration in Management*, London: Heinemann.
11. Miller, A. (2008) A Critique of Positive Psychology – or "The New Science of Happiness", *Journal of Philosophy of Education*, 42 (3–4): 591–608.
12. Harper, D. (2012) Being Happy Isn't Only Down To The Individual, *Guardian*: 22nd February.

13. Davies, W. (2015) *The Happiness Industry: How the Government and Big Business Sold Us Well-Being*, London: Verso.
14. Edmonstone, J. (2019) *Systems Leadership in Health and Social Care*, Abingdon: Routledge.
15. Wilkinson, R. and Pickett, K. (2018) *The Inner Level: How More Equal Societies Reduce Stress, Restore Sanity and Improve Everyone's Well-being*, London: Allen Lane.
16. Wilkinson, R. and Pickett, K. (2009) *The Spirit Level: Why More Equal Societies Almost Always Do Better*, London: Allen Lane.
17. Dorling, D. (2017) *The Equality Effect: Improving Life for Everyone*, Oxford: New Internationalist Publications.
18. Dorling, D. (2014) *Inequality and the 1%*, London: Verso.
19. Dorling, D. (2010) *Injustice: Why Social Inequality Persists*, Bristol, MA: Policy Press.
20. Tucker, R. (1978) *The Marx-Engels Reader*, New York: Norton.
21. Terry, D. and Hogg, M. (1996) Group Norms and the Attitude-Behaviour Relationship: A Role for Group Identification, *Personality and Social Psychology Bulletin*, 22 (8): 776–793.
22. Huczynski, A. (1978) Approaches to the Problem of Learning Transfer, *Journal of European Industrial Training*, 2 (1): 26–29.
23. Edmonstone, J. (1995) Managing Change: An Emerging New Consensus, *Health Manpower Management*, 21 (1): 16–19.
24. Ibarra, H. (2015) *Act Like a Leader, Think Like a Leader*, Boston, MA: Harvard Business School Publishing.
25. Pentland, A. (2014) The Death of Individuality, *New Scientist*, 5 April.
26. Ehrenreich, B. (2009) *Smile Or Die: How Positive Thinking Fooled America and the World*, London: Granta Publications.
27. Burrell, G. and Morgan, G. (1979) *Sociological Paradigms and Organisational Analysis*, London: Heinemann.
28. Eliot, T. (1944) Little Gidding, in *Four Quartets*, London: Faber and Faber.

Who Should Read This Book?

This book has great relevance for those OD practitioners who are working in healthcare in both the public and private sectors, both as internal and external consultants; for academics in Higher Education institutions offering Master's level and Doctoral programmes of study targeted at OD practitioners or providing shorter courses and for practitioners working in consultancy organisations.

Figures

Tables

Chapter 1

What Is OD?

This chapter explores the early representations of Organisation Development (OD) and its embodied humanistic values before identifying a set of key underlying assumptions. It notes a major sea change in the evolving context from the 1980s onwards which has transformed OD from an end to be pursued to a set of means towards pre-prescribed ends.

There is no shortage of definitions as to what OD is or is about. One the one hand, and simplistically, it is about what all organisations do – they are created, evolve, expand and contract; become more simple or more complex; are sometimes merged with other organisations and eventually go out of existence. Organisations are the formal structures within which most people accomplish their work and conduct their careers. However, OD has also come to be used as a description of the attempts to plan and implement organisational change using the insights and methods of the behavioural or social sciences which began in the late 1940s and continues to this day. OD was thus variously described in its early days as:

> An effort which is planned, organisation-wide and managed from the top, to increase organisational effectiveness and health through planned interventions in the organisation's processes using behavioural science knowledge [1].
>
> A response to change, a complex educational strategy intended to change the beliefs, attitudes, values and structure of organisations so that they can better adapt to new technologies, markets and challenges, and the dizzying rate of change itself [2].
>
> A long-range effort to improve an organisation's problem-solving and renewal processes, particularly through a more effective and

DOI: 10.1201/9781003167310-1

collaborative management of organisation culture – with special emphasis on the culture of formal work teams – with the assistance of a change agent or catalyst, and the use of the theory and technology of applied behavioural science, including action research [3].

What these definitions have in common is a clearly humanistic value base aimed at changing organisations in a quite particular direction. For example, Bennis, Benne and Chin [4]. identified a series of overarching value commitments dedicated to more collaborative ways of working, the basing of plans for change on valid data and the reduction of power differentials in work settings. Likewise, Beckhard [1] identified a set of "relatively universal" values which he claimed underlay OD:

That man is, and should be, more independent and autonomous.

That man has, and should have, choices in his work and leisure.

That man should be striving to meet higher-order needs for self-worth and for realising his own potential.

If man's individual needs are in conflict with organisational requirements, then he may, and perhaps should, choose to meet his own needs, rather than submerge them in the organisation's requirements.

That the organisation should so organise work that tasks are meaningful and stimulating and thus provide intrinsic rewards plus adequate extrinsic (money) rewards.

That the power previously invested in bosses is reducing and should be further reduced. With choices in work and leisure, managers should manage by influence, rather than through force or the giving or withholding of financial or other rewards.

Leaving aside the overtly gendered language, it is clear that this represents an expression of a humanistic viewpoint which takes the human being as the measure of all things and demonstrates a respect for human dignity and the value and agency of all human beings, both individually and collectively. It has been described as "closing the gap between the human condition and the human potential" [5]. The attention to the place of people in change, the importance of individual dignity and the need to hear the voices of all, and not just the powerful, are all key features of this early OD. However, Beckhard's use of the term "universal" was most likely at the time, and in practice, largely confined to Anglo-American cultures and organisations, given the origins of OD, which are addressed in Chapter 2. The extent to which OD may be culture-bound is also addressed in Chapter 7.

There appear to be a number of key assumptions underlying this initial approach to OD. They are:

An action research model: An action research approach to OD [6] involves the systematic collection of data on organisational problems and then the taking of a set of actions as a function of what the analysed data indicates. This process has become embedded in both internal and external OD consultancy and is based on a well-known consultancy framework [7] of:

> **Contracting**: Agreeing the technical, financial and interpersonal arrangements needed for an internal or external OD practitioner to work within or with a client organisation, including the interpersonal expectations of each party and the shared values underlying the work. Contracting would therefore cover the identification and delineation of the client system and the key stakeholders within it; an initial definition of the work to be done, covering its scope, aims, boundaries and timescales; the major issues to be addressed; the extent of the financial and human resources available; a clarification of mutual expectations regarding intended outcomes and a description of roles, responsibilities, accountabilities and reporting arrangements – effectively a mutually agreed set of ground rules.

> **Data collection**: The collection, from within the client organisation, its clients, customers or service users and suppliers, of relevant data of both "hard" (usually quantitative) and "soft" (usually qualitative) nature, which are pertinent to the issues being addressed and which seek to identify the major areas in need of change. This would involve, for example, the mapping of the organisational structures, processes and relationships within the client system and would be undertaken by a variety of means, such as document analysis (including reports, minutes and audit data), focused interviews, focus groups, observation of meetings, questionnaire-based surveys, conferences and workshops. It would be conducted against agreed timescales and with appropriate attention paid to confidentiality matters. Such data could be collected by the OD practitioner and/or the client.

> **Diagnosis**: The analysis and use of the data collected to jointly diagnose the causes and effects of organisational problems. This might involve the use of diagnostic models or frameworks on which the collected data could be "hung". There is no shortage of such frameworks, but there are dangers that they can oversimplify the complex and dynamic nature of the situation and that diagnosis may privilege one set of views over others.

Data feedback: The feeding back into the wider client system of the collected data and the resulting diagnosis by the OD practitioner in such a way as to enable ownership and sharing across all professions/ functions and all organisational levels. This might involve any combination of, for example, a written report, a presentation, a workshop event or an organisational conference. The provision of such feedback is, of course, itself an OD intervention and would need to be accomplished in a sensitive manner, not least because it might well provoke a degree of anxiety within the client system.

Design/action planning: This involves the OD practitioner working with representatives of the client system to design a series of actions or interventions aimed at tackling the problems which were highlighted by the data collection and diagnosis activity. Such action planning is a collaborative process and is based on the valid information previously collected.

Change interventions: A range of actions, some involving the OD practitioner, some undertaken by the client system alone, some with other assistance brought in, but all aimed at tackling the diagnosed problems. Some of these interventions would be focused on developing sustainability – the capacity of the client system to handle similar future problems itself, thereby lessening the degree of dependency on the OD practitioner.

Evaluation: A review of the entire change process with a view to informing and improving all the previous activities and ensuring that client self-sufficiency is established, maintained or enhanced, thus guaranteeing the "institutionalisation" of change, both in an immediate and continuing sense.

Personal development enhances organisation development: It was assumed by early OD that by actively pursuing the development of self-fulfilling individuals, organisational effectiveness would therefore almost automatically be guaranteed. The personal development of individuals would lead inexorably to improved organisational learning, and so, in addition to the development of personal human capital, would inevitably lead to the creation of social capital or the "goodwill available to individuals and groups with its source in the structure and content of social relations" [8]. This meant that much early OD work was education and training-based using a range of normative/re-educative strategies, and, as a result, it tended to ignore many of the structural, technological and political aspects of organisational change.

Shared values: There was a basic assumption that both the OD practitioner and the client system ultimately shared a set of values which were essentially democratic and about broad power equalisation between individuals and groups within and across organisations (and also by implication within and across the wider society). Such humanistic values insisted that organisations both could and should be shaped for people and not the reverse – that people should be shaped for organisations [9].

A pluralistic frame of reference: Early OD embodied a sense of moving away from a previous, and possibly unconscious, unitary frame of reference [10], which implied one single source of organisational authority and one focus of organisational loyalty, with common organisational objectives and an integration of functions. The unitary perspective saw management alone as the legitimate foundation of organisational control and authority. It assumed that everyone subscribed to, and was dedicated towards, all organisational goals.

The more sophisticated pluralistic frame of reference suggested instead that organisations were, in practice, loose "federations" of subcultures with differences and conflicts of interest (some of them possibly even intractable) between individuals and groups. This was because organisations were made up of diverse groups of people with different cultures, values and beliefs. As a result, some form of conflict was both rational and inevitable. The challenge was to manage this pluralism through a "negotiated order" – a state of dynamic equilibrium – of "antagonistic cooperation" [11] or "regulated pluralism" [12].

In healthcare, this was typified as "domain theory" [13,14]. This proposed that healthcare was made up of three separate but loosely coupled domains. Each domain operated by different and contrasting principles, success measures and work modes – and interactions between domains created conditions of disjunction and discordance. The domains were:

A policy domain or the level at which strategic-level governing policies were formulated and pursued by elected or appointed representatives and which highlighted the importance of corporate governance and probity. The structure was one of representation, the success criteria were those of equity and economy and the work mode was one of voting and/or bargaining.

A service domain comprised the healthcare professionals who considered themselves capable of some form of self-governance and so emphasised their autonomy and self-regulation – and who had the requisite clinical expertise to respond to the needs and demands of patients/service users. The structure was collegial, the success criteria were quality and good practice and the work mode was patient-specific.

A management domain based on principles of hierarchical control and coordination and which attempted to mirror the ideology and approach of industrial and commercial management. The structure was bureaucracy, success was based on notions of efficiency and effectiveness and the work mode was one of planning and control.

Each domain was seen as being internally consistent but incongruent with each of the other domains. Interaction between these domains with separate and distinct identities produced an organisational form which was internally somewhat disjunctive and discordant, with a limited sense of overall coherence and connectedness. People in each domain collected only that information which was needed to pursue their own purposes and to perform their own roles and selectively ignored or discounted information produced from other sources, and thus frequently arrived at incompatible conclusions. "Problems" were only those things affecting one's own measures of success – so one domain's solution to that problem could well result in being a problem for another domain [13].

From this perspective, a healthcare organisation was viewed as a loose coalition, a diverse plurality of powerholders, drawing their power from a variety of different sources. Some degree of conflict was inherent and ineradicable – and indeed might even, in some respects, be both positive and functional [15].

Internal and externals: OD practitioners could operate from within organisations ("internals") or from outside them ("externals") and there were advantages and disadvantages to both.

Internal practitioners would know the client system well, including the local culture and history, so might well have a good understanding with regard to the client's issues. They would most likely share the same values as the client and might also be able to see beyond the "presenting problem" in order to see what the real issue was (and perhaps also even who the real client was). They might well have established an excellent reputation or track record for their previous work within the organisation, would know where to go to extract relevant information and might be able to organise assistance from other internal sources. However, internal practitioners might themselves be part of the culture that could need to be changed or might even be part of the problem themselves. They might have been imposed upon or "pointed at" the client system by senior leaders and managers, with a brief to "fix" matters, and might know things about the client that could not be publicly disclosed, so there might be problems over questions of confidentiality. The perceived status of the internal OD practitioner might also be problematic. They might fear delivering bad news to the client because it might affect their own position and career prospects, or they might have difficulty in working either above or below their status level, especially when it might involve "speaking truth to power" and confronting people who might take offence in the face of such feedback.

External OD practitioners also come with advantages and disadvantages. They might, for example, possess specialist expertise and experience and so come with a well-established reputation. They might have a wider pool of talent upon which to draw for an assignment and could appear to be independent, neutral and objective in relation to the internal organisational dynamics of the client system. Using externals also, paradoxically, provides the client system with a high degree of control, as they would be able to define the work to be done and also be able to terminate the working relationship quite easily. However, the external practitioner might well have little or no real understanding about the internal organisational culture, micropolitics and history. Given that externals often work with multiple clients at one time, their availability to provide a continuing focus on the local client system might be an issue. Moreover, external OD practitioners often have delivered data collection and diagnosis only, leaving the taking of action and evaluation to the client system itself. There is also the danger of externals providing one-size-fits-all, off-the-peg "solutions" which worked effectively elsewhere but which might not be applicable in the particular local context. Finally, there is the issue of cost – external OD practitioners tend to be more expensive to use than internals.

Overall then, early OD demonstrated a set of common aims that set out to:

Improve an organisation's "health" and effectiveness.

Systematically introduce planned behavioural science interventions.

Apply top-down strategies and seek to get all employees committed to change. This is embodied in such notions as "cascading" change down existing managerial hierarchies and "scaling-up" change from early pilot activity.

Introduce change incrementally and base planned change on collected empirical data.

Use an OD practitioner as a specialist change agent working to help to manage the change process.

Achieve permanent and sustained, rather than temporary, change within an organisation.

The "founding principles" of early OD [16] could therefore be described as:

A fundamental belief that the needs and aspirations of human beings provide the prime reason for the existence of organisations within society. This involved treating each human being as a person with a complex set of needs, all of which were important to their work and to their life more generally.

That organisations should provide opportunities for people to function as human beings, rather than simply as resources. This involves consideration of their feelings as well as their thoughts.

That opportunities should exist for each organisational member, as well as the organisation itself, to develop to its full potential.

Attempting to create the work itself and a work environment in which it was possible to find exciting and challenging activities through decentralised decision-making.

The seeking after of social justice, with a high value placed on the democratisation of organisations through power equalisation.

Ensuring authentic interpersonal relations through an equality of voice by creating open communication and empowering employees to act.

Enabling a set of diverse viewpoints to be considered and then actioned. This involved providing opportunities for people in organisations to influence the ways in which they relate to work, the organisation and society.

The use of action research approaches as the main methodology, as a means of continuous learning.

Change driven by data, as a means of increasing the effectiveness of an organisation in terms of all of its goals.

Organisational change reflected by these historical and ethical roots was considered to be something which was rational, orderly, episodic, top-down, linear, incremental and data-driven.

Some years later what was branded this "love/trust" model and allegedly individual-centred form of OD which embodied the valuing of personal growth, autonomy, trust, openness and emotional expression was strongly critiqued [17,18] as being an approach to organisational change which blurred together the personal and professional values of the OD practitioner and rejected any data which did not support its underlying humanistic values. While Tranfield [18] identified that most of the early OD practitioners in his study had emerged from well-educated middle-class backgrounds and often from socially mobile one-parent families, he also was clear that the conclusions of his research were both tentative and transitory and therefore very much a product of their time. The original humanistic OD values were even eventually labelled "a nirvana that was never to be in a capitalist-driven world" [19]. These commentators were perhaps early precursors of changes to the evolving context within which OD was practiced and the subsequent ways in which it changed.

From the 1980s onwards, in particular, this was marked by:

Changes in the employment environment: This included the downsizing of the numbers of employees working in many organisations and the delayering of some hierarchical organisational levels. This change was accompanied, for many, by the gradual ending of guaranteed job security, the resultant growth of precariousness and the increasing introduction for many of performance-related pay. The notion of the core and periphery or flexible firm staffing model became widespread, enhancing a growing sense of insecurity amongst employees. The growth of the gig economy of self-employed people on short-term or zero-hour contracts, part-time working, internships and spurious "self-employment" has led to the expansion of the "flexiforce" [20] or "precariat" [21], which in turn has led to uncertainty over future employment and impedes the ability for many people to make any long-term life plans [22].

The dominance of the neoliberal ideology: This world view originated in the 1930s and spread widely from the 1950s and permeated political and social judgements quite dramatically from the 1980s onwards following the end, in the 1970s, of the long global economic boom that followed the Second World War. It is an outgrowth of liberalism – the political and moral philosophy based on liberty, consent of the governed and equality before the law. Liberalism is generally supportive of free markets, free trade, limited government, individual rights (including civil and human rights), democracy, secularism, gender and racial equality, freedom of speech and the press, and it originated the development of the Welfare State in the UK, through the work of William Beveridge and John Maynard Keynes.

Neoliberalism is a "pure" or essentialised emanation from liberalism [23] and has displaced liberalism as the dominant political ideology. It became entrenched as the default orthodox political, economic and social perspective, especially in the Anglo-American sphere, but also more widely across the world through the influence of the so-called "Washington Consensus" led by the International Monetary Fund and the World Bank [24]. In the 1960s and 1970s, the notion of individual freedom resonated widely, appealing to and co-opting the progressive social movements and popular culture of the era. With its emphasis on individual liberty, the proponents of neoliberalism were well placed to channel the palpable discontent with the status quo which marked this period in their preferred direction [25].

Neoliberalism sought to replace all political and social norms and judgements with economic evaluation, especially that evaluation which was provided by markets [23]. It was hostile to the supposed ambiguity of politics and was committed instead to a reliance on quantitative economic indicators. The idea that everything could be captured in monetary terms was seductive because it seemed to offer a way of making political choices without making any of the hard and controversial moral and ethical decisions [26]. So, instead of an economy being seen to be embedded in social relations, social relations were seen as being embedded in the economic system [27].

As a result, economic value and financial calculation were now privileged over all other forms of value [28] and the relationships between people were seen as being fundamentally grounded in a transactional business case – as being instrumental – a means towards an (economic) end. People thus came to be seen as commodities, valued for their place in the market, rather than for their intrinsic worth [26]. Long [29] suggests that where people in organisations are used in this way, as a means to an end, as tools and commodities rather than as respected citizens, then such instrumental relations indicate an organisational culture of "perversion", which is concerned with seeking individual gain and pleasure at the expense of the common good, often to the extent of not even recognising the existence of others or of their rights. Such commodification poses a direct threat to any culture of kinship, a responsibility to each other and to kindness, which is exemplified in healthcare generally and quite specifically embodied in the UK's National Health Service (NHS) [30].

While this perversion premise was based upon a study of large private corporations, the idealisation of those entities and the injunction through the New Public Management (NPM) to healthcare organisations to mimic them [31] meant that such an analysis has huge and continuing relevance. Such commodification includes the work of healthcare professionals, and this serves to undermine the intrinsic value, job satisfaction and enjoyment associated with their work and threatens dangerously to undermine the concept of a vocation to serve others. The uncritical substitution of economic measures for political, moral and ethical judgements thus fractures the bonds between human beings.

Campling [32] identifies four closely intertwined processes at work in the UK's NHS:

First, the active promotion of a competitive market economy, on the basis of a commodified view of need, skills and service. This works against the idea of an integrated service that prioritises the needs of vulnerable people and so can insidiously affect the attitudes, feeling and relationships of staff.

Second, the huge increases over time in the complexity, clinical interventions and diagnostic technologies have heightened the need to manage limited resources well and, as a result, have shifted the focus in healthcare from caring for individuals and their families to organising and managing care to meet the needs of the many. This process of industrialising healthcare via what is, in effect, a manufacturing model has the potential to undermine the healthcare system as comprising work undertaken by skilled individuals in relationships with patients and service users and turn it into the mechanical delivery of processes and systems.

Next, Campling cites the framework and currency of specifications, regulations and performance management. How services are specified, monitored and evaluated (and also funded) has a profound effect on the day-to-day clinical work of professional staff.

Finally, the inexorable rise of consumerism and the promotion of patient "choice" have further advanced commodification. Healthcare has become the business of planning and delivering fragmented and costed inputs of time, skills and interventions by clinical professionals to deliver equally fragmented outcomes, outputs or results. As a result, the need to be able to organise, ration, cost and plan healthcare moves insidiously into colonising the thinking and attitudes of healthcare staff, with the danger that different parts of the system may feel they are in competition with other parts, generating anxiety and directing attention away from the patient.

One example of neoliberalism in action is the Return on Investment (ROI) approach to the evaluation of activities and programmes which is treated as if it were a science rather than simply a subjective conceptual model. The key feature of ROI is the calculation of the monetary value of the costs of investing in a particular programme or activity, the results or outcomes of which are then converted into a financial value, enabling a cost–benefit analysis to take place. Those results which cannot be so monetised are called "intangibles" or "externalities", and in the ROI approach, these have only a secondary importance. With ROI, only financial quantitative data matters and intangibles/externalities, as evidenced by qualitative data, are relegated to this secondary role. The ROI approach risks either minimising such qualitative results or forcing an essentially hypothetical and subjective financial value onto them. Yet such intangibles or externalities can potentially lead to significant benefits over time. This is because there are no side effects, just effects, and the very notion of side effects is a sign that the mental model underlying ROI is too narrow and the time horizons too short [33] because it is rooted completely in the neoliberal paradigm.

With neoliberalism, organisations of all kinds (including healthcare organisations) were seen as economic entities in a competitive world. Competition rather than collaboration was considered as the only basis for personal and organisational survival and success [34], and every attempt to constrain such competition was seen as an infringement upon "liberty". Where everything in life was seen to be driven by competition, then this could best be fostered by constant and universal quantified measurement and comparison [35]. Mautner [36] noted that the market had now become the overarching social principle, as social discourse had become almost wholly marketised by influence from the business world. In the NHS, the marketisation of care is now embodied, for example, in such language as "care packages" which are "delivered" to patients [37], together with language like "financial envelopes" and "purchasing" (later softened to "commissioning").

So prevalent, pervasive and internalised has this viewpoint spread that it has now become regarded as being just a neutral background factor and described as the "common sense furniture of everyday life" [38]; "everyday neoliberalism" [39]; "capitalist realism" [40]; "as a kind of biological law" [41] or even as the final stage of human history, where the only plausible plans are business plans and the only source of innovation is seen to be entrepreneurship [42,43]. It has become an unquestionable orthodoxy that operates as if it were the objective truth [44]. As Monbiot [45] asked "What greater power can there be than to operate namelessly?" and Thompson [46] maintained:

In most societies we can observe an intellectual as well as institutional hegemony, or dominant discourse, which impacts a structure of ideas and beliefs – deep assumptions as to social priorities and economic processes; as to the legitimacy of relations of property and power, a general "common sense" as to what is possible and what is not, a limited horizon or moral norms and practical probabilities beyond which all must be blasphemous, seditious, insane or apocalyptic fantasy – a structure which serves to consolidate the existing social order, reinforce its' priorities, and which is itself enforced by rewards and penalties, by notions of "reputability".

Neoliberalism is also marked by the atomisation of all social phenomena because the autonomous individual operating alone is seen as the primary focal point, so that organisational and social change could not be achieved through any collective action but only through the atomised actions of individuals. This is what Giroux [47] termed "dis-imagination" – an imperative for people to only look inwards, to better manage their self, to abandon new possibilities, to accept the status quo and to use self-discipline in order to become more personally effective – a narcissistic search for a "perfect" self [48].

Under neoliberalism many employees in healthcare organisations experience a growing gap between senior leadership and management rhetoric and their day-to-day experienced reality, especially in three areas. There is the rhetoric of empowerment which emphasises that individuals can expect to be given greater autonomy at work, when in their experience they are often increasingly expected to be much more compliant, to stick quite rigidly to the rules and to be ever more closely monitored and controlled. Second, there is the rhetoric of equity and justice, which emphasises fair treatment and a single and favourable employment relationship for all, when in reality many employees are now expected to accept significant differences with respect to that relationship and that some individuals and groups will be treated less well than others. Finally, there is the rhetoric of continual change as being necessary, evolutionary and rational and as offering employee opportunities to learn and increase their "employability", when in reality such initiatives may be mere play-acting and the outcomes are likely to mean even more work for exactly the same rewards [49]. It is perhaps unsurprising, therefore, that Zuboff [50] has described neoliberalism in its organisational manifestations as an anti-democratic and anti-egalitarian social force.

The performativity within: As Western society has become more fragmented, there has been a gradual breakdown of a sense of community and a growing domination of neoliberal values [51]. With the decline of identification with local neighbourhoods, civic groups, churches and other places of worship, and of extended families, the workplace has increasingly come to be seen as a primary source of such a sense of community and hence as a place for people to feel connected with each other. Yet, as implied by Pentland [52], at work people often feel that they need to be acceptable to others through acquiring the "right" qualifications, wearing the "right" clothes and driving the "right" car in order to fit in with their peer group. Individual self-image and self-esteem are undermined by people feeling the need to comply with such external criteria without question and without any questioning of what would be "right". At its most extreme, people can experience feelings of superiority or isolation, wanting to impose their will and opinions on, or to blame, others; doubting their own abilities or being part of a "performance", rather than behaving in an authentic manner.

As a feature of this, Edmonstone [38] noted the development of a "performativity within" in which individuals take on a form of self-discipline and a personal responsibility for working harder, faster and better as a means of seeking to enhance their personal worth in the eyes of others. The "self-managing" individual or "quantified self" is created within the interstices of targets, audits, inspections, appraisals and reviews and takes on responsibility for enhancing their own performance. Employees calculate about themselves, "add value" to themselves, improve their productivity, strive for excellence and live a whole existence as "enterprising subjects" [53]. Human relationships accordingly degenerate into "calculations of self-interest" [54] with the ideal employees being those who see themselves as "reservoirs of competence" and consider it their responsibility to self-monitor, self-develop and self-optimise those skills [55]. The onus is placed on the individual to be economically self-interested [56] and self-regulating [57]. Mirowski [39] describes this neoliberal self as:

a jumble of assets to be invested, nurtured, managed and developed, but equally an offsetting inventory of liabilities to be pruned, outsourced, shorted, hedged against and minimised.

As day-to-day work practice is increasingly flooded with sets of figures, indicators and comparisons, an individual's purposes may seem to be contradictory, their motivations may become blurred and their self-worth may become uncertain. People become unsure about exactly what aspects of their work are valued and how to prioritise their efforts. They become uncertain about the reasons for their own actions – are they doing something because it is important? Because they believe in it? Because it is worthwhile? Or is it being done simply because it will be measured and compared and so make themselves and the organisation look good? The result is one of self-doubt and destabilising personal anxiety [30] and a questioning of whether people are doing things for the "right" reasons – and how can this be known? [58]. Crowley and Hodson [59] have noted this negative consequences of neoliberalism on employee well-being, especially on those working relationships and everyday behaviours, that underwrite successful organisational functioning. Such consequences include increases in employee turnover and a reduction in previously informal on-the-job training, coaching, mentoring and assistance.

The impact on OD: The extent to which this advance of the neoliberal ethos has permeated the OD community in the USA is illustrated by a 2014 survey [60] which indicated that among the lowest-ranked OD values were:

Promoting autonomy and freedom

Promoting democratic systems and policies

Establishing systems based on equality

Giving back to society

Protecting the natural environment

so that these OD practitioners were seemingly no longer as committed to the original core values of the field and that these values were therefore no longer located at the centre of their OD practice. In a less explicit fashion, in the UK the Human Resource professional body the Chartered Institute of Personnel and Development (CIPD) promoted a "profession map" [61] featuring OD and learning and development, but drilling down into these areas reveals a substantial emphasis on cognitive skills only, such as analysis, strategy development and designing solutions. Inquiry-based OD skills were subsumed into areas such as "facilitation of learning events" and "managing change", rendering them less explicit, less nuanced and potentially less valued [62]. Gillon [63] describes this as a predatory "land grab" on the part of the CIPD as a means of owning OD and incorporating it within the Human Resource function. In this respect, it is worth noting that Human Resource's philosophy of commitment to existing organisational goals and to a mutuality of interests is completely based upon a unitary perspective [64]. This involves the Human Resource function attempting to square the circle between a set of individual-focused activities, such as recruitment, selection, promotion and performance appraisal on the one hand, and collective activities such as developing and promoting an organisational vision, mission, values and enabling team building on the other.

The shattering of shared values: Rather than organisations being shaped for people as early OD intended, as a result of the spread of neoliberal values, people increasingly began to be shaped for organisations, including the growth in the use of psychometric tests for selection and promotion purposes [65] and the growth of "talent management", seeking to identify future "hi-po" (high potential) individuals. Success in organisational life increasingly came to be defined solely in "business" terms, so that short-term pressures (typically of a financial nature) gradually took precedence over any longer-term needs. As a result, all change activity became less open-ended and more directed towards a set of prescribed short-term goals. Rather than any form of power equalisation, the unitary frame of reference was reinforced, promulgating and fostering a belief that there should be:

Only a single and hierarchical authority source within organisations.

Likewise, a single loyalty focus – to the employing organisation, not to a profession or occupation or to the local or national community.

Adherence to a set of common organisational objectives expressed through mission statements and via performance management and accountability systems.

Greater integration of organisational functions through regular restructuring and team building.

Morgan [66] has noted that such over-tight accountability systems only serve to foster low levels of trust and an inability to tolerate high levels of uncertainty. This revival of the unitary movement eventually solidified into organisational systems of command and control [67], a top-down perspective in which:

The emphasis is on the "holy trinity" of management – planning, organising and controlling.

All work within organisations is necessarily divided into functional or professional specialisms which require to be integrated by managerial actions.

Performance targets and short-term metrics dominate.

"Strategic" decision-making is completely separated from the day-to-day work itself.

Measures in use are always related to the budget and are often experienced as being arbitrary.

Management's role is to "make the numbers" and to "manage the people".

Conflict and diversity are seen as problems that need to be managed, while compliance is rewarded.

Employees' motivation is assumed to be extrinsic (involving the use of both the carrot and the stick), rather than intrinsic.

The attitude towards patients or service users is effectively transactional and contractual.

Underlying the command-and-control approach is an essentially military model which embodies an unstated expectation that the directives and even suggestions of senior leaders and managers should be complied with without any challenge, debate or even discussion. Decisions ought to be carried out as instructed, just because of the seniority of the leader [68]. Should this be challenged and debated, then defensive and offensive reactions are likely to be triggered and status anxiety generated [69].

In the UK's NHS from the 1980s, this was manifested in increasing demands for greater "accountability" in healthcare by national politicians. The introduction of annual accountability reviews and of a complex range of performance management measures such as performance indicators, performance appraisal and performance-related pay all served to emphasise the desire for a stronger line of direct control from UK Government ministers to the front-line point at which healthcare services were finally delivered.

Increasingly the policy domain was staffed by appointed people who, consciously or unconsciously, subscribed to a neoliberal ideology. This policy domain then appointed the key managers (from the 1980s onwards general managers, often at the time recruited from across the private sector generally and also from the armed forces) and shaped the priorities of the management domain. Developments such as the introduction of clinical directorates in hospitals which covered individual or grouped medical specialties sought to incorporate the service or professional domain, with doctors being encouraged to take on the role of Clinical Director with responsibilities for managing staff and budgets – a part-time managerial role – in addition to their existing clinical commitments. As this became the norm, McGivern et al. [70] noted the emerging distinction between such "willing" and "incidental" hybrid manager professionals. Thus, over time, a clear hierarchy was developed, whereby the service/professional domain became beholden to the management domain, which in turn was appointed and directed by the policy domain made up of Government appointees.

Locked into conformist innovation: Legge [71] made a useful distinction between what she described as conformist and deviant innovation. The former meant buying completely into the prevailing current organisational values and norms; working within the system and pursuing incremental organisational change within a set of prescribed boundaries, which minimised costs and risks. The latter meant questioning those prior assumptions upon which that value system was based; the challenging and reframing of the status quo against values and ethical standards and, when necessary, "speaking truth to power". It assumed that the existing system could be changed, both in terms of what was done and how it was done.

Conformist innovation would focus, for example, on how to produce a healthier workforce in order to increase productivity, while deviant innovation would consider how to support the well-being of the workforce because this was a desirable end in itself. Likewise, conformist innovation would concentrate on how to modify a performance management system in order to improve it, while deviant innovation would ask what the point or purpose of such a system really was. Increasingly, OD seemed to become confined to conformist innovation only and by definition addressing only "tame" organisational problems, while ignoring "wicked" ones [72,73].

As an example, a more recent (and healthcare-related) initiative Taylor-Pitt and Dumain [74] asked NHS OD practitioners what their purpose was, with the responses being:

"Change", "Patients", "Enabler", "Diversity", "Growth", "People", "Strategic", "Supporter", "Disrupter", "Improvement", "Connector" and "Innovating".

OD practitioners were also asked what the healthcare system thought OD's function was, and the responses were:
"Change", "Underground", "Culture", "Transformation", "Training", "Unknown", "Helpers", "Connectors", "Fixers", "Team Builders", "Magic Wands" and "Whatever".
From this, rather than a definition, an "ambition statement" was derived:

We make positive change which all staff engage with to make services better for patients. Our work is integrated in the day-to-day business of our organisations. OD is systematic, innovative, proactive and enabling. We work across whole systems to support effective transformation. We are catalysts for change. Our practice is evidence-based, inclusive and strategic.

This statement of course raises a whole series of important questions, such as:
"Make" – Is it truly the role of OD practitioners to "make" change themselves?
"Positive change" – Positive from whose viewpoint? The patient or service user? The healthcare employees? The local community? The Government? The assumption would seem to be that these are all simply compatible, while this might or might not be the case. Indeed, it is more likely that there are real tensions in existence between these different stakeholders.
Truly "all staff" or confined only to managers? Most OD work has historically involved a prime focus only on managers from the middle to the top of organisational hierarchies, rather than with front-line staff. Do all stakeholders truly have equality of voice?
"Integrated into the day-today business of our organisations" – What does such integration mean in practice if OD is about change to the status quo? The use of the term "business" also still remains anathema to many clinical professionals.
"Systematic" – Systematic as an OD process or as addressing the entire healthcare (or health and social care) system?
"Innovative" – Innovative within pre-prescribed parameters or much wider-ranging? How much challenge to be really innovative is actually permissible (and by whom)?
"Effective transformation" – Effective for whom? Transformation to where or towards what?
"Evidence-based" – Who chooses what evidence is permissible?

"Inclusive" – Exactly who is included, and who is then excluded?

"Strategic" – Does this imply only working at senior hierarchical levels, which have historically always claimed "strategy" as their own?

The blandness and ambiguity of the ambition statement cannot disguise the conclusion that the OD being described is essentially conformist in nature. Using an analogy, it is as if these OD practitioners, either consciously or unconsciously, were content to paddle around in the organisational, leadership and management waters of a river delta, rather than concerning themselves with the underlying assumptions and behaviour emanating from the original headwaters of that same river.

From ends to means: It can therefore be argued that healthcare OD has, over time and especially from the 1980s onwards, been gradually transformed from a value-rich **end** to be pursued – one of open organisations with enabling systems making a contribution to the larger society and providing support and challenge through meaningful work for all staff – to a series of **means** towards a set of pre-defined ends [75]. Bushe and Nagaishi [76] suggest that organisational leaders and managers gradually came to see OD as something about implementation (or the journey) but not about what to change (the destination). As a result, much of the theory and practice of OD in the UK's NHS has adopted an emphasis on pre-determined policy and strategic imperatives and the requirements which are associated with specific organisational initiatives and roles. From these, it develops an "ideal" state of affairs and related role models and then constructs processes of appraisal, audit and assessment against this ideal in order to identify the deficit or gap. OD activity is then seen as a means of filling that deficit or gap. This transformation of OD has also taken place in many other economic and social sectors, but specifically in the UK's NHS, it has been noted by Spurgeon [77] that:

OD has tended to become a largely reactive process attempting to implement, accommodate and at times ameliorate the impact of a range of externally-driven policy initiatives [78].

The NHS management community is so accustomed to a programmatic approach to change that they have become deskilled and are dependent on tools and programmes to improve things. Within such a culture of dependence, where all change is micromanaged and centrally-programmed, NHS managers are not at liberty to evaluate change, reframe experience and develop reflexive processes.

Hardacre concluded that there was little evidence that the NHS approach to OD was underpinned by any central set of values, principles or assumptions; that the NHS used OD only as a set of tools and techniques for planning and implementing change quickly in a way that demonstrated results in the short term; that the desired outcomes of OD were in achieving against performance indicators, targets and processes; that evaluation processes did not feature strongly and that the embedding and sustainability of change was neglected.

As a result, change agendas were "chunked" unilaterally by client healthcare organisations into definable needs and ends, rather than jointly with an OD practitioner, and then OD behavioural science expertise was targeted towards those specific client-defined "chunks" only. This is an example of anthroposcission – the breaking down of work activity into pieces, an action which fosters a process of differentiation, rather than integration. There was little or no room within this essentially adversarial and transitory model to challenge or renegotiate the ends or to modify the means in the light of emerging client and OD practitioner shared understanding as the work progressed. Gilpin-Jackson [79] noted that this phenomenon was still very prevalent in much recent OD activity in healthcare where even such "post-Lewinian" OD interventions as Appreciative Inquiry or Open Space events were conducted with little consideration of any longer-term direction but rather as a short-term and "technicist" activity [80]. Such approaches did little to foster longer-term working relationships but rather emphasised smaller and bounded (i.e., by client organisation definition) pieces of work [81]. What appeared to be lacking was the kind of "partnership team" suggested by Edmonstone and Flanagan [82] which actively sought to learn from experience and to modify and steer the work, allowing for greater flexibility and responsiveness over a longer time period.

The purpose of OD in healthcare has thus become the development of the organisation solely in prescribed directions, because data collection and diagnosis, together with evaluation, might potentially be politically sensitive and elicit an "unacceptable finding" – and so has largely tended to be avoided or contracted-out to external OD practitioners with a defined and limited brief. The only variety of data collection which is permissible is that which supports current policy and confirms previously prescribed directions – an example of a search for policy-based evidence, rather than the evidence-based policy which was central to the original rationale of early OD.

This shrinks OD to a collection of behavioural science tools and techniques, often captured in "recipe books" [83] and turns the OD practitioner from a "professional" to a "technician" or "hired hand" [84]; perhaps even to an "organisational social worker" or "agony aunt" as the custodian of the (shrinking) softer organisational values [85]; as a source of rest and refreshment or even as a kind of wartime stretcher-bearer, taking people out from the organisational battlefield, patching them up through activities like coaching and mentoring and sending them back into the fray. Burnes and Cook [86] express concerns that the core values of OD (an emphasis on the value of democracy, equality and listening to and engaging with the voices of the less powerful) that underpin the drive for real social corporate responsibility (rather than an espoused version) are being increasingly lost.

A profession or a field of practice? While a movement regarding OD to be a profession has certainly prospered in the USA [87], equivalent attempts to create a similar national professional body in the UK in 2018–2019 foundered. The contrast with the related field of coaching offers an interesting comparison, as the latter has become increasingly professionalised and codified, with the creation of a number of professional bodies, credentials, competency grids and supervisory regimes [88]. This avoidance of professionalisation may reflect the fact that OD is best regarded as an open field of practice, rather than as a functional discipline or profession [89], not least because it borrows from many other fields in social or behavioural science which gives it added depth and complexity. It is unusual, to say the least, for someone to make an early career choice to work in healthcare OD in the UK. Rather, people typically move into the OD field in mid-career (usually from beyond the age of 30) from a range of other professions and occupations, such as Human Resources (especially education and training, leadership and management development), improvement science or even from professional and managerial positions. The dangers associated with this open and boundary-less state of affairs have been noted by Bradford and Burke [90], who comment that:

When there is a lack of clarity as to the boundaries of the field and corresponding confusion about what the appropriate role of an OD practitioner is, then anybody can hang out a shingle claiming he or she is an OD consultant.

Such open boundaries to the field of OD have also made it vulnerable to capture by other more professionalised areas of work, such as the Human Resources function, as Gillon [63] has suggested.

Bradford and Burke's view can also, of course, be interpreted as an elitist approach, but such blurred or "fuzzy" boundaries may also be seen as a strength, as well as a weakness, as they prevent OD from becoming a completely bounded or restricted area of understanding and practice. Instead, OD as an open field of practice is perceived as being incapable of being put into any kind of single fixed competency framework; as being facilitative and challenging and as valuing both intuition and reflexivity. This may be why there appears to be a preference on the part of many OD practitioners in both the UK and USA for the network form of association, rather than a more formal institutional one. This certainly seems to be the case with OD in the UK's NHS [91].

References

1. Beckhard, R. (1969) *Organization Development: Strategies And Models*, Reading, MA: Addison-Wesley.
2. Bennis, W. (1969) *Organisation Development: Its Nature, Origins and Prospects*, Reading, MA: Addison-Wesley.
3. French, W. and Bell, C. (1978) *Organization Development: Behavioural Science Interventions For Organization Improvement*, Englewood Cliffs, NJ: Prentice-Hall.
4. Bennis, W., Benne, K. and Chin, R. (1969) Some Value Dilemmas of the Change Agent, in Bennis, W., Benne, K. & Chin, R. (Eds.) *The Planning of Change*, New York: Holt, Rinehart & Winston, 33–42.
5. Levy, A. and Merry, U. (1986) *Organisation Transformation: Approaches, Strategies, Theories*, Westport, CT: Greenwood Publishing Group.
6. Clark, P. (1972) *Action Research and Organisational Change*, London: Harper & Row.
7. Kolb, D. and Frohman, A. (1970) An Organisation Development Approach to Consulting, *Sloan Management Review*, 2 (2): 51–65.
8. Adler, P. and Kwon, S. (2002) Social Capital: Prospects for a New Concept, *Academy of Management Review*, 27 (2): 17–40.
9. Zand, D. (2010) An OD Odyssey: In Search of Inward Light, *Journal of Applied Behavioural Science*, 46 (4): 424–435.
10. Fox, A. (1973) Industrial Relations: A Social Critique of Pluralistic Ideology, in Child, J. (Ed.) *Man and Organisation*, London: Allen & Unwin, 65–78.
11. Strauss, A., Schatzman, L., Erlich, D., Bucher, R. and Sabshin, M. (1963) The Hospital and Its Negotiated Order, in Friedson, E. (Ed.) *The Hospital in Modern Society*, New York: Macmillan, 54–73.
12. Bate, P. (2000) Changing the Culture of a Hospital: From Hierarchy to Networked Community, *Public Administration*, 78 (3): 485–512.
13. Kouzes, J. and Mico, P. (1979) Domain Theory: An Introduction to Organisational Behaviour in Human Service Organisations, *Journal of Applied Behavioural Science*, 15 (4): 449–469.

14. Edmonstone, J. (1982) Human Service Organisations: Implications for Management and Organisation Development, *Management Education and Development*, 13, Part 3, (Autumn).
15. Blackler, F. and Kennedy, A. (2006) The Design and Evaluation of Leadership Programme for Experienced Chief Executives from the Health Sector, in Rigg, C. & Richards, S. s(Eds.) *Action Learning, Leadership and Organisational Development in Public Services*, Abingdon: Routledge, 79–100.
16. Margulies, N. and Raia, A. (1988) The Significance of Core Values on the Theory and Practice of Organisation Development, *Journal of Organisational Change Management*, 1 (1): 6–17.
17. Goodge, P. (1975) The Love/Trust Model and Progress in OD, *Journal of European Training*, 4 (3): 179–184.
18. Tranfield, D. (1978) *Some Characteristics of Organisation Development Consultants*, Doctoral thesis, Sheffield Hallam University.
19. Sherrit, D. (2016) Is OD Just a Big Bag of Interventions? In Burnes, B. and Randall, J. (Eds.) *Perspectives on Change: What Academics, Consultants and Managers Really Think about Change*, Abingdon: Routledge, 245–265.
20. CBI (2009) *The Shape of Business: The Next Ten Years*, London: Confederation of British Industry.
21. Standing, G. (2011) *The Precariat: The Dangerous New Class*, London: Policy Network.
22. Thomas, P., McArdle, L. and Saundry, R. (2020) Introduction to the Special Issue: The Enactment of Neoliberalism in the Workplace: The Degradation of the Employment Relationship, *Competition and Change*, 24 (2): 105–113.
23. Davies, W. (2017) *The Limits of Neoliberalism: Authority, Sovereignty and the Logic of Competition*, London: Sage.
24. Williamson, J. (2004) The Strange History of the Washington Consensus, *Journal of Post Keynesian Economics*, 27 (2): 195–206.
25. Martinez, R. (2016) *Creating Freedom: Power, Control and the Fight for Our Future*, Edinburgh: Canongate Books.
26. Sandel, M. (2009) The Reith Lectures 2009, Lecture 1: *Markets and Morals*, broadcast 9 June, BBC Radio 4.
27. Polanyi, K. (2001) *The Great Transformation: The Political and Economic Origins of our Time*, Boston, MA: Beacon Press.
28. Earle, J, Moran, C. and Ward-Perkins, Z. (2017) *The Econocracy: The Perils of Leaving Economics to the Experts*, Manchester: Manchester University Press.
29. Long, S. (2008) *The Perverse Organisation and Its' Deadly Sins*, London: Karnac Books.
30. Ballatt, J. and Campling, P. (2011) *Intelligent Kindness: Reforming the Culture of Healthcare*, London, RCPch Publications.
31. George, M. (2017) The Effect of Introducing New Public Management Practices on Compassion Within the NHS, *Nursing Times*, 113 (7): 30–34.
32. Campling, P. (2014) Reforming the Culture of Healthcare: The Case for Intelligent Kindness, *BJPsych Bulletin*, 39 (1):1–5, February.

33. Sterman, J. (2012) Sustaining Sustainability: Creating a Systems Science in a Fragmented Academy and Polarised World, in Weinstein, M. and Turner, R. (Eds.) *Sustainability Science: The Emerging Paradigm and the Urban Environment*, New York: Springer Science, 84–103.
34. Day, A. (2019) *Disruption, Change and Transformation in Organisations: A Human Relations Perspective*, Abingdon: Routledge.
35. Verhaghe, P. (2014) *What About Me? The Struggle for Identity in a Market Based Society*, London: Scribe Publications.
36. Mautner, G. (2010) *Language and the Market Society: Critical Perspectives on Discourse and Dominance*, Abingdon: Routledge.
37. Bunting, M. (2020) *Labour of Love: The Crisis of Care*, London: Granta Books.
38. Edmonstone, J. (2019) Beyond Critical Action Learning: Action Learning's Place In The World, *Action Learning: Research and Practice*, 16 (2): 136–148.
39. Mirowski, P. (2013) *Never Let a Serious Crisis Go to Waste*, London: Verso.
40. Fisher, M. (2009) *Capitalist Realism: Is There No Alternative?* Winchester: Zero Books.
41. Pell, C. and Caulkin, S. (2016) Foreword, in Pell, C., Wilson, R. and Lowe, T. (Eds.) *Kittens Are Evil: Little Heresies in Public Policy*, Axminster: Triarchy Press, 7–8.
42. Davies, W. (2020) *This Is Not Normal: The Collapse of Liberal Britain*, London: Verso.
43. Fukuyama, F. (1992) *The End of History and the Last Man*, New York: Free Press.
44. Chopra, R. (2003) Neoliberalism as Doxa: Bourdieu's Theory of the State and the Contemporary Indian Discourse on Globalisation and Liberalisation, *Cultural Studies*, 17 (3/4): 419–444.
45. Monbiot, G. (2016) Neoliberalism: The Ideology at the Root of All Our Problems, *Guardian*, April 15.
46. Thompson, E. (1993) *Witness Against the Beast: William Blake and the Moral Law*, Cambridge: Cambridge University Press.
47. Giroux, H. (2014) *Neoliberalism's War on Higher Education*, Chicago: Haymarket Books.
48. Storr, W. (2017) *Selfie: How We Became So Self-Obsessed and What It's Doing to Us*, London: Picador.
49. Edmonstone, J. (2013) *Personal Resilience for Healthcare Staff: When the Going Gets Tough*, London: Radcliffe Publishing.
50. Zuboff, S. (2019) *The Age of Surveillance Capitalism: The Fight for a Human Future at the New Frontier of Power*, London: Profile Books.
51. Putnam, R. (2000) *Bowling Alone: The Collapse and Revival of American Community*, New York: Simon & Schuster.
52. Pentland, A. (2014) The Death of Individuality, *New Scientist*, 5 April.
53. Rose, N. (1989) *Governing the Soul: The Shaping of the Private Self*, London: Routledge.
54. Bunting, M. (2016) *Love of Country: A Hebridean Journey*, London: Granta Publications.
55. Brinkmann, S. (2017) *Standing Firm: Resisting the Self-Improvement Craze*, Cambridge: Polity Press.
56. Olssen, M. and Peters, M. (2005) Neoliberalism, Higher Education and the Knowledge Economy: From the Free Market to Knowledge Capitalism, *Journal of Education Policy*, 20 (3): 313–345.

57. Phillips, L. and Ilcan, S. (2004) Capacity-Building, the Neoliberal Governance of Development, *Canadian Journal of Development Studies*, 25 (3): 393–409.
58. Ball, S (2012) The Making of a Neoliberal Academic, *Research in Secondary Teacher Education*, 2 (1): 29–31.
59. Crowley, M. and Hodson, R. (2014) Neoliberalism at Work, *Social Currents*, 1 (1): 91–108.
60. Schull, A., Church, A. and Burke, W. (2014) Something Old, Something New: Research on the Practice and Values of OD, *OD Practitioner*, 46 (4): 23–30.
61. CIPD (2013) *CIPD Profession Map*, London: Chartered Institute of Personnel & Development.
62. Tosey, P. and Marshall, J. (2017) The Demise of Inquiry-Based HRD Programmes in the UK: Implications for the Field, *Human Resource Development International*, 20 (5): 393–402.
63. Gillon, A. (2016) *Conceptualising Organisation Development: Practitioner and Academic Perspectives: A UK Study*, PhD thesis, Nottingham Trent University.
64. Armstrong, M. (1999) *A Handbook of Human Resource Management Practice*, London: Kogan Page.
65. Macabasco, L. (2021) "They Become Dangerous Tools": The Dark Side of Personality Tests, *Guardian*, 4 March.
66. Morgan, G. (1993) *Imaginisation: The Art of Creative Management*, Newbury Park, CA: Sage.
67. Seddon, J. (2019) *Beyond Command And Control*, Oxford: Mayfield Press.
68. Milgram, S. (1974) *Obedience to Authority*, New York: Harper Collins.
69. de Botton, A. (2004) *Status Anxiety*, London: Hamish Hamilton.
70. McGivern, G., Currie, G., Fitzgerald, L., Ferlie, E. and Waring, J. (2015) Hybrid Manager-Professionals' Identity Work: The Maintenance and Hybridisation of Medical Professionalism in Managerial Contexts, *Public Administration*, 93 (2): 412–432.
71. Legge, K. (1978) *Power, Innovation and Problem-Solving in Personnel Management*, Maidenhead: McGraw-Hill.
72. Rittell, H. and Webber, M. (1973) Dilemmas in a General Theory of Planning, *Policy Sciences*, 4: 155–169.
73. Edmonstone, J., Lawless, A. and Pedler, M. (2019) Leadership Development, Wicked Problems and Action Learning: Provocations to a Debate, *Action Learning: Research and Practice*, 16 (1): 37–51.
74. Taylor-Pitt, P. and Dumain, K. (2018) The Role of Organisational Development in the NHS: A Do OD Paper for Discussion, Debate, Reflection and Action, NHS Leadership Academy/NHS Employers.
75. Furedi, F. (2004) *Where Have All The Intellectuals Gone?: Confronting Twenty-First Century Philistinism*, London: Continuum Press.
76. Bushe, G. and Nagaishi, M. (2018) Imagining the Future Through the Past: Organisation Development isn't (just) about Change, *Organisation Development Journal*, Fall: 23–36.
77. Spurgeon, P. (1999) OD: From A Reactive To A Proactive Process, in Mark, A. and Dopson, M. (Eds.) *Organisation Behaviour in Health Care*, London: Macmillan, 66–78.

78. Hardacre, J. (2005) *How Does The NHS Interpret And Use OD?* MSc thesis, University of Birmingham.
79. Gilpin-Jackson. Y. (2013) Practising in the Grey Area between Dialogic and Diagnostic Organisation Development, *OD Practitioner*, 45 (1): 60–66.
80. Grey, C. and Mitev, N. (2004) Management Education: A Polemic, in Grey, C. and Antonacopoulou, E. (Eds.) *Essential Readings in Management Learning*, London: Sage, 104–123.
81. Edmonstone, J. (2011) The Tender Trap: Back to the Future? *British Journal of Healthcare Management*, 17 (8): 272–275.
82. Edmonstone, J. and Flanagan, H. (2007) A Flexible Friend: Action Learning in the Context of a Multi-Agency Organisation Development Programme, *Action Learning: Research and Practice*, 4 (2): 199–209.
83. Bunker, B., Alban, B. and Lewicki, R. (2004) Ideas in Currency and Organisation Development Practice: Has the Well Gone Dry? *Journal of Applied Behavioural Science*, 40 (4): 403–422.
84. Edmonstone, J. and Havergal, M. (1995) The Death (And Rebirth?) of Organisation Development, *Health Manpower Management*, 21 (1): 28–33.
85. Edmonstone, J. (1982) From Organisational Social Work to Organisation Design, *Leadership and Organisation Development Journal*, 3 (1): 24–26.
86. Burnes, B. and Cooke, B. (2012) The Past, Present and Future of Organisation Development: Taking the Long View, *Human Relations*, 65 (11): 1395–1429.
87. Minahan, M. (2016) OD: Sixty Years Down, and the Future to Go, *OD Practitioner*, 48 (1): 5–10.
88. Doherty, D. (2016) The Evolution of One Practitioner's Coach Approach: Taking the Coaching Turn, *Philosophy of Coaching: An International Journal*, 1 (1): 21–34.
89. Garrow, V., Varney, S. and Lloyd, C. (2009) *OD: Past, Present and Future*, Working Paper 22, Institute for Employment Studies, University of Brighton.
90. Bradford, D. and Burke, W. (2004) Is OD in Crisis? *Journal of Applied Behavioural Science*, 40 (4): 369–373.
91. Malby, B. and Anderson-Wallace, M. (2016) *Networks in Healthcare: Managing Complex Relationships*, Bingley: Emerald Group Publishing.

Chapter 2

The Historical Development of Early OD

This chapter identifies two historical modernities and locates Organisation Development's (OD's) emergence in the second, before noting the major strands of activity which came together to form the notion of planned organisational change based on behavioural science theory and practice.

As the Introduction has argued, attention to context is crucial for understanding the genesis of OD, especially in both the USA and the UK. Zuboff [1] has usefully identified what she calls two key "modernities", the first being located in the late 19th and early 20th centuries, as globalisation and migration became increasingly common and when life gradually became more individualised for greater numbers of people as they separated away from their historical and traditional social norms, meanings and rules. Each individual life became instead an open-ended reality to be discovered, rather than a predefined certainty to be enacted. People became convinced that they could begin to shape the kind of person that they wanted to be and the kind of life that they wanted to live. This represented a flowering of the original enlightenment values from their origins in the 18th century [2].

The second modernity dates roughly from after the Second World War and was stimulated by democratic politics, distributional economic policies (especially by progressive taxation), an increased investment in, and access to, education, health and social care and by the creation and enhancement of strong civil society institutions [3]. It was part of an ethos of a need to rebuild, reorganise and manage a new post-war world and tended to stress the importance of common good above individual gain and of state regulation above market forces [4,5]. Increasing numbers of people gained access to those experiences which had once been solely the preserve of a tiny social elite – university education, domestic and foreign travel, increased life expectancy, disposable income, rising living standards, access to consumer goods and intellectually demanding work. Improved access to education and the development of "knowledge work" in particular led to an increased mastery of language and thought. Improved communication, access to information and travel fostered individual self-consciousness and imagination. Improvements in health and a longer lifespan provided time for self-life to deepen and mature.

As one example, the 1950s and 1960s especially saw professional and managerial jobs as a proportion of the UK labour market double, spurring a concomitant dramatic growth in upwards social mobility [6], although the major beneficiaries from this were the growing middle class, rather than the poorest part of the population, whose share of the total wealth has always been miniscule, generally around 5% [3].

This second modernity viewed the past as something which was unfolding progressively into the present and saw the future as a space which was wide open for new possibilities to emerge and to flourish [7]. It was from this second modernity where there was a growing belief in progress, a growing interest in progressive education, where the social hierarchy was being challenged and where democracy was being extended, that OD began to emerge.

One of the most powerful influences, especially in the USA, was the reaction to the Second World War Holocaust, as many of the leading early OD thinkers, such as Kurt Lewin, were expatriate German Jews who were horrified by the inhumanity witnessed in the Second World War and who sought to understand how human beings came to do such terrible things to one another in such a mechanistic manner. While some would also trace the origins of OD even further back to the Hawthorne studies of 1924 [8]; the realisation from the 1930s that organisational structures and processes influenced individual behaviour and motivation, and the growing reaction against the dehumanising effects of scientific management and the work of F.W. Taylor [9], this post-war period in particular saw the emergence of a number of interrelated initiatives that taken together can be described as the sources for OD's emergence. They were:

Sensitivity training (or T-groups) at the National Training Laboratory in the USA from 1946: This was a form of small group training (sometimes also called laboratory training) where the participants learnt more about themselves and about small group processes in general through their interactions with each other, using personal feedback to gain insights into themselves, into others and about the dynamics of small group working. The term "sensitivity training" was used because it sensitised the participants to their own behaviour. It was focused on the way that individuals in groups understood how their behaviour in the "here and now" made an impact on the other group members and thus on the overall group processes. The purpose of such groups was for the members to learn about themselves from their spontaneous responses to an ambiguous situation, because the groups met without any specific agenda. Problems of leadership, structure, status, communication and self-serving behaviour typically arose and were addressed in such groups. Group members had opportunities to learn something about themselves and to practice such skills as listening, observing others and functioning as an effective group member. As such, T-groups have been described as one of the most important, and contentious, social inventions of the 20th century [10,11].

The group was seen as the key vehicle for achieving individual behavioural change, as it kept individuals aligned with each other and provided the forum for the group decision-making that could facilitate change. It also concentrated on personal development through the enhancing of self-awareness. Its longer-term impact in OD was to place an emphasis on such activities as team building and teamwork development as a means of improving the working relationships and communication between team members [12], together with attention to intergroup dynamics and the coaching and mentoring of individuals [13,14]. This is due to the fact that, while the original assemblies were "stranger groups", this led eventually to a changed focus on intra-organisational "family groups" – and hence towards the emergence of a set of activities which, taken together, contributed to early OD. This emphasis on individual and small group development is one of the prime reasons that OD was seen by some critics to be so closely linked with the education and training function, especially in relation to leadership and management development.

The development of survey methodology and feedback at the Institute of Social Research at the University of Michigan in the same year: This is a process in which the employees of organisations complete questionnaires on various organisational issues, receive feedback on the questionnaire results, then take appropriate actions to address the emergent critical needs and concerns. The use of perception and attitude surveys aimed at employees, with the results fed back and discussed to them became known as survey feedback and sought to align the aspirations of staff with organisational success [15]. The collection, analysis and feedback of such data became a key part of emerging OD and the annual National Health Service (NHS) staff survey (the largest survey of employee opinion in the UK) is an example of survey feedback in action, as a means of focusing attention on such matters as health and well-being, work/life balance, performance appraisal, employee engagement and career planning.

The refining of action research by Kurt Lewin and colleagues also in the 1940s: This emerged in the 1940s as an interactive inquiry process that balanced problem-solving actions undertaken in a collaborative way with data-driven analysis and research (also done in a collaborative way) in order to understand the underlying causes of a situation, so enabling the direction of organisational and personal change. Human behaviour in a social system was seen to be shaped by two sets of forces – the driving forces that operated for change and the restraining forces that attempted to maintain the status quo. In order to bring about change, there was a need to either increase the strength of the driving forces or decrease the strength of the resisting forces, or to do both.

Often simplified into three stages, such as Unfreezing (awareness of the need for change), Changing (diagnosis and exploration of new ways of working) and Refreezing (evaluation and reinforcement) or as Planning, Action and Review [16,17], this was an essentially humanistic approach that very much focused on the group, as well as the individual, viewed change as a learning process and strongly advocated the need for organisational change to be both voluntary and fully participative.

The strength of these action research models lies in their simplicity, which makes them easy to understand and use, but this is also a potential weakness, as it presents a unidirectional view of change, solidifying dynamic and complex processes and promoting stable (or refrozen) cultures and structures that are not conducive to continuous change. It suggests that organisations are static entities that can be moved neatly from one state to another with the right amount of planning and managerial skill, so it does not really capture the complexity, unpredictability and volatility of the interactions between people and groups. It also ignores power and organisational politics. In its simplistic form, it therefore serves to reinforce existing mechanistic, management-driven and top-down approaches to change [18]. It led to early OD focusing largely on participative and consensual decision-making, improving teamwork and communication and the management of transformation [19], and as such, all the associated learning tends to reinforce the status quo as a means of maintaining equilibrium.

Action research has also been strongly critiqued by Cooke [20] as prioritising means over ends; privileging a managerial agenda; focusing on intra-organisational (individual and group) processes and ignoring the external social context, and while control over some micro-level organisational processes are indeed ceded, broader organisational strategies and imperatives are seen as being "givens". These features most likely relate to the Cold War context in which early action research proponents worked and to the "paranoid style" in American politics [21]. Indeed, Burnes and Cooke [22] assert that in the era of post-war McCarthyism, the term "social science" was considered as sounding too much like socialism and so was best avoided – and hence behavioural science became the default term instead.

Nonetheless, action research has subsequently been a major strand in the development of OD [23] and has continued to be extended, improved and refined [24]. Action research now is regarded as a cyclical and iterative research approach, conducted within specific and practical organisational contexts, undertaken with rigour and understanding, so as to generate new knowledge and to refine practice. It is deliberate, systematic, rigorous, scrutinised, verifiable and always made public through publication and/or oral reports [25].

More or less in parallel with these development, in the UK, the Tavistock Institute of Human Relations, which embodied a psychodynamic orientation, increasingly came to see:

Organisations as sociotechnical systems: Insightful linkages were made by the Tavistock Institute between the operation of group dynamics in a therapeutic context [26] with those in a work and organisational setting. In this way, the Tavistock developed its own OD practices in parallel with, rather than derived from, US experience [27]. The notion of a workplace system made up of two interacting parts – human (people and their non-linear relationships with each other) and technical (the linear structure, processes, tools, techniques and procedures necessary for task accomplishment) emerged [28]. Change initiatives that focused on either the purely technical or social aspects of work were deemed as likely to have limited success, as they created a situation where the whole system was sub-optimised for developments in one dimension only. The interdependency of the social and technical elements encouraged consideration of such aspects as the design of work, including individual jobs; the operation of autonomous work teams as the basis of improved productivity; the degree of autonomy and discretion, and hence of meaningful work, available to employees as a means of both problem-solving and improved performance on the one hand

and the quality of working life on the other. Out of this strand were also to later emerge some aspects of action learning [29] and the concept of emotional labour, the latter being important in understanding the work of clinical professionals in healthcare organisations [30,31]. There is also a powerful case made that the Tavistock Institute was, in fact, much more influential in relation to the origins of OD than most US-based accounts have proposed [32].

As these strands interacted, so gradually emerged what has been variously called "diagnostic", "classical", "first-generation" or "traditional" OD – the notion of planned organisational change based upon behavioural science theory (especially derived from social and organisational psychology, sociology, anthropology, theories of motivation, personality and learning, together with systems theory) – so very much an inter-disciplinary phenomenon – and also on collaborative consultant/client practice – OD was seen as being grounded in participation, reflection, feedback and empowerment. It assumed that organisational change could be orchestrated by objectively identifying and quantifying problems and correcting them with solutions that people in the system adopted and implemented. Objective data or valid information was sought out and used as the basis for diagnosing deficiencies, uncovering the discrepancies between desired and actual behaviours and outcomes and recommending solutions. The underlying values emphasised the need to promote democratic working and participation in order to tackle social conflict, personal growth, emotional expression and a challenge to bureaucracy. This confluence was largely embodied in the first Addison-Wesley series of books on OD published in 1969 [33–36]. This flowering was the legacy of Kurt Lewin in particular [37]. The underlying assumption was that "individuals learn as individuals, but that their experience is shaped and understood in social contexts" [38].

References

1. Zuboff, S. (2019) *The Age of Surveillance Capitalism: The Fight for a Human Future at the New Frontier of Power*, London: Profile Books.
2. Soares, C. (2018) The Philosophy of Individualism: A Critical Perspective, *International Journal of Philosophy and Social Values*, 1 (1): 11–34.
3. Piketty, T. (2014) *Capital in the Twenty-First Century*, London: Belknap Press of Harvard University Press.
4. Gillon, A. (2016) *Conceptualising Organisation Development: Practitioners and Academic Perspectives: A UK Study*, PhD thesis, Nottingham Trent University.

5. Marlow, J. (1996) *Questioning the Post-war Consensus Thesis: Towards an Alternative Account*, Aldershot: Dartmouth.
6. Bukodi, E. and Goldthorpe, J. (2018) *Social Mobility and Education in Britain: Research, Politics and Policy*, Cambridge: Cambridge University Press.
7. Davies, W. (2020) *This Is Not Normal: The Collapse of Liberal Britain*, London: Verso.
8. Mayo, E. (1949) *Hawthorne and the Western Electric Company: The Social Problems of an Industrial Civilisation*, London: Routledge.
9. Mintzberg, H. (1989) *Mintzberg On Management*, New York: The Free Press.
10. Back, K. (1972) *Beyond Words: The Story of Sensitivity Training and the Encounter Movement*, New York: Russell Sage Foundation.
11. Cooper, C. and Bowles, D. (1977) *Hurt or Helped?: A Study of the Personal Impact on Managers of Experiential, Small Group Training Programmes*, Training Information Paper 10, Training Services Agency, London: HMSO.
12. Marrow, A. (1969) *The Practical Theorist: The Life and Work of Kurt Lewin*, New York: Basic Books.
13. Hardacre, J. and Peck, E. (2005) What is Organisational Development? In Peck, E. (Ed.) *Organisational Development in Healthcare: Approaches, Innovations, Achievements*, Abingdon: Radcliffe Publishing.
14. Edmonstone, J. (1981) Using Inter-Group Training Methods to Break Down Barriers, *Health Services Manpower Review*, 7 (4): 4–7.
15. Baumgartel, H. (1959) Using Employee Questionnaire Results for Improving Organisations: The Survey (Feedback) Experiment, *Kansas Business Review*, 12: 2–6.
16. Lewin, K. (1958) Group Decision and Social Change, in Maccoby, N., Newcomb, T. and Hartley, E. (Eds.) *Readings in Psychology*, New York: Holt, Rinehart and Winston, 163–226.
17. Adelman, C. (1993) Kurt Lewin and the Origins of Action Research, *Educational Action Research*, 1 (1): 7–24.
18. McMillan, E. (2008) *Complexity, Management and the Dynamics of Change*, Abingdon: Routledge.
19. Shaw, P. (1997) Intervening in the Shadow Systems of Organisations: Consulting from a Complexity Perspective, *Journal of Organisational Change Management*, 10 (3): 235–250.
20. Cooke, B. (2006) The Cold War Origins of Action Research as Managerialist Co-optation, *Human Relations*, 59 (5): 665–693.
21. Hofstadter, R. (1965) *The Paranoid Style in American Politics: And Other Essays*, New York: Knopf.
22. Burnes, B. and Cooke, B. (2013a) Kurt Lewin's Field Theory: A Review and Re-Evaluation, *International Journal of Management Reviews*, 15 (4): 408–425.
23. Clark, P. (1972) *Action Research and Organisational Change*, London: Harper & Row.
24. Sharp, C. (2005) *The Improvement of Public Sector Delivery: Supporting Evidence-Based Practice Through Action Research*, Edinburgh: Research for Real for Scottish Government.
25. Edmonstone, J. (2018) *Action Learning in Health, Social and Community Care: Principles, Practices, Resources*, Boca Raton, FL: CRC Press.
26. Bion, W. (1984) *Attention and Interpretation*, London: Karnac Books.

27. Neumann, J. (2005) Kurt Lewin at the Tavistock Institute, *Educational Action Research*, 13 (1): 119–136.

28. Trist, E. and Bamforth, K. (1951) Some Social and Psychological Consequences of the Longwall Method of Coal-Getting: An Examination of the Psychological Situation and Defences of a Work Group in Relation to the Social Structure and Technological Content of the Work System, *Human Relations*, 4 (1): 3–38.

29. Boshyk, Y. (2011) Ad Fontes – Reg Revans: Some Early Sources of His Personal Growth and Values, in Pedler, M. (ed.) *Action Learning in Practice*, 4th edition, Farnham: Gower.

30. Menzies-Lyth, I. (1959) The Functioning of Social Systems as a Defence Against Anxiety: A Report on a Study of the Nursing Service of a General Hospital, in Menzies-Lyth, I. (Ed.) *Containing Anxiety in Institutions: Selected Essays: Volume 1*, London: Free Association Books, 43–88.

31. Hayward, R. and Tuckey, M. (2011) Emotions in Uniform: How Nurses Regulate Emotions at Work Via Emotional Boundaries, *Human Relations*, 64 (11): 1501–1523.

32. Burnes, B. and Cooke, B. (2013b) The Tavistock's 1945 Invention of Organisation Development: Early British Business and Management Applications of Social Psychiatry, *Business History*, 55 (5): 768–789.

33. Beckhard, R. (1969) *Organisation Development: Strategies and Models*, Boston, MA: Addison-Wesley.

34. Schein, E. (1969) *Process Consultation: Its Role in Organisation Development, Volume 1*, Boston, MA: Addison-Wesley.

35. Galbraith, J. (1969) *Developing Complex Organisations*, Boston, MA: Addison-Wesley.

36. Lawrence, P. (1969) *Developing Organisations: Diagnosis and Action*, Boston, MA: Addison-Wesley.

37. Burnes, B. (2007) Kurt Lewin and the Harwood Studies: The Foundations of OD, *Journal of Applied Behavioural Science*, 43 (2): 213–231.

38. Marsick, V. and O'Neil, J. (1999) The Many Faces of Action Learning, *Management Learning*, 30 (2): 159–176.

Chapter 3

The Development of OD in Healthcare in the UK

This chapter explores the development of Organisation Development (OD) in healthcare in the UK, from its unlikely origins in the coal industry through early proto-OD projects in the 1960s and early 1970s, before locating the real origins of OD in the UK's National Health Service (NHS) in Sheffield, with the creation of the first internal OD practitioner posts. The growing national interest in OD led, over time, to a form of "colonisation" by the Human Resource function. The notion of a third modernity which challenges OD's original assumptions is also identified.

As the Second World War ended, the UK General Election of 1945 brought into power a Labour Government with radical economic and social aims which led, in the six years to 1951, to a wide range of institutional changes, including the creation of the NHS and the development of what came to be known as the Welfare State. This set of extensive and comprehensive changes was later labelled "Britain's New Deal" [1] and was clearly part of the second modernity highlighted in Chapter 2. One of the policies of that Government was the nationalisation of certain key industries, and the coal industry was one of those which was taken into public ownership. A National Coal Board (NCB) was created and, strangely enough, contained within it some of the early shapers of OD in the UK's healthcare system.

At the creation of the NCB, an acute shortage of high-quality management was evident across the coal industry, made worse by an exodus of a complete level of previously private sector managers at the moment when, because of the

DOI: 10.1201/9781003167310-3

great size of the new undertaking, managerial and administrative talent was seen as being needed as never before [1,2]. At a national level, therefore, a series of appointments were made to key national positions in the NCB. The Chief Economic Adviser was Fritz Schumacher, who later developed the concept of intermediate technology [3] and was the predecessor to, and stimulus towards, later-day challenging economic thinking [4]. The Director of Research was Jacob Bronowski, later the renowned author of a history of science, *The Ascent of Man* [5]. The Director of Education was Reginald Revans, who subsequently went on to develop action learning in a way that linked together employee relations, human relations, technological change and the question of organisational scale with information processing, problem-solving and learning [6]. Revans undertook this role from 1945 to 1950 and worked closely with Fritz Schumacher and with Eric Trist of the Tavistock Institute. He began his NCB role by spending several weeks working at the coalface in a colliery in County Durham.

The NCB as a new organisation was required to increase coal production in order to help the UK recover from the debilitating effects of the Second World War. When faced with this challenge, Revans eschewed the standard staff management training programmes with their learning from experts and lecturers and introduced instead the process which he had found to be so effective in his earlier career in the Cavendish Laboratory at Cambridge University where colleagues "shared their ignorance", worked together on problems and moved beyond textbook learning into those areas of work where there were no experts and no prefabricated answers. The process encouraged twenty-two local pit managers in the coal industry to research their own problems as encountered in their pits and then to meet together in small groups in order to share their experience, ask each other penetrating questions and so learn with and from each other [7]. As a result of this application of what might be termed proto-action learning, productivity in the coal industry increased by some 30% in the period from the 1940s to the 1960s [8] and the safety record improved significantly.

Finally, the NCB's Director of Staff Training was one Duncan Smith who was to be an early seminal figure in the development of OD in the NHS. Smith worked closely with Revans to employ the use of these early forms of action learning as part of the transformation of the NCB into a modern coal industry, which consistently then featured excellent employee relations until the eventual advent in the UK of cheap natural gas as a competitive energy source and later of privatisation of the industry.

The UK's Wilson Government, which began in 1964, ushered in a further period of innovation. It attempted to respond to the "What's Wrong with Britain" critique which had developed in the early 1960s [9] and the promised "white heat of technology" emphasised the importance of science, technical expertise and management. Wilson's Government was keen to support scientific advancement and professionalism in both public and private sectors [10]. Among the manifestations of this were the Fulton Report of 1968 on the UK's Civil Service and the Salmon Report of 1966 which created a hierarchical nursing management structure in the NHS for the first time.

Against this backdrop, in 1965, Duncan Smith was appointed to the Department of Health and Social Security (DHSS) as a researcher investigating the training needs of hospital porters, cleaners and other poorly paid staff. The eventual success of this work was then instrumental in his next appointment as Principal Training Officer in the DHSS in 1968 and then as Chief Training Officer in 1972. He remained in this post until his retirement in 1976, but his term in office was important for the introduction of two important development programmes in 1973–1974, Training of Training Officers (TOTO) and Training of Personnel Officers (TOPO), both of which were provided by an external consultancy agency, Industrial Training Service (ITS), and had a strong OD orientation.

Also central to this period was the Hospital Internal Communications (HIC) action research project which ran from 1965 to 1968. This was probably the first large-scale OD intervention initiated in the NHS, although the term "OD" was still not in common use. The ten London teaching hospitals concerned had experienced a set of common problems – high nursing staff turnover rates, high patient mortality rates, long hospital stays and demoralised staff. Designed and led by Reg Revans, the project aimed to improve communications, morale and performance in the participating hospitals. Revans' earlier operational research studies in hospitals using techniques of direct observation and statistical analysis had found that low morale, especially in the nursing profession, was associated with communication problems [11]. This operational research focus to addressing organisational problems fitted in well with the ideal of scientific professionalism promulgated by the Wilson Government. The HIC was therefore based on the extensive use of attitude surveys and on the pursuing of change through self-help teams [12].

Each hospital in the project nominated a two-tier team – a senior or supporting team of three (a hospital nursing matron, a senior administrator and a medical consultant) and a junior or operational team (a deputy matron, administrator and medical registrar or consultant). The operational teams, having received four weeks of training in data collection and survey methods, instead of addressing problems in their own hospital, addressed problems in one of the other hospitals, so that each hospital had a team drawn from elsewhere working on their issues. Learning across the participating hospitals was arranged via project meetings involving all of the ten participating organisations [13].

Thirty-eight projects were tackled over the three years of the project's duration. Many of the individual hospital projects involved a greater degree of close consultation and cooperation between medical, nursing and other staff [14]. The approach adopted was to collect data, write a report and then take action on the report. Action was taken on over 50% of projects, with the remainder not getting beyond the report stage [15]. Evaluation of the project in 1980–1981 by US academics demonstrated significant improvements over and above what might have been expected to occur "naturally" and a total cost-saving of US$5 million (or £2.47 million) over the project's duration was calculated [16]. The evaluation results also included reductions in the length of patient stay, improved employee morale, reduced staff turnover and improved communications. When the participants returned to their own hospitals, they took their insights with them and then applied them locally. Additionally, there was a major improvement in the self-confidence of all participants. While the HIC project evinced both successes and failures [12], from the perspective of the evolution of OD in healthcare it emphasised:

- ◼ A rejection of a theory-led and top-down approach to organisational change and a preference instead for a form of "bottom-up" or "inside-out" organisational learning.
- ◼ An early indication of the many problems associated with such large-scale and "programmatic" organisational change and renewal projects [17].
- ◼ The need to give the learning from the project an equal status with the taking of action, and hence the need, on the one hand, for early investment in the education and training necessary to equip the project participants with the requisite expertise, and on the other, with the building-in of adequate time, space and support in order to discuss questions and address concerns on the part of the operational teams – and hence to capture and spread the learning.
- ◼ The need for continuing and sustained interest and support from the senior management in the participating organisations.
- ◼ The importance of adequate "steering" arrangements to tie together the disparate activities and to promote the shared learning.

Following the HIC project, a further **action research/action learning project concerned with coordination of services for people with learning disabilities** took place between 1969 and 1972 across seven local authorities and associated hospitals [10]. This followed a number of high-profile scandals across this field in the 1950s and 1960s in both hospital and social care services which led to a number of official inquiries and to recommendations for change and improvement. These inquiries produced very similar findings on such aspects as the disempowerment of professional staff, inadequate leadership, ineffective systems and processes and poor communication [18]. The project, once again led by Revans, involved over a hundred patients, parents, clinical professionals in hospital and community settings, social care professionals, administrators and statutory and voluntary organisations. Data was gathered from six sets of questionnaires, and the resulting analysis was used to promote discussion amongst the care providers [19].

Among the challenges which the project encountered were:

A minority of professionals who felt that the project researchers alone should do the work, rather than those who were working in the field.

A degree of complacency among those professional and administrative staff who saw little or no need for any evaluation or review of their services.

A strong sense of managerial and professional hierarchy which felt that the involvement and voice of more junior staff would only serve to "weaken authority".

Defensiveness and an emotional attachment to more established ways of doing things.

An official national policy stance which did not recognise the pressing need for change in the learning disabilities field.

Nevertheless, the project recorded a number of quite specific positive outcomes, including a greater sharing of knowledge and expertise between professionals, administrators and families; a major overhaul of record-keeping and referral procedures; the identification of the need for training programmes for service providers; generally improved levels of cooperation and coordination and a better understanding of the various roles of organisations and individuals. It also identified a series of emerging needs, such as to equip the staff concerned with the analytic tools needed in order to carry out their own service investigations and evaluations; to foster a more honest sharing of any "chronicles of failure" and to encourage a climate of openness in which the urge to speak out and challenge what was already known and believed was more fully supported [20]. This project was also influential in stimulating further project work in the same learning disabilities field [21].

In OD terms, the project was significant in that it emphasised that those who were working in the learning disabilities field – the service providers, together with the service users – should design, conduct and evaluate the search for improvements in their services. This illustrated a major movement away from the earlier operational research and quantitatively based approach and towards a more participative path which placed equal value on qualitative and subjective data. There was a growing recognition that the issues which OD addressed in healthcare were often "wicked" problems [22] that crossed both professional and organisational boundaries and which were not solvable by statistical analysis, scientific professionalism and reasoning alone. Wicked problems were fundamentally social (and often paradoxical) in nature and so were not susceptible to being worked on by the rational-empirical scientific method [23] which the original operational research orientation had embodied.

Meanwhile, in Sheffield in the early 1970s something was stirring. The Regional Training Officer of the Sheffield Regional Hospital Board (SRHB) – an organisation serving a population of about 4.5 million people – was strongly influenced by psychodynamic insights drawn from the work of the Tavistock Institute of Human Relations and attempted to incorporate these into regional management training programmes run across a geographical area covering South Yorkshire and the East Midlands. Unfortunately, this initiative was extremely countercultural to the local mainstream healthcare culture of the time and the training staff concerned were moved sideways to a Special Schemes Training Unit and tasked instead to run national training programmes for staff in hospital support services. A mainstream administrator was then appointed to the Regional Training Officer role as a "safe pair of hands" and the education and training provision reverted to more conventional and didactic lines.

Nevertheless, the zeitgeist of the times could not be completely denied [24]. In both the education and training and the management services work of the SRHB, important developments did occur in the early 1970s. In the former, management training programmes targeted at healthcare middle managers were contracted out for delivery to a local Polytechnic and the academic staff delivering the programmes introduced a variety of experiential training methods into their design and delivery, something which was also initially viewed as being somewhat countercultural by mainstream healthcare management and by many of the clinical professionals who were participants in the programmes, although this view gradually softened over time.

In the management services field, as early as 1967, there had been evidence of a growing interest in the seeking of the participation of front-line staff in striving for productivity improvements and in the early 1970s a post of Management by Objectives (MBO) Adviser was created, in the light of interest in MBO by senior SRHB management. In 1972 and 1973, the same local Polytechnic ran project management training courses for work study team leaders and began an OD intervention in the Management Services Division of the SRHB. During 1973, some persuasive writing by the MBO Adviser on the practical difficulties he had experienced in undertaking his role and the need for the development of a more comprehensive OD approach led to the creation in 1973 of three OD Adviser posts based within the management services function. One Adviser came from a work study background, another had been a computer systems analyst and the third had previously worked in the management training field.

In 1974, representatives of both the education and training and management services functions of the newly created organisational successor to the SRHB – the Trent Regional Health Authority (TRHA) – attended a nationally run training programme on OD, together with staff of the DHSS training function. This then stimulated internal action in the form of a seminar for the senior management team of the TRHA focused on the nature and role of OD in healthcare. This event was designed and delivered by the external ITS consultancy working with the internal OD Advisers. Following the seminar, it was decided to bring together all the interested parties in TRHA to form an OD Advisory Team (ODAT) to promote and monitor OD work. Recognising the need for investment in the newly created resource, the TRHA decided to sponsor and pay for the attendance of the three OD Advisers on a two-year Master of Science programme in OD at the local Polytechnic, and from 1975 to 1977, the three individuals concerned engaged in a course of study and the resulting project work for their dissertations. It is worth noting that in the mid-1970s, there was no recognisable OD career pathway, so this action was entirely exploratory for the three individuals concerned, as well as for their employing organisation. Subsequently, the OD Advisers were designated, from 1977, as the OD Unit, and the life of this group is the subject of Chapter 4 [25].

The OD Advisers were strongly influenced by the humanistic ethos of the times – seeking to go beyond the need to make both public and private sector bureaucracies "work better" [26]; were strongly influenced by the Addison-Wesley series of OD books emerging from the USA, the client-centred and non-directive themes of unconditional positive regard in the writings of Carl Rogers [27] and by Revans' work on action learning in healthcare [28]. They viewed themselves as essentially process consultants, where process consultation was seen as:

> The creation of a relationship with the client that permits the client to perceive, understand and act on the events that occur in the client's internal and external environment in order to improve the situation, as defined by the client. [29]

Process consultation was based on the assumption that all organisational problems were fundamentally problems involving human interactions and processes. Learning and change were seen as being interrelated – the client had to learn about themselves and their organisation before they could change it. In order to assist in this, the OD practitioner had to establish a dialogue that allowed the client to explore their situation and learn more about it.

As a result, a description of the OD Unit and its work produced in these years concluded that:

> Members of the Unit help client organisations to diagnose organisational problems, identify development needs and the form that changes might take, and assist in the implementation of these changes. [30]

This description adheres closely to the picture of early OD as outlined in Chapter 1.

The Trent healthcare region was not the only part of the NHS interested in OD, although such interest was largely confined to the NHS in England, with the system in other parts of the UK – Scotland, Wales and Northern Ireland – simply watching on such developments with a growing interest. Indeed, it was not until the mid-1980s that another major OD intervention took place at the Grampian Health Board in Scotland and, while this did involve the use of an external management consultancy, it also featured the recruitment and development of a group of internal change agents [31]. In the Wessex healthcare region of England, the Regional Personnel Officer and the Regional Training Officer were also both equally concerned with fostering attention on the importance of the management of change during the mid-1970s and early 1980s.

At a national level, one part of the legacy of Duncan Smith after his retirement was the creation of a Training Advisory Group (TAG) in the DHSS which worked with NHS "field" organisations in a collaborative manner and which reported to a National Training Council (NTC). Central to the enhancement of OD was the appointment by the newly appointed Chief Training Officer, Geoff Perkins, of Dr Michael Walton, a development-minded former NHS personnel manager to the TAG in 1979. Dr Walton had a remit which centred on management education and training. Part of that remit included oversight of the "National Education Centres" – a number of university centres which delivered management development programmes targeted at senior NHS managers. The NTC had a subcommittee – the Standing Committee on Management Education and Training (SCMET) – which had already decided in 1978 that it wished to review "organisation-based management training", by which they meant those training and development activities for managers which took place within healthcare organisations as opposed to those which took place externally on management training courses.

Accordingly, and orchestrated by Dr Walton, a **working conference on organisation-based management training in the NHS** took place in October 1979 and which can, with hindsight, be recognised as the point at which OD began to have a higher profile in the NHS, although the term "OD" was still not yet in widespread use. The three-day event, in which over sixty key people drawn from across the NHS in England participated, had as its objectives:

To hear at first hand details of some of the organisation-based training initiatives being undertaken within the NHS.

To enable the process of informing the NHS of such activities and the emerging alternatives to course-based training.

To inform the SCMET members about such developments.

The conference had a keynote address given by Professor Elliott Jaques, whose work had strongly influenced the most recent 1974 reorganisation of the NHS [26,32] and whose concepts remained highly influential. Among the accounts of practice which the conference featured were those of teamwork development for senior management teams and primary healthcare teams, the application in healthcare of action learning and the developing work of the Trent Regional Health Authority OD Unit [33].

From this point on OD began to exhibit an increasingly higher profile in healthcare, and national conferences played a major part in this process. Lancaster University's Department of Management Learning ran a series of annual conferences on education and development in organisations from 1980 onwards and the NHS itself began a series of National Trainers' Conventions which ran from 1983 to 1989. These events all regularly featured examples of OD work. A UK-wide OD Network, which originated with OD practitioners drawn from the multinational company, Imperial Chemical Industries (ICI) (at the time the largest single manufacturer in Britain), was active both nationally and locally, especially in both South Yorkshire and Wessex, with NHS OD practitioners being prominent and active members, including on the national coordinating executive. One of the Trent OD Advisers became the editor of the Network's monthly newsletter.

These developments highlight that the stimuli for moving towards OD in healthcare were not confined solely to the education and training function but also grew out of management services activity, including work study and MBO.

The innovative activity which led to OD's emergence largely came from needs expressed from the front line – from those organisations which were concerned with the planning and delivery of healthcare – rather than being cascaded in a centralised and top-down manner from a Government department.

There was anxiety about what OD was or might be from both mainstream healthcare management and clinical professionals. It is noteworthy, for example, that the Trent Regional Health Authority OD practitioners were known as "Advisers", rather than consultants, not least because the term "consultant" was confined to senior hospital doctors. Likewise, the term "organisation-based management training" was deemed to be safer than the term "Organisation Development", which may have been perceived as something radical and possibly scary – and certainly as being new and countercultural. The creation of an OD "Advisory Team" to monitor OD activity was perhaps indicative of the prevalent hesitancy. This hesitancy may have represented a form of "organisational drag" – of entering backwards into the future with eyes fixed firmly on the way that things were conducted in both the recent past and the present – rather than envisioning and anticipating what the future might hold or need.

Key individuals such as Duncan Smith and Dr Michael Walton played a crucial role in fostering the emergence of OD in the NHS, being located in position at the right place and at the right time to purposefully influence events. Despite the prevalent anxiety, brave decisions were made to invest in the venture of training of OD practitioners at Master's degree level.

However, as the 1980s turned into the 1990s, a major change took place within OD in healthcare in the UK. As the profile of OD gradually rose, a multitude of people across the healthcare system in the UK now claimed to be "doing OD", as Human Resources Directors re-badged themselves as Directors of Human Resources and OD and many Training Officers did likewise, now calling themselves OD Managers [34].

Historically condescended to as junior partners by their Director peers in charge of core corporate functions, such as Medicine, Nursing and Finance, Human Resource Directors saw the opportunity to now "get a seat at the top table" and to extend their remit away from their traditional regulatory and legalistic work areas like employee relations and workforce planning and towards leadership and management development activity, and then towards OD. In this they were often inspired by the putative "war for talent" which was popularised by the management consultants McKinsey [35] and by the creation and influence in the mid-1980s of a national (for England) NHS Training Authority, with an emphasis on management development and vocational training (because clinical professional education was considered to be a "sacred grove" and not to be included in the remit).

The renaming of the former Personnel function which took place at this time as "Human Resources" and the re-titling of people working in the function as "Human Resource Business Partners" indicated that the people who were working within healthcare organisations were now increasingly regarded as a cost and the entire evolving performance management system was seen as a means of minimising such a cost and of maximising what could be extracted from the remaining "resource". As part of this sea change, staff and their salaries, together with their education and training, were seen as a burden to be at least challenged, and possibly shrunk, rather than an asset to be developed. Despite the stark philosophic differences between the developmental orientation of OD, with its behavioural science roots, process orientation and long-term focus on the one hand, and the more regulatory mandate of the Human Resource function, content-driven with its developing short-term "business" orientation [36,37], OD gradually became colonised by the Human Resource function and became increasingly concerned solely with conformist innovation [38]. As one commentator at the time asserted:

> Human Resources should be defined by what it delivers – results that enrich the organisation's value to customers, investors and employees. [39]

Yet another observer commented that:

> The HR function is monopolising the OD function at an unprecedented pace, blunting effectiveness and compromising the role. [37]

The emergence of OD in healthcare in the UK was clearly part of the second modernity mentioned in Chapter 2. Kershaw [40] posits the development of a third modernity in which the spirit of the age is that of "post-modernism", marked by a transition from a society which was previously dominated by industry to one which is increasingly shaped by information technology. This third modernity challenges the belief that there is an objective reality which is independent of the observer. Rather, it claims that reality is an illusion constructed by the human mind and can never therefore be described objectively. It asserts that all knowledge is insecure because it is historically contingent; that there are no verifiable truths because the things that we think that we know now might well be proven wrong later, just as things that people thought that they knew for certain in the past (such as the legitimacy of slavery or eugenics) might now seem wrong, odd or simply illogical. All meaning, words and action, post-modernism asserts, arise in social contexts and so cannot be separated from them. The "truths" that we believe that we know about the world are shaped by who we are and by the particular societies and times that we live in.

Post-modernism is characterised by a general distrust of grand theories, narratives and ideologies that attempt to put all knowledge into a single framework – and so should be abandoned. It is signified by divergence, dissonance, a pluralism of interpretations and the absence of any claim to an authoritative voice. It features an "incredulity towards meta-narratives" [41]. Meta-narratives are overarching single stories that attempt to sum up the whole of human history or put all knowledge into a single frame of reference. In the case of OD, the meta-narrative is the idea that humanity's story is one of progress towards deeper knowledge and enhanced social justice, brought about by greater scientific understanding. Lyotard [41] asserts that knowledge has become disconnected from all questions of truth and is now being judged, not in terms of how true it is, but in terms of how well it serves certain ends. The result is a pervasive knowing sense of scepticism verging on cynicism, relativism, irony, doubt, uncertainty, fragmentation and pastiche, a distrust of truth and a disrespect for evidence. As long ago as the 1970s, Schon [42] anticipated this and labelled it as "epistemological nihilism", a view that nothing is true or can be known or that one opinion is just as good as another [43].

Notions of progress and rationality (both key assumptions of OD), of truth or any single way of grasping where society has come from and where it may be going have, under post-modernism, evaporated or splintered into a myriad of individualistic, subjective approaches or "discourses", none of which can claim superiority over others. Previous dominant discourses are seen to be reflective of the power relations, which were then extant in society. It has involved a collapse of the idea of historical progress into a perpetual present, a constant series of "mash-ups" or a rehashing and recombining of existing ideas, which would claim to put an end to any hope that the future might possibly be radically different from what exists now [44,45], so any attempt at resistance to the present is futile [43]. Higgs [46] contrasts what he terms as the solid ground of the second modernity with the "swamp" or "quicksand" of post-modernism.

Kershaw [40] suggests that this reflects the increasing breakdown of the collective and the dominance of the individualistic in society (and hence also in organisations), typified by the glorification of political strong men and perhaps even also by the journey in organisational life from a concern with management towards a focus on supposedly "transformational" leadership. The rise of the neoliberal ideology mentioned in Chapter 1 has its roots in this post-modern world view. Indeed, Mason [43] has described post-modernism as anti-humanist and the "slave ideology" for neoliberalism because it rationalised the existence of social atomisation and frenzied consumption as being inevitable. The original Enlightenment notion of individualism has been incorporated into this post-modern viewpoint [47] but, despite the individualistic emphasis of this third modernity, Zuboff [48] has asserted that, paradoxically:

> the neoliberal economic paradigm's aim is to reverse, subdue, impede and even destroy the individual urge towards psychological self-determination and moral agency

She claims that the aim of the post-modern/neoliberal project is to contain, rechannel or even reverse the second modernity, where:

> the absolute authority of market forces should be enshrined as the ultimate source of imperative control, displacing democratic contest and deliberation with an ideology of atomised individuals sentenced to perpetual competition for scarce resources. The discipline of competitive markets promises to quiet unruly individuals and even transform them back into subjects too preoccupied with survival to complain.

As an example of where this sense of direction leads, in the late 1990s, it was confidently predicted that:

Lifetime adult employment would gradually disappear as jobs increasingly became a series of discrete tasks rather than managerial positions or professional roles.

Many members of professions (including the clinical professions) would be replaced by interactive information-retrieval systems. (A precursor of developments in artificial intelligence or AI).

There would be a decline in the status and power of the more traditional political and economic elites, as well as a diminution in the respect accorded to the symbols and beliefs that justified the individual nation state.

There would be a growing popular hatred of the information elite, rich people and the well-educated and increasing complaints about disappearing jobs [49].

This view sees any form of government or collective activity as a brake on personal ambition and success. It regards "welfare" as something that the rich are forced to fund for the less bright, less successful and less ambitious. It maintains that Governments would increasingly be forced to do less and less and that what they would still do would be done more and more according to the values of the market. Governments would treat people as "customers", rather than as citizens, and market forces, rather than political majorities, would compel societies to reconfigure themselves in ways that public opinion would neither comprehend nor welcome. Such changes, it suggested, were immutable. Social democracy, which marked many of those changes embodied in the second modernity, was seen as an anachronism, "as much an artefact of industrialisation as a rusting smokestack". Such a perspective would have no interest in, or time for, OD, unless it was seen as a means of advancing this direction of travel.

References

1. Hennessy, P. (1992) *Never Again: Britain 1945–51*, London: Jonathan Cape.
2. Kynaston, D. (2007) *Austerity Britain: 1945–51*, London: Bloomsbury Publishing.
3. Schumacher, F. (1973) *Small is Beautiful: A Study of Economics as if People Mattered*, London: Blond and Briggs.
4. Raworth, K. (2017) *Doughnut Economics: Seven Ways to Think Like a 21st Century Economist*, London: Random House Business Books.
5. Bronowski, J. (1973) *The Ascent of Man*, London: British Broadcasting Corporation.
6. Lessem, R. (1982) A Biography of Action Learning, in Revans, R. (Ed.) *The Origins and Growth of Action Learning*, Bromley: Chartwell-Bratt, 4–17.
7. Revans, R. (1982a) A Consortium of Pitmen, in Revans, R. (Ed.) *The Origins and Growth of Action Learning*, Bromley: Chartwell-Bratt, 39–55.

8. DBEIS (2013) *Coal Data: Coal Production, Availability and Consumption*, London: Department of Business, Energy and Industrial Strategy.
9. Hennessy, P. (2019) *Winds of Change: Britain in the Early Sixties*, London: Allen Lane.
10. Brook, C. (2020) An Instrument of Social Action: Revans' Learning Disabilities Project (1969–1972) in a Politico-Historical Context, *Action Learning: Research and Practice*, 17 (3): 292–304.
11. Revans, R. (1964) *Standards for Morale: Cause and Effect in Hospitals*, London: Nuffield Provincial Hospitals Trust.
12. Pedler, M. (2006) Review of Organisational Change in Hospitals: The Hospital Internal Communications Project, 1965–68, *Action Learning: Research and Practice*, 3 (1): 107–122.
13. Revans, R. (1982b) Action Learning Takes a Health Cure, in Revans, R. (Ed.) *The Origins and Growth of Action Learning*, Bromley: Chartwell-Bratt, 272–279.
14. Leigh, H., Weiland, G. and Anderson, J. (1971) The Hospital Internal Communication Project, *The Lancet*, 297 (7707): 1005–1009.
15. Wieland, G. and Leigh, H. (Ed.) (1971) *Changing Hospitals: A Report on the Hospital Internal Communications Project*, London: Tavistock Publications.
16. Weiland, G. (1981) *Improving Health Care Management: Organisation Development and Organisation Change*, Ann Arbor, MI, Health Administration Press.
17. Beer, M., Eisenstadt, R. and Spector, B. (1990) *The Critical Path to Corporate Renewal*, Boston, MA: Harvard Business School Press.
18. Powell, M. (2019) Learning from NHS Inquiries: Comparing the Ely, Bristol and Mid-Staffordshire Inquiries, *The Political Quarterly*, 90 (2): 229–237.
19. Revans, R. (1982c) Helping Each Other to Help the Helpless, in Revans, R. (Ed.) *The Origins and Growth of Action Learning*, Bromley: Chartwell-Bratt.
20. Revans, R. and Baquer, A. (1972) *I Thought They Were Supposed to be Doing That: A Comparative Study of Coordination of Services for the Mentally Handicapped in Seven Local Authorities, June, 1969 to September, 1972*, London: Kings Fund.
21. Collin, A. and Sturt, J. (1978) *Report Of An Evaluation Study Of An Action Learning Project In Hospitals For The Mentally Handicapped, North Derbyshire Health District*, Sheffield, Trent Regional Health Authority Organisation Development Unit.
22. Grint, K. (2008) Wicked Problems and Clumsy Solutions: The Role of Leadership, *Clinical Leader*, 1 (2): 54–68.
23. Sarason, S. (1978) The Nature of Problem-Solving in Social Action, *American Psychologist*, 33 (4): 370–380.
24. Berkowitz, E. (2006) *Something Happened: A Political and Cultural Overview of the Seventies*, New York: Columbia University Press.
25. Edmonstone, J. (1989) Return to Go: Renewal Processes in an Internal Organisation Development Unit, *Industrial and Commercial Training*, 21 (6): 26–30.
26. Jaques, E. (1976) *A General Theory of Bureaucracy*, London: Heinemann.
27. Rogers, C. (1961) *On Becoming a Person: A Therapist's View of Psychotherapy*, London: Constable.
28. Revans, R. (1976) *Action Learning In Hospitals: Diagnosis And Therapy*, Maidenhead, McGraw-Hill.

29. Schein, E. (1988) *Process Consultation: It's Role in Organisation Development*, Reading, MA: Addison-Wesley.
30. Edmonstone, J. (1979) Leadership in an Organisational Context: An Experiential Learning Design, *Health Services Manpower Review*, 5 (1): 13–16.
31. Mabey, C. and Mallory, G. (1994) Structure and Culture Change in Two UK Organisations: A Comparison of Assumptions, Approaches and Outcomes, *Human Resource Management Journal*, 5 (2): 28–45.
32. Jaques, E. (1978) (Ed.) *Health Services: Their Nature and Organisation and the Role of Patients, Doctors and the Health Professions*, London: Heinemann.
33. Walton, M. (1979) *Proceedings of the Working Conference on Organisation-Based Management Training*, Occasional Paper, National Training Council for the NHS.
34. Edmonstone, J. and Havergal, M. (1995) The Death (and Rebirth?) of Organisation Development, *Health Manpower Management*, 21 (1): 28–33.
35. Michaels, E., Handfield-Jones, H. and Axelrod, B. (2001) *The War for Talent*, Boston, MA: Harvard Business Review Press.
36. Gillon, A. (2016) *Conceptualising Organisation Development: Practitioner and Academic Perspectives: A UK Study*, PhD thesis, Nottingham Trent University.
37. Minahan, M. (2010) OD and HR: Do We Want the Lady or the Tiger? *OD Practitioner*, 42 (4): 17–22.
38. Legge, K. (1978) *Power, Innovation and Problem-Solving in Personnel Management*, Maidenhead: McGraw-Hill.
39. Ulrich, D. (1998) A New Mandate for Human Resources, *Harvard Business Review*, January-February.
40. Kershaw, I. (2019) *Roller-Coaster: Europe 1950–2017*, London: Penguin.
41. Lyotard, J. (1984) *The Postmodern Condition: A Report on Knowledge*, Manchester: Manchester University Press.
42. Schon, D. (1973) *Beyond the Stable State: Public and Private Learning in a Changing Society*, London: Pelican.
43. Mason, P. (2019) *Clear Bright Future: A Radical Defence of the Human Being*, London: Allen Lane.
44. Davies, W. (2020) *This Is Not Normal: The Collapse of Liberal Britain*, London: Verso.
45. Jameson, F. (1991) *Postmodernism, or the Cultural Logic of Late Capitalism*, Durham, NC: Duke University Press.
46. Higgs, J. (2016) *Stranger Than We Can Imagine: Making Sense of the Twentieth Century*, London: Weidenfeld and Nicolson.
47. Soares, C. (2018) The Philosophy of Individualism: A Critical Perspective, *International Journal of Philosophy and Social Values*, 1 (1): 11–34.
48. Zuboff, S. (2019) *The Age of Surveillance Capitalism: The Fight for a Human Future at the New Frontier of Power*, London: Profile Books.
49. Davidson, J. and Rees-Mogg, W. (1997) *The Sovereign Individual: The Coming Economic Revolution and How to Survive and Prosper in It*, London: Simon and Schuster.

Chapter 4

An NHS Case Study: The Trent Regional Health Authority Organisation Development Unit

This chapter is a case study of the first ever internal Organisation Development (OD) Unit ever created in the National Health Service (NHS). It tracks the evolution of this resource over a seventeen-year period, from being an early adopter with ever-present issues of legitimacy, anxiety, the tension between reactive and proactive modes of working and the growing realisation that OD in healthcare was somewhat unique. The eventual demise of the OD Unit is related to the onset of the third modernity.

When the three Trent Regional Health Authority OD Advisers returned to work in 1977 following their immersion in a two-year Masters-level programme in OD, one of them wrote a paper proposing to his colleagues that:

> the creation of an OD Unit would be the next obvious step both to consolidate the work undertaken to date and to prove a sound basis for the development of OD in future years. [1]

DOI: 10.1201/9781003167310-4

A number of reasons were advanced for the proposal. One was to "market" OD to local healthcare organisations in the Trent region of the NHS. It was noted that OD activities were unlikely to be successful if OD was sold to potential clients as a package or a commodity which was intended as a panacea for organisational problems. Yet there was clearly a need to let people know what OD was and what it could do. The concept of "visibility" was eventually adopted – letting the potential clients know of the kind of expertise that was available, the sorts of problems which could be tackled and how to obtain such assistance.

The paper went on to deal with the question of the credibility of the OD Advisers. It was considered to be important for senior people in their employing organisation, the Regional Health Authority, to regard the OD resource as being both legitimate and useful, but it was suggested that such credibility would be enhanced by developing a unique capability or capabilities. This could be achieved by a variety of means, such as developing a high level of skill in a particular area of work, such as teamwork development, or in a specific aspect of healthcare, such as community health services. Noting that the OD Advisers were organisationally located within a management services function, the paper identified that there were few linkages with the Regional Health Authority's education and training function and it was proposed to remedy this.

Agreement was quickly reached on the formation of an OD Unit, but questions were then begged as to the purpose and task of such an entity. The OD Advisers spent a day trying to address these issues in some depth. This was a frustrating and exhausting exercise but did achieve some measure of understanding and an agreement about a limited number of issues. There was, however, an awareness of some conflict over larger questions, such as whether the Unit existed to help healthcare organisations make optimum use of their resources (very much a management services outlook) and whether this made sense in relation to such other change goals as increasing the understanding, choice and control of client organisations over their environment.

The task of the Unit was perceived by the OD Advisers as being an exceedingly difficult one. It had to meet at least some of the conflicting wants and needs of its operating environment in order for it to survive and prosper. An analogy was drawn between the challenge faced by the OD Advisers in reaching an agreement on such matters with the difficulties associated with getting a group of General Medical Practitioners to agree on the purpose and goals of a multi-professional primary health care team. It seemed that the OD Unit was engaged in a new kind of challenge – to create novel and innovative types of intervention for healthcare organisations – and it seemed important to avoid a goal trap and not to force the OD work into a straightjacket of overspecific goal statements which might then inhibit achievement. Rather than a strategy of "comprehensive rationality", the Unit would be best served by one of "disjointed incrementalism" [2] – step-by-step development as an issue unfolded.

One of the core tenets of early OD was to work with whatever emerged from the client organisation in a more holistic manner, which was always contextually dependent. The existence of predefined problems (and predefined intervention methods) therefore seemed to the OD Advisers to be anathema to the very essence of their understanding of OD. The purpose of the Unit thus became one of continually finding and developing common ground between the expressed wants of client organisations (which often varied from what the underlying needs might be), the developing expertise and experience of the OD Advisers themselves and the interests of their employer, the Regional Health Authority, and to use this common ground to move towards trying to realise the needs of all the parties concerned.

Over the next two years (1977–1979), the OD Advisers became heavily involved in a wide range of project work in such areas as the organisation and management of mental health services [3,4], issues of integration and industrial relations in ambulance services [5] and developments in primary health care [6]. In 1979, a further period of reflection and review ensued, aimed at producing a public statement on what OD in the Trent region was and what it could do for potential clients. Perhaps because 1979 was an election year, the terminology used for this statement was a "manifesto". The work on the manifesto revealed some fundamental differences of perspective within the OD Unit. For example, it became clear that all developmental activities in organisations were difficult to relate to the conventional indicators of successful organisational functioning (what later became known as performance indicators), not only because of the problems of measuring results but also because the time-scale for OD often did not mesh with those over which mainstream organisational indicators were measured. OD could therefore be seen as an act of faith in times of relative economic and social buoyancy, but that faith would only be sustained by results reflecting organisational survival and success criteria in the more difficult times.

The manifesto work also revealed distinctive changes in the Unit's aims and methods since its creation. While the OD Advisers view of themselves was still principally one of non-directive, client-centred process consultants with a commitment to developing open, honest and caring communication, the variety of strategies and goals in their work reflected a range of competing organisational realities in the NHS. The Unit had explicitly recognised the need for political support and safety and had developed strategies of action research and networking as part of a change towards operating as links in a wider network of influence, rather than only on a one-to-one client–consultant model. This change involved greater interdependence, and the

OD Advisers found this somewhat challenging, given a history of independence in relation to clients, type of project and choice of methods.

One useful conceptual model which emerged from this process was that of the "three-legged stool". The management services base and the process consultant role contained notions of working which were essentially reactive in nature. By the late 1970s, consultancy work had led the OD Unit to develop a number of useful ideas, especially related to the human aspects associated with the commissioning of new district general hospitals, which the OD Advisers desired to test out in an action research mode. They had also accumulated learning on healthcare organisations which they felt would be useful to share with others in the NHS. This prompted a move towards becoming more proactive and an expansion of action research and training activity as a complement to consultancy projects. OD work was thus conceived as involving three aspects, the three legs to the stool – consultancy, action research and training – in some unspecified and changeable mix.

By 1981, the development of an action research role seemed an even more significant turning point. In retrospect, the continuing lack of a productive relationship with the Regional Health Authority's education and training function was seen as instrumental in confining the Unit to reactive consultancy in its early years of existence. There was now, however, a growing interest in the Unit as a national, rather than just a regional, training resource and this effectively by-passed the local deadlock. A national NHS restructuring exercise in 1982 not only produced greater involvement of the OD Unit by the Regional Health Authority on a range of policy issues but also produced "restructuring blight" in relation to local consultancy work.

Once again the OD Advisers took time out to reflect on its present and future role, this time using two pieces of OD technology. The first involved the use of the open systems planning approach [7] in order to map out the key environmental factors impinging on the NHS in general and the OD Unit in particular. Among the predictions which this exercise made for the NHS in the 1980s was the effect of increased unemployment, reduced funding available for healthcare and a growing political perception of welfare services as a burden on the employed. An increased critique of professions was predicted and an accentuation of social conflict was forecast. In terms of the OD Unit over the next period, less experimentation and risk-taking were predicted and more clients were forecast as coming from outside the Trent region. Moreover, the OD literature was now perceived, at least in part, as being somewhat misleading and related more to the problems of industrial and commercial enterprises and less to those of human services organisations [8]. Its derivation from OD practice in the USA did not automatically mesh with the lived experience of undertaking OD work in a UK healthcare context. Overall, the day spent on mapping the future was a fairly gloomy one, particularly when once again the OD Advisers were unable to agree on a single core process for the Unit.

Shortly afterwards a further review, this time using the demands, constraints and choices model [9] was undertaken. While this was more successful in agreeing on some immediate next steps, it also revealed a desire on the part of the OD Advisers to work towards greater congruence in terms of purpose and visibility, while working methods and desired outcomes of the work were more likely to remain as individual matters.

Around this time, there were doubts raised at a national policy level over the continuing existence of the Regional Health Authorities themselves. The idea of charging or cross-charging for services was also being mooted, and the OD Unit was seen to be an obvious candidate for a more commercial approach. As a result, once again a number of options for the future development of the Unit were opened up, including an internal transfer from the management services to the Human Resource function within the Regional Health Authority; a location in the newly created national NHS Training Authority or a relocation to an academic base in higher education. There was also the "do nothing" option. None of these options were ultimately taken up.

In 1983, one of the original three OD Advisers departed to take up a role as Regional Training Manager with another Regional Health Authority. In Trent region, a new Regional Training Manager with a previously successful career track record in the management development field was appointed by the Regional Health Authority. He fairly quickly created within his structure two posts of Management Development Adviser and thus established what was seen to be potentially a rival grouping to the OD Unit. A form of financial discipline was then imposed on the OD Advisers with the requirement to recover at least part of their costs by charging for their services. They were also (and finally) retitled as OD consultants. In 1986, the OD consultant resource was merged with that of the Management Development Advisers to form a Management and Organisation Development Unit (MODU), accountable to the Regional Training Manager and located in the Human Resource function. This was part of a wider trend for OD and management development to be treated as if they were a single entity [10].

Another national reform of the NHS was initiated by the "Working for Patients" White Paper [11], which resulted in the creation of a split between the purchasers or commissioners of healthcare services and the operational providers of those services – the creation of an internal market in healthcare. Functions were to be delegated to the lowest possible local organisational level, and this meant that the Management and OD Unit was now transferred from a regional position to a local District Health Authority (DHA). The role and activity of the Management and OD Unit was not perceived as being central to the purchaser role which the DHA was then assuming, so in 1990, the budget and some of the staff of the Management and OD Unit were transferred into the Centre for Professional and Organisational Development at Sheffield Hallam University, while the remaining two of the original OD Advisers were given an early retirement package.

What lessons can be learnt from this pioneering seventeen-year experience?

The Trent Regional Health Authority was an early adopter [12] of OD in the NHS, and there were therefore no significant previous role models for the employing organisation and for the OD Advisers themselves to follow. The literature sources that were available to them were largely derived from experience in industrial and commercial enterprises, mostly in the USA, and the learning available from previous UK healthcare OD exercises such as the HIC project (see Chapter 3) was limited. Similarly, the Masters programme that the OD Advisers had followed also relied significantly on USA-sourced material. As a result, continuing individual and shared group concern on the part of the OD Advisers and anxiety on the part of their employing organisation were major features across the seventeen-year existence of the OD Unit. This was perhaps an early example of the imposter syndrome in practice [13] – feelings of inadequacy on the part of the OD Advisers that persisted despite evidence of successful activity, leading to continuing self-doubt and a sense of intellectual fraudulence that overrode any feelings of success or external proof of competence. However, recent research [14] suggests that people who experience such imposter syndrome are also encouraged to improve their interpersonal behaviour, through listening well and collaborating and, through demonstrating extra effort, are spurred to improve their performance.

This meant that the question of the legitimacy of OD was a perennial issue, given that, at that time, it appeared to many to be countercultural to the mainstream of both healthcare management on the one hand and to the ongoing concerns of the clinical professions on the other. While in practice the OD Advisers themselves believed that they effectively straddled the line between conformist and deviant innovation [15], they were largely viewed as being located in the latter by both healthcare managers and clinical professionals. The anxiety and concerns of healthcare managers were particularly manifested in the preference for the term organisation-based management training rather than OD and by the creation of an OD Advisory Team to "monitor" the work of the OD Advisers. The worries of the OD Advisory Team were obvious in the nomenclature which they insisted be used to describe the OD practitioner role – an adviser, rather than a consultant – because the only consultants in a healthcare setting were deemed to be senior hospital doctors.

This meant that the credibility of the OD Advisers had to be grown from the work which they undertook with their clients and from the ways in which learning from this was captured, recorded and publicised. Issues of visibility and the marketing of OD and of the OD Unit were therefore constantly on the agenda, as was the most appropriate location or base for work of this kind. This vulnerability was eased to an extent by the networking linkages established by the OD Advisers with the DHSS nationally and with emergent interested parties elsewhere in the healthcare system and in higher education, by the publicising of their work through the writing of journal articles and by conference presentations, although this, in turn, produced certain tensions within the OD Unit, between "locals" and "cosmopolitans" [16] with the former emphasising loyalty to the existing and prevailing organisational culture and the latter highlighting the importance of more humanistic values and of external networking and publicising.

The career background of the OD Advisers was both a positive and a negative factor in the OD Unit's development. There was a continuing dynamic tension between the management services background of two of the Advisers (placing an emphasis on formal systems and structures) and the education and training background of the third (emphasising people issues). There was perhaps also a more fundamental divergence between those individuals subscribing to a "functionalist" view of society and organisations and those adhering to more radical interpretations [17]. These differences emerged in the continuing search for a common agreed purpose or core process for the Unit. While the tension between the OD Advisers was one element of this, the others were the expressed needs and wants of the healthcare clients that the Advisers were working with and the views of their employer – the Regional Health Authority. On reflection, what the OD Advisers undertook in practice was to establish a "working path" [18] – that is, just getting on with some joint actions without fully agreeing on any ultimate purpose or aims, not least because, in practice, it may not always be possible to get complete agreement on such matters at the outset or even on the way. The OD Advisers implicitly agreed to walk together without agreement on a final destination, not least because the path that they were following was likely to change over time as they learnt more and found new ways to do things. The shared endeavour was the journey. This involved the pursuit of an iterative reflexive process, similar to that of Kolb's learning cycle [19] as shown in Figure 4.1. Parallels were also drawn by the OD Advisers themselves with the movement around a Monopoly board, so much so that an earlier account of the OD Unit's journey was titled "Return To Go" [1].

There were continuing tensions between the concerns of OD with real and sustained, rather than rapid and cosmetic, change and a recognition that such change necessarily took a long time to achieve. This was set against a rapidly changing political, economic and social backdrop which increasingly valued quick results and was sceptical about commitment to any longer-term and continuous investment of resource, time and effort.

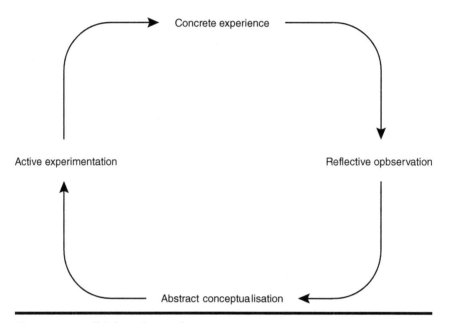

Figure 4.1 Kolb's learning cycle.

Likewise, there was a continuing dynamic between the initial reactive process consultancy role which had been adopted by the OD Advisers and the gradual accumulation of experience and learning in particular areas of work, which led to demands from clients on the one hand and from within the Advisers themselves on the other, to move towards a more proactive, perhaps even a more "expert" stance. One example of this was work undertaken by the OD Advisers on the human and organisational aspects associated with the commissioning of new District General Hospitals, which led to a published journal article on the topic and a series of innovative national workshops for local commissioning teams run at the NHS Training and Studies Centre in Harrogate [20].

The relationship between the OD Unit and the Regional Health Authority's education and training function continued to be problematic for over half of the seventeen years of the Unit's existence. This was perhaps indicative of an inability or unwillingness on the part of the Regional Health Authority as an employer to address this perennial issue, as well as of defensive and competitive behaviour on the part of both the OD Unit members and those who were employed in the education and training resource. The issue was finally resolved by the eventual creation of a Management and OD Unit which absorbed the original OD Unit.

The OD Advisers came to realise, over time and in the light of experience, that OD work in healthcare was somewhat different from that in most other kinds of organisations, given that healthcare was a human service [21] and that people working in healthcare (especially the clinical professionals) were subject to "emotional labour" [22], unlike those in more conventional employment. The work of Revans [23] in describing a hospital as an "institution cradled in anxiety" and of Menzies Lyth [24] in identifying how social systems in healthcare operated as a defence against such anxiety was key here. Gillon [10] noted that the US scholars and practitioners had largely dominated both thinking and practice in early OD but that increasingly their rhetoric did not reflect the emerging nature of OD in the UK – and this was experienced by the OD Advisers as being especially true in the healthcare field.

Finally, the importance of the political, economic and social context against which the creation, development and demise of the OD Unit took place is vital for understanding and learning from this experience. As the Chapter 3 indicated, the roots of OD lay within the second post-war modernity, but as the 1970s became the 1980s, the spread of neoliberal ideas into healthcare, marked nationally by the concept of the internal market in the NHS and the requirement to charge for OD services which had previously been available at no cost to clients, was indicative of the changing times. The ideas of progress and improvement and the ability to plan organisational change which were originally central to OD seemed anathema to the post-modern third modernity which emphasised divergence, dissonance, a pluralism of interpretations and the absence of any claim to any authoritative voice.

References

1. Edmonstone, J. (1989) Return to Go: Renewal Processes in an Internal Organisation Development Unit, *Industrial and Commercial Training*, 21 (6): 26–30.
2. Lindblom, C. (1959) The Science of "Muddling Through", *Public Administration Quarterly*, 19: 79–88.
3. Edmonstone, J. (1979) OD In Health Care: The Special Problems Of The Psychiatric Hospital, *ODMAG: Journal of the UK OD Network* (June).
4. Edmonstone, J. (1980) Changing Hospital Organisation Using Outside Consultants: Evaluation Of One Example, *Hospital and Health Services Review*, (January).
5. Collin, A. (1979) An Outsider's View of the Ambulance Service, in *Need for an Ambulance: Purpose, Provision and Use of the Out-Patient Ambulance Service*, National Corporation for the Care of Old People.
6. Sturt, J. (1980) So What About the Workers? *Health and Social Services Journal*, 11th January.
7. Kleiner, B. (1986) Open Systems Planning: Its Theory and Practice, *Behavioural Science*, 31 (3): 189–204.

8. Edmonstone, J. (1982) Human Service Organisations: Implications For Management And Organisation Development, *Management Education and Development*, 13 (3) (Autumn).

9. Stewart, R. (1982) *Choice for the Manager: A Guide to Managerial Work and Behaviour*, Englewood Cliffs, NJ: Prentice-Hall.

10. Gillon, A. (2016) *Conceptualising Organisation Development: Practitioner and Academic Perspectives: A UK Study*, PhD thesis, Nottingham Trent University.

11. Department of Health and Social Security (1989) *Working for Patients*, London: HMSO.

12. Rogers, E. (1962) *Diffusion of Innovation*, New York: Macmillan.

13. Langford, J. and Clance, P. (1993) The Imposter Phenomenon: Recent Research Findings Regarding Dynamics, Personality and Family Patterns and their Implications for Treatment, *Psychotherapy: Theory, Research, Practice, Training*, 30 (3): 495–501.

14. Tewfik, B. (2019) *Imposter Thoughts as a Double-Edged Sword: Theoretical Conceptualisation, Construct Measurement and Relationships with Work-Related Outcomes*, PhD dissertation, Wharton School, University of Pennsylvania.

15. Legge, K. (1978) *Power, Innovation and Problem-Solving in Personnel Management*, Maidenhead: McGraw-Hill.

16. Gouldner, A. (1957) Cosmopolitans and Locals: Towards an Analysis of Latent Social Roles, *Administrative Science Quarterly*, 2 (3): 281–306.

17. Burrell, G. and Morgan, G. (1979) *Sociological Paradigms and Organisational Analysis*, London: Heinemann.

18. Huxham, C. and Vangen, S. (2005) *Managing to Collaborate: The Theory and Practice of Collaborative Advantage*, Abingdon: Routledge.

19. Kolb, D. (1984) *Experiential Learning: Experience as the Source of Learning and Development*, Englewood Cliffs, NJ: Prentice-Hall.

20. Edmonstone, J., Collin, A. and Sturt, J. (1981) Commissioning DGHs: The State of the Art, *Hospital and Health Services Review*, October: 268–271.

21. Stein, H. (1981) The Concept of the Human Service Organisation: A Critique, *Administration in Social Work*, 4 (2): 1–13.

22. Tallis, R. (2005) *Hippocratic Oaths: Medicine and its Discontents*, London: Atlantic Books.

23. Revans, R. (1964) *Standards for Morale: Cause and Effect in Hospitals*, Oxford: Oxford University Press.

24. Menzies-Lyth, I. (1959) The Functioning of Social Systems as a Defence Against Anxiety: A Report on a Study of the Nursing Service of a General Hospital, in Menzies-Lyth, I. (Ed.) *Containing Anxiety in Institutions: Selected Essays: Volume 1*, London: Free Association Books, 43–88.

Chapter 5

The Changing Context for OD Activity – A VUCA/RUPT World

This chapter takes a more comprehensive look at the changing context in which OD operates, including globalisation, technological advancement and climate change. A volatile, uncertain, complex and ambiguous setting has become the new normal. A major strategy to address this has been competency-based education and training, while a case is made that a more important and relevant requirement for such times is the development of enhanced capacity.

It has been argued [1] that we are living through a time of major historical transition where disruptive and discontinuous change is the norm. Kershaw's notion of a third modernity [2] is based on the belief that a developing post-industrial information age economy is one of dynamic complexity marked by permanent change, turbulence and uncertainty, to the extent that it can be experienced by many as chaotic. This has been described as "liquid modernity" [3] as a time:

> in which social forms (structures that limit choices, institutions that guard repetitions of routines, patterns of acceptable behaviour) can no longer (and are not expected) to keep their shape for long, because they decompose and melt faster than the time it takes to cast them, and once they are cast for them to set. Forms, whether already

present or only adumbrated, are unlikely to be given enough time to solidify, and cannot serve as frames of reference for human actions and long-term life strategies because of their short life expectation.

This was also prefaced as early as 1848 by Marx and Engels [4] in reviewing social and organisational change in the 19th century as:

> All fixed, fast-frozen relations, with their train of ancient and venerable prejudices and opinions are swept away, all new-formed ones become antiquated before they can ossify. All that is solid melts into air.

In our times, social and economic change consistently disrupts the existing social and organisational order, generating high degrees of ambiguity, uncertainty and insecurity for organisations and for the people who work in them, as the future becomes increasingly unknowable and the consequences of personal and organisational actions become increasingly unpredictable. Technological change and automation are re-shaping working practices and so-called "culture wars" are re-casting the very meaning of work, among other identities, for millions of people. The influence of trade unions is in decline, and the labour market continues to de-socialise and fragment, eroding worker protections and creating an employment landscape characterised by instability and uncertainty.

Globalisation in particular stretches social transactions across both time and space. The local is now shaped by the distant, and vice versa. Multinational corporations (MNCs) view the whole world as a single entity and the entire planet as a market. Their impact transcends all national boundaries, and they do not make decisions based on terms of what is good for countries but only on what is best for the corporation [5]. Population movement has now become endemic. Ongoing political turmoil around the planet has escalated both forced and voluntary migration into more politically stable countries. Increased movement across national state borders (both legally and illegally) fosters an increasingly global society and, as a result, many institutions and organisations face major challenges to their traditional ways of doing things. Accelerating technological advances like artificial intelligence (AI) and the use of advanced computerised decision-making systems such as algorithms will increasingly have significant impacts on employment and the anxiety and sense of threat which they generate for existing employees. The instability of the earth's climate as a result of corporate and human behaviour is closely related to the current economic and social systems, so all organisations are both central to the issue of climate change and to the potential solutions, which are likely to be disruptive to many existing personal and organisational expectations [6].

This chapter explores the world in which healthcare organisations now find themselves, where the acceleration of the interdependence between social, political, economic, climate and technological dynamics is increasing dramatically [7]. This is a state of affairs where change and complexity are the so-called "new normal" and where volatility, uncertainty, complexity and ambiguity dominate the context. It will examine the notions of competence and capability as means of addressing this world and will consider the different kinds of problems which such organisations face.

A VUCA/RUPT world: Certain characteristics are now manifest in some form or another across public, private and third sector organisations on both a national and international basis and certainly affect healthcare organisations. They are summarised by the notion of "VUCA", which stands for:

Volatility: The type, speed, volume and scale of economic, social and organisational change forces and catalyses events in and around organisations to an extent never experienced before.

Uncertainty: There is a lack of predictability with regard to the future and therefore a much greater likelihood of surprises occurring without people in organisations having any early or enhanced awareness and understanding of both issues and events.

Complexity: There are multiple forces and factors in play, and as a result, many issues become confounded, with no simple and obvious cause-and-effect sequence to events and activities being observable.

Ambiguity: There is a lack of precision, and there are multiple meanings of the same event possible. Reality can appear "hazy" with a greater potential for misreading and misunderstanding exactly what is going on.

Social pressures and trends, heightening expectations, the power of social media, globalism on the one hand and localism on the other affect people and their communities – and all contribute to volatility, uncertainty, complexity and ambiguity.

The practical implications of these characteristics are:

Volatility: People in organisations face challenges that, while not necessarily hard to understand, may be unstable, unexpected or last for an unknown length of time.

Uncertainty: People face challenges where the original cause may possibly be known, but a lack of supplementary information serves to shroud the process of change management and hence the effects can appear diffuse.

Complexity: People face challenges in dealing with a multitude of interdependent and interacting variables within, across and beyond the boundaries of their organisations.

Ambiguity: People face the challenges of "unknown unknowns" where there are unclear relationships between cause and effect.

An alternative concept is that of a "RUPT" world, which is rapid, unpredictable, paradoxical and tangled:

Rapid: People in organisations face a series of overlapping challenges, across multiple domains, which occur and reoccur and need to be addressed and overcome at pace.

Unpredictable: People face unexpected challenges which, despite thorough and well thought-out strategies and governance, can rapidly challenge their underlying assumptions and so cause a reframing of their thinking.

Paradoxical: People face challenges in located polarities. Rather than providing a single solution (either this **or** that), challenges now need to be embraced as polarities (both this **and** that) in order to be addressed in both the short and long term.

Tangled: People face interdependent challenges within, across and beyond the existing boundaries of their system.

Within this often chaotic environment, rapid and unpredictable paradoxes are embedded in tangled multi-causal relationships. In order to work effectively in such contexts, people need to develop (both within themselves and also across their organisation) a learning capability (see below) where the majority of learning occurs in association with real-life challenges [8].

Despite this, the still dominant worldview in organisational life is often best characterised as "LUMO" – that is:

Linear: Causal and sequential modes of thinking predominate.

Anthropocentric: Regarding human kind as the central or most important element of existence, with little or no wider regard for nature.

Mechanistic: Regarding organisations as working like machines.

Ordered: Carefully arranged or controlled through categories and hierarchies.

Change and complexity as the new normal: As a result of operating in a VUCA/RUPT world, anyone faced with the reality of working in organisations, particularly healthcare organisations, in the early 21st century faces a whole series of challenges. These include:

Working in the face of the Covid-19 pandemic and the short- and long-term impact it has made (and will continue to make) on all societies and organisations. There is a growing realisation that healthcare (and related social care) cannot simply return to the previous established ways of working and that major changes are needed [9,10] Culpin [11], for example, identifies that the

VUCA/RUPT world will be a continuing reality; that virtual working (or at least hybrid working) is here to stay and that leadership capability, rather than competence, will be increasingly necessary.

Working in the continuing aftermath of the 2008 global financial crisis, with the austerity and employment uncertainty which that has entailed in healthcare. It has meant working in a harsh resource climate where both financial and political demands focus attention largely on short-term targets, yet the need for more creative and longer-term thinking is probably greater than ever, but where short-term pressures and expectations actually generate and encourage pre-existing "silo" working.

High and growing levels of public expectation of what healthcare and social care services could and should deliver to local and national populations, in terms of quality, choice and accessibility. In this respect, the public has become increasingly less tolerant of the range, quality and accessibility of current provision and more demanding of future provision. There is therefore an urgent requirement to balance the short-term operational delivery of healthcare and social care services with longer term and more strategic innovation in those services. Yet there is little or no time or space available for the much-needed long-term horizon-scanning activity which could identify exactly what is and is not possible in terms of service delivery.

Significant social and cultural change, including the growth of multicultural communities in some parts of the UK, and changing (and often contested) attitudes towards such issues as obesity, alcohol and drug abuse, HIV/AIDS, abortion and towards welfare provision more generally.

Changing demographics, with an increasingly ageing population (often exhibiting long-term health conditions and combinations of those long-term conditions) and a major shrinking of the younger workforce recruitment pool from which healthcare professionals and other staff have historically been drawn. In the UK, three out of every ten employees are over fifty years of age, and there are more people in the population over the age of sixty-five than there are under sixteen [12]. Frozen or capped salaries available for front-line staff and resultant staff shortages make recruitment and retention much more difficult, and taken together with negative media coverage, consistently generate a public "crisis" image.

An increase in the numbers of dual earner couples and of workers with family care-giving responsibilities. Despite this, an increase in reported loneliness, especially in the case of both the elderly and the young, but not confined only to those age groups. While this sense of loneliness has inevitably been exacerbated by Covid-19 lockdowns, loneliness can also be about feeling alone even when surrounded by other people and is about the quality of connections which people have with others, rather than just the number of social relationships. It is something of a paradox that in a modern, densely populated urban society, there is a shortage of friendship and good relationships, because although people are physically closer together, they are also socially separate [13]. A danger is that, as a consequence of the Covid-19 pandemic and austerity, the reduction or closure of local services providing such a sense of community and providing vital support may further enhance such loneliness.

For those in full-time work, the UK has some of the longest working hours in Europe and the least public holidays. There is also an unusually high percentage of part-time workers for whom their average working hours may be short but many of whom appear to want full-time work but simply cannot access it. This relates to the growth of the gig economy of self-employed people on short-term or zero-hour contracts, with around 25% of the UK employed population being identified as part of this "precariat" [14]. This insecure cohort is less qualified, has limited job autonomy and significantly less financial security [15]. They are potentially vulnerable to fluctuations in working time (and therefore also of pay levels), short notice of working schedules and experience a degree of precariousness in terms of a lack of employment rights [16].

A blurring has taken place of the boundaries between work time and leisure time, with some sections of employed society feeling that they are always on call, even if their contract of employment does not actually demand it. There is a constant possibility that their personal and private time gets interrupted by work. People now regularly and reflexively check their mobile phones for new work-related messages and also reply to work emails in non-work time [17].

Social mobility has become so frozen that it has been estimated that it would take at least five generations for the poorest families in the UK to reach the average income, while higher earners already get bigger rewards and consolidate their own and their families' wealth for the next generation [18]. As an example, the Chief Executives of the UK's FTSE 100 companies are paid a median average of £3.6 million a year, which is 115 times the £31,461 average pay of UK full-time workers [19]. Such growing inequality in UK society produces powerful psychological effects. When the gap between richest and poorest increases, so does the tendency for people to self-define and to define others in terms of superiority and inferiority. Low social status is typically associated with elevated levels of personal stress, and the rates of anxiety and depression are intimately related to the inequality that increasingly makes that status paramount [13].

A decline in a previous culture of deference to both authority and expertise, largely fuelled by an explosion in the availability and usability of information, much of it digitally-based. A corresponding collapse of confidence and trust in any kind of traditional authority, but especially with those institutions and individuals with claims to expertise [20].

A growing emphasis on the importance of diversity and equality at work and in society as a whole and a growing intolerance of sexism, misogyny and racism.

Alongside this, there is also evidence of a growing intolerance of minorities of all kinds and of increased polarisation within society seeming to verge, at times, on xenophobia. This can be sustained and amplified by what some observers consider a "toxic" media, especially via certain newspapers and also by social media.

Powerful drives to consistently increase efficiency and to improve quality simultaneously – to do "more for less".

Continuing intra-organisational restructuring or reconfiguration, often known as "re-disorganisation", and typically involving processes of de-layering, down-sizing and the merging of individual roles or of whole organisations, often resulting in job losses, enhanced uncertainty and a sense of heightened anxiety for the staff concerned [21].

Where previously healthcare employees could acquire, through the relevant educational and training institutions, a single set of professional skills and would then expect to progress upwards through a fairly rigid and self-contained professional and managerial hierarchy, they are now required to periodically re-skill through "continuing professional development" as they move from one employer to another and from one role to another. Individuals are expected to take responsibility for their learning throughout their entire career while demonstrating an adaptable approach to job seeking and re-skilling in an employment market which is increasingly characterised by uncertainty and career instability [22]. As the organisation of work is in some instances decentralised, with lateral networks gradually replacing previous pyramidal hierarchies, a premium is increasingly put on "flexibility" [23]. Such flexibility also potentially implies elements of the workforce being casualised, with an ever-increasing number of healthcare workers being employed on a temporary basis or being outsourced to agencies. The creation of new roles, such as healthcare assistant and advanced clinical practitioner, serves to blur previously well-defined professional boundaries.

The "psychological contract" – the unwritten and implicit relationship between the employer and the employee and involving such key factors as job security, appropriate training and development, career and promotion prospects, job satisfaction and social support in return for organisational commitment – has changed. Employees can no longer count on continuing job security, even if they do their jobs well and are loyal to their organisation. Increasingly, the terms of the psychological contract have been changed unilaterally by the employer, as employees are expected to work longer hours, take work home, take on greater responsibility, be more flexible and tolerate continual change and ambiguity [24].

It has been argued [25] that the focus of the psychological contract should now be on the notion of "employability" – the development of those skills needed in order to find work when individuals need it, wherever they can find it. In this approach, the employer offers the employee the tools and the opportunities for assessing and developing their skills. In return, employees accept responsibility for, and have loyalty to, their own careers – and offer the organisation an adaptive and responsible skill base and commitment to the organisation's success. There is an underlying assumption and acceptance by both employee and employer that their relationship will terminate when such a win/win basis is no longer possible. Traditional expectations of loyalty and security are absent from this revised psychological contract, as employees are expected to be more entrepreneurial and pursue their own self-managed or boundary-less careers. However, this focus is one which has been developed by and for the advantage of the employer, rather than for the employee, who has never been consulted over such a change. Indeed, historically employees have valued the meeting of basic "deficit" needs (physiological, safety, love and belonging, esteem) prior to those of self-actualisation, and there is nothing to suggest that this has changed in any way [26].

Uncertainty with regard to the future associated with the developing impact of Brexit – the UK's departure from the European Union. This includes the ending of free movement and the reluctance of people from the EU to now consider any full or part-time employment in the UK, and this is particularly important where historically healthcare services have been reliant on them. This is especially challenging in respect of the nursing profession and of related social care employees [27].

As a consequence, there is an increased experience of complexity and ambiguity within healthcare organisations, and all this produces a sense of being caught in a perfect storm of increasing public need, demand and expectation, coupled with a decreasing resource and staffing capacity.

Faced with this, senior organisational leaders in healthcare have sought to exercise and reassert clarity and control – to "hold things together" in the face of the volatile and virtual environments of the 21st century organisations – such new organisational forms as strategic alliances, joint ventures, partnership arrangements, remote working, matrix working – all of which lead to a blurring of single organisational identity as organisational boundaries became more porous and gave rise to feelings on the part of such senior leaders of fragmentation and loss of control [28–30].

As a result, healthcare organisations seem to be on a journey for an old to a new world, as Table 5.1 reveals.

Competence and capability: The most popular means which has been adopted to deal with this omnipresent VUCA/RUPT reality has been an emphasis on increasing the competence of key people in healthcare organisations – and hence to the recent and continuing popularity of competency-based approaches to education and training.

Table 5.1   Moving from an Old to a New Order

Old World	New World
Low complexity, slow change	High complexity, rapid change
Learning has a long shelf-life	Learning has a short shelf-life
Senior people know most and best	Knowledge and understanding are scattered
Someone, somewhere, knows	No individual can pretend to know
Doing more of the same is the rule	Innovation is the rule

Competence is concerned with what individuals know or are able to do, in terms of their knowledge, skills and attitudes, as expressed in their observable behaviour. Much work has been undertaken to analyse, define and publicise what organisations, functions, professions or whole sectors of society deem to be desirable competences. Competence obviously works well with "tame" issues (see Chapter 6) where the challenges concerned are both clear and unambiguous and where tried and tested solutions can be applied. It suffices when there are high degrees of certainty and agreement and where the tasks to be done and the contexts or settings in which they are to be accomplished are both familiar. It also reflects an "instrumentalist" and reductive view of learning where, for every predetermined role, there are agreed competences that need to be defined and then achieved.

Critiques of the competency approach [31–35] identify the problems with the approach as:

It is essentially past and present-oriented: Inevitably, lists of competences reflect what has been done in the past or is done currently and, while some of this will continue to be valid in the future, there is no predictive basis on which to decide what will and will not be relevant then. As a result, the use of competency frameworks involves "walking backwards into the future". This runs the danger of "competency traps" [36] when an organisation's previously entrenched expertise ruins its capacity to deal with a changing and uncertain world. Organisations become locked into particular ways of doing things simply because they are already skilled at doing things that way.

It assumes a particular kind of organisational culture: Typically, competences are associated with traditional bureaucratic forms, where levels and jobs are tightly prescribed, while increasingly many organisations seem to be more concerned with devolved responsibility and, in some cases, with increased degrees of discretion.

It is individualistic: The focus is on the isolated individual leader or manager and ignores the context within which that person works. It struggles to take account of situational or complex organisational factors. Even more fundamentally, it assumes that competences exist in a detached and abstract state. The idea that managers can learn, for example, about communication skills separated from the context in which they communicate is quite unrealistic.

It is reductionist and fragmentary: The assumption is that people can learn each single competence in isolation, without reference to the other competences – and then un-problematically integrate them.

Professional and functional differences are ignored: Generic and standardised competence frameworks do not recognise the differences between a host of different professions and occupations and, while the importance of reducing professional and functional barriers is obviously important, enforced generic competence lists are not necessarily the most appropriate way in which to do so.

It ignores diversity: Most competence lists tend, either explicitly or implicitly, to reflect the assumptions and norms of able-bodied, heterosexual, white, middle-class, middle-aged bureaucratic male managers – "pale, male and stale". The intention of the competency approach seems to be to produce "identikit" managers.

It supports and reinforces the personality trait or "right stuff" view of leadership: It embodies assumptions that leadership and management is an elite practice and a rational endeavour arising from a set of characteristics possessed only by a few special and gifted individuals [37].

In reality, however, there can be no single set of competences that can realistically capture everything that people at work do, because working in organisations generally (and in healthcare organisations in particular) is as much a collective as an individual activity; is surrounded by complex emotions and politics [38] and is context-specific. It is therefore somewhat contentious to claim that there could be a single generic competency-based model of desirable behaviour to work in such complex contexts. It may even be, therefore, that the very act of prescribing such a set of competences, as outlined above, actually limits the potential emergence of capability (see below).

The picture painted above with regard to competence is certainly not an accurate description of a VUCA/RUPT world, and increasingly both individuals and organisations in healthcare find themselves in situations where there is little certainty and agreement; where both the managerial and professional tasks and the settings in which they are undertaken are unfamiliar and where applica-tion of the old and familiar solutions simply does not work. What is required here instead is a form of learning agility which has been called capability [39], which is effectively a form of future-orientated potential and which is concerned with the extent to which individuals as learners can cope with uncertainty; can adapt to changing situations; can generate new knowledge and can continue to improve their performance [40].

It involves a psychological flexibility or mind-set, which can react and change swiftly and energetically in response to changing circumstances. It implies continuous renewal and reinvention – learning, unlearning and relearning. It embodies an emphasis on independence in terms of self-esteem, self-confidence, the ability to make judgements and the power to respond flexibly, both reac-tively and proactively [41]. Learning which builds capability takes place when individuals engage with an uncertain and unfamiliar context in a meaningful way. Capability cannot therefore be taught in any formal sense or even passively assimilated. It is reached through a personal transformation process in which existing competences are adapted and tuned to new circumstances. Anticipating this, some years ago it was noted [42] that:

> Now we need people who can flex and adapt quickly, who develop complex and personal repertoires of skills and responses which enable them to get by and survive and prosper. People who can forget skills as quickly as they can learn them are more likely to be valued in a world where organisations are formed and dissolved in half a generation, rather than over generations of seemingly predictable progression.

The distinction between competence and capability is shown in Figure 5.1.
For people working in healthcare such capability entails [43]:

A primary concern for, and an understanding of, service users and their carers.
An ability to read and analyse a particular situation and to respond creatively to what is seen.
The ability to draw upon a number of different approaches and to discrimi-nate between them, based upon the merits of each – a personal repertoire of responses.
A willingness to continuously learn by experiment, reflection and review of personal and group experience.
A concern to work by trial and error – but in a systematic manner.
The ability to theorise about practice during practice itself – to turn instinct into insight by thinking about what one is doing as one works and arguing about it in one's head and with others.

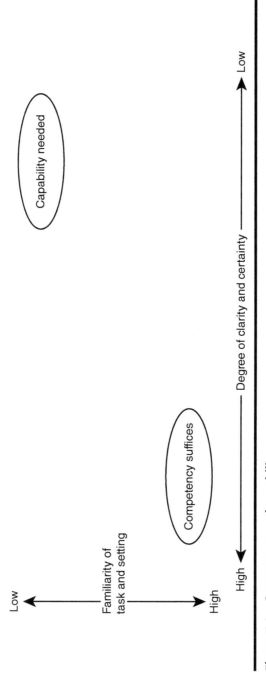

Figure 5.1 Competence and capability.

From this, the ability to draw out the theory which underlies actions.

The ability to relate personal theory and practice to wider considerations of theory and practice – to self-evaluate personal and professional practice in order to improve it.

A concern with the knowledge currently in use and the creation of future knowledge.

An understanding of, and a concern with, the role of the profession or occupation in society.

Increasingly people and organisations in healthcare have to cope on a regular basis with complex and uncertain situations where all the previously operated knowledge and both the related and preferred routines fall short, or simply do not fit, with what is happening. In such cases, what works is clearly not a simple adherence to the previously known and trusted procedures, a pretence that surprise elements just do not exist or an expansion of the current practices in order to "nail down" the problems. Instead it implies attention to effective working relationships and to the specifics of the particular setting or context within which people work. Accordingly, all learning needs to reflect the lived reality where action transpires and where people can be found engaging with their colleagues on real problems.

As a result, in working in a VUCA/RUPT world, the defined technical and explicit knowledge that is associated with competence is simply not enough and the development of that learning agility called capability involves also valuing practical and tacit knowledge. Explicit knowledge, for example, is appropriate for "technical" challenges, while tacit or implicit knowledge is more relevant for "adaptive" challenges, which involve negotiating a way through ambiguity with other people [44], a point which is further pursued below. This is shown in Table 5.2.

Table 5.2   Technical (Explicit) and Practical (Tacit) Knowledge

Technical (Explicit) Knowledge	Practical (Tacit) Knowledge
Typically codified and written into policies and rules	Typically expressed in practice and learned only through experience
Based on established practice	Based on established practice modified by idiosyncratic understanding and technique
In accordance with prescription	Loosely, variably, uniquely. In a discretionary way based on personal insight
Used in clearly defined circumstances	Used in both expected and unexpected circumstances

(Continued)

Table 5.2 (*Continued*)   Technical (Explicit) and Practical (Tacit) Knowledge

Technical (Explicit) Knowledge	Practical (Tacit) Knowledge
To achieve an envisaged and familiar result	To achieve an indefinite or novel result
Emphasis on routine – method, analysis, planning	Emphasis on non-routine – variety, invention, responsiveness
Focus on well-defined problems	Focus on poorly defined problems
Generalisable	Locally relevant

References

1. Giddens, A. (2002) *Runaway World: How Globalisation is Reshaping our World*, 2nd edition, London: Profile Books.
2. Kershaw, I. (2019) *Roller-Coaster: Europe 1950–2017*, London: Penguin.
3. Bauman, Z. (2000) *Liquid Modernity*, Cambridge: Polity Press.
4. Marx, K. and Engels, F. (2015) *The Communist Manifesto*, London: Penguin.
5. Irogbe, K. (2013) Global Political Economy and the Power of Multinational Corporations, *Journal of Third World Studies*, 30 (2): 223–247.
6. Thunberg, G. (2019) *No One Is Too Small To Make A Difference*, London: Penguin Books.
7. Day, A. (2020) *Disruption, Change and Transformation in Organisations: A Human Relations Perspective*, Abingdon: Routledge.
8. Till, A., Dutta, N. and McKimm, J. (2016) Vertical Leadership in Highly Complex and Unpredictable Health Systems, *British Journal of Hospital Medicine*, 77 (8): 471–475.
9. Malby, R. and Hufflett, A. (2020) *Ten Leaps Forward: Innovation in the Pandemic*, London: School of Health and Social Care, London South Bank University.
10. Abbott, C. and Bloodworth, M. (2020) *UK Social Work in the Time of Covid-19: A Six-Week Research Study into the Impact of the SARS-Cov-2 Pandemic on the Social Work Profession*, York: Centre for Action Learning.
11. Culpin, V. (2021) *Leadership in the 21st Century: Lessons from a Pandemic*, Berkhamsted: Hult Ashridge Executive Education.
12. Dorling, D. and Thomas, B. (2011) *Bankrupt Britain: An Atlas of Social Change*, Bristol, MA: The Policy Press.
13. Wilkinson, R. and Pickett, K. (2018) *The Inner Level: How More Equal Societies Reduce Stress, Restore Sanity and Improve Everyone's Well-Being*, London: Allen Lane.
14. Standing, G. (2011) *The Precariat: The Dangerous New Class*, London: Policy Network.
15. Williams, M., Broughton, A., Meager, N., Spiegelhalter, K., Johal, S. and Jenkins, K. (2017) *The True Diversity of Self-Employment*, Brighton: Centre for Research on Self-Employment, Institute of Employment Studies.

16. Broughton, A., Gloster, R., Marvell, R., Green, M., Langley, J. and Martin, A. (2018) *The Experiences of Individuals in the Gig Economy*, Brighton, Institute for Employment Studies for Department for Business, Energy and Industrial Strategy.
17. Hammond, C. (2019) *The Art of Rest: How to Find Respite in the Modern Age*, Edinburgh: Canongate Books.
18. OECD (2018) *A Broken Elevator?: How to Promote Social Mobility*, Paris: Organisation for Economic Cooperation and Development.
19. Shand, L., Kay, R. and Hildyard, L. (2020) *FTSE 100 CEO Pay in 2019 and During the Pandemic*, London: Chartered Institute for Personnel and Development.
20. Peston, R. (2017) *WTF*, London: Hodder and Stoughton.
21. Ballatt, J. and Campling, P. (2011) *Intelligent Kindness: Reforming the Culture of Healthcare*, London: RCPsych Publications.
22. Down, B. (2009) Schooling, Productivity and the Enterprising Self: Beyond Market Values, *Critical Studies in Education*, 50 (1): 51–64.
23. Sennett, R. (1998) *The Corrosion of Character: The Personal Consequences of Work in the New Capitalism*, New York: W.W. Norton and Co.
24. Edmonstone, J. (2013) *Personal Resilience for Healthcare Staff: When the Going Gets Tough*, London: Radcliffe Publishing.
25. Hiltrop, J. (1996) Managing the Changing Psychological Contract, *Employee Relations*, 18 (1): 36–49.
26. Maslow, A. (1998) *Towards a Psychology of Being*, New York: Wiley.
27. Dayan, M., Fahy, N., Hervey, T., McCarey, M., Jarman, H. and Greer, S. (2020) *Understanding the Impact of Brexit on Health in the UK*, London: Nuffield Trust.
28. Bolden, R. and Gosling J. (2006) Leadership Competencies: Time to Change the Tune? *Leadership*, 2 (2): 147–163.
29. Kallinokos, J. (2003) Work, Human Agency and Organisational Forms: An Anatomy of Fragmentation? *Organisation Studies*, 24 (4): 595–618.
30. Child, J. and Rodrigues, S. (2002) *Corporate Governance and New Organisational Forms: The Problem of Double and Multiple Agency*, Paper presented at Joint Symposium on Renewing Governance and Organisations: New Paradigms of Governance? Academy of Management meeting, Denver, CO.
31. McKimm, J. and Swanwick, T. (2011) Leadership Development for Clinicians: What Are We Trying to Achieve? *Clinical Teacher*, 8: 181–185.
32. Bolden, R., Wood, M. and Gosling, J. (2006) Is the NHS Leadership Qualities Framework Missing the Wood for the Trees? In Casebeer, A., Harrison, A. and Mark, A. (Eds.) *Innovations in Health Care: A Reality Check*, New York: Palgrave Macmillan, 47–66.
33. Alimo-Metcalfe, B. and Alban-Metcalfe, J. (2008) *Engaging Leadership: Creating Organisations That Maximise the Potential of Their People*, London: Chartered Institute for Personnel and Development.
34. Walmsley, J. and Miller, K. (2008) *A Review of the Health Foundation's Leadership Programmes: 2003–2007*, London: The Health Foundation.
35. NHS Confederation (2009) *Reforming Healthcare Leadership Development – Again*, London: NHS Confederation.
36. Kuhl, S. (2019) *The Rainmaker Effect: Contradictions of the Learning Organisation*, Princeton, NJ: Organisational Dialogue Press.

37. Rogers, C. (2007) *Informal Coalitions: Mastering the Hidden Dynamics of Organisational Change*, Basingstoke: Palgrave Macmillan.
38. Vince, R. (2004) Action Learning and Organisational Learning: Power, Politics and Emotion in Organisations, *Action Learning: Research and Practice*, 1 (1): 63–78.
39. Goh, S., Elliott, C. and Quon, T. (2012) The Relationship Between Learning Capability and Organisational Performance: A Meta-Analytic Examination, *The Learning Organisation*, 19 (2): 92–108.
40. Edmonstone, J. (2011) The Challenge of Capability in Leadership Development, *British Journal of Healthcare Management*, 19 (11): 541–547.
41. Reeve, S. (1999) Action Learning and Capability: A Search for Common Ground, in O'Reilly, D., Cunningham, I. and Lester, S. (Eds.) *Developing the Capable Practitioner*, London: Kogan Page, 68–85.
42. Boydell, T., Leary, M., Megginson, D. and Pedler, M. (1991) *Developing The Developers*, London: Association for Management Education and Development.
43. Eraut, M. (1994) *Developing Professional Knowledge and Competence*, London: Falmer Press.
44. Heifitz, R., Grashow, A. and Linsky, M. (2009) *The Practice of Adaptive Leadership: Tools and Tactics for Changing Your Organisation and the World*, Boston, MA: Harvard Business Publishing.

Chapter 6

The Unusual Nature of Healthcare Organisations

This chapter explores the unusual nature of healthcare organisations, noting that they provide public services for human beings; are staffed by clinical professionals who operate as street-level bureaucrats and experience emotional labour. The impact of the latter is both individual and organisational. Healthcare organisations face wicked problems which are not amenable to being worked on by rationalistic and linear problem-solving approaches. A further important factor is the culture which has evolved in the UK's National Health Service (NHS).

Conventional wisdom tends to treat healthcare organisations in exactly the same way as all other kinds of organisation. Yet there is a powerful case to be made that healthcare organisations are very different from most industrial, commercial and financial enterprises, while having some parallels with other public sector organisations.

Public service organisations: Healthcare organisations are largely public service organisations [1] with three distinctive characteristics:

First, they do not just operate under a single hierarchy but also feature multiple professional hierarchies, co-existing and in parallel with a bureaucratic managerial hierarchy. Often the needs of service users within a local community cannot just be addressed by a single organisation working alone, so each organisation also has to constantly engage with the professional

DOI: 10.1201/9781003167310-6

and managerial hierarchies of other local organisations, both statutory and voluntary, at every level in order to deliver those services that meet peoples' complex needs.

Second, they provide services (typically personal services), rather than products. The quality of such services is largely determined by the face-to-face work which is conducted between an individual service provider working as a clinical professional and an individual service user or patient, where the latter always wants to be treated as an individual and not as a condition, case, type, number or statistic.

Third (and perhaps most importantly), they have an overarching purpose to serve the common good – the good of the public as a whole, based on notions of equity or fairness and of social solidarity. This makes them different from most industrial, commercial or financial organisations located in the private sector in that they are not subject to the "reconciling function" of profit [2]. For public service organisations, there is typically, for most, no such reconciler, not least because they are located in, and are part of, a much wider system. The purpose of these organisations is therefore not primarily to make money (although some may aim to do so) but instead to make a practical difference in terms of social change and improvement.

In organisational terms, they are dominated by a largely programmatic approach, which assumes that they are like machines and can be "fixed" by top-down imposed change, the instigators of which are typically politicians, senior leadership and management and Human Resources staff and rarely by local initiative. Such programmes are often experienced by front-line staff as being "led by different individuals, detached from each other and divorced from any connecting bigger picture" [3].

Human service organisations: Healthcare organisations are also human service organisations [4]. These are organisations whose principal function is to protect, maintain or enhance the personal well-being of individual members of society by defining, shaping or enhancing their personal attributes, such as good health or better education [5]. Such a term covers, in addition to healthcare, local authority social work and housing services, the entire education sector (schools, colleges, further and higher education), probation and aftercare services and the police.

In human service organisations, the professional staff typically learn a particular discipline as the content of their education and training, while the process (which is seldom explicit) also inculcates a value for more autonomous decision-making and the importance of constantly improving their own performance, rather than necessarily that of their employing institution. As a result, they identify much less with a specific employing organisation and much more with a professional culture – with a set of values, skills and knowledge quite independent of any specific work setting, and so the rewards which are of major significance to them – such as the respect of their peers and their personal reputation – are derived more from this larger arena than from their local organisational affiliation. In this respect, they are "cosmopolitans" rather than "locals" [6]. Their ultimate loyalty is to the profession, rather than to the employing organisation; their commitment is to professional values and skills, and their reference group is made up of their professional colleagues, located across many different organisations.

Professional organisations: Healthcare organisations are also primarily professional organisations [7] where the front-line clinical professionals possess a high degree of day-to-day control over their practice. Clinical professionals form what Mintzberg [8] has called the "operating core" of healthcare organisations. What clinical professionals control in healthcare is what Marxism would typify as the "means of production". There is what has been described as the disconnected hierarchy in healthcare – a disjunction between those who carry corporate responsibility in leadership and management positions and those clinical professionals who deliver front-line services [9]. It is, in effect, an inverted power structure in which people at the front-line generally have greater influence over clinical decision-making on a day-to-day basis than do those who are nominally in control at the "top". Leaders and managers take a corporate view and are appointed to their roles. They operate within given policies and procedures in order to achieve targets. They are engaged in "superior–subordinate" relationships with their followers who are managerially accountable to them [10].

Much clinical leadership is, by contrast with management, elective or representative and starts from an essentially non-hierarchical premise – that members of a professional group are theoretically equal – and equally valuable. Most decision-making within clinical professions is typically collegiate in nature, with debate, persuasion and negotiation seen as being crucial if a consensus or majority view is to be reached. Such elective or representative leadership can be a fragile commodity and the incorporation of clinical leaders within an essentially hierarchical framework always runs the risk of diminishing their credibility vis-à-vis their peers over time. There is therefore a premium placed by healthcare management on leaders with professional clinical backgrounds leading any change, not least because attempts at innovation based solely within the formal managerial system of healthcare, defined by hierarchical superior–subordinate relationships can be aided or thwarted by interactions within the more informal clinical leadership systems [11].

Such professional organisations are notoriously varied and fractured internally by different clinical specialties, occupational groupings and intra-professional hierarchies. There is ongoing competition for resources and status with various groupings being more (or less) able to articulate their own interests and hence to align themselves with the organisation's current direction of travel. Such competition is quite an overt political process. These organisations are dynamic mosaics which are made up of multiple, complex and overlapping groupings with variably shared assumptions, values, beliefs and behaviours [12].

As a result, the ability of corporate leaders and managers in such organisations to influence directly clinical decision-making is much more constrained and contingent than in other kinds of organisations [13] and the role of managers (particularly at, or close to, the front-line) can often therefore, in practice, be to lend support to the clinicians in making changes, through the provision of finance, time and other resources. Nonetheless, there are clearly two different (and competing) views of professional practice [14], as shown in Table 6.1.

Street-level bureaucrats: Many healthcare employees (just like other public service workers such as social workers, the police, firefighters and people working in education) have been described as street-level bureaucrats [15,16] who engage in direct communication and interaction with the general public as patients and clients, in contrast to the policy makers, managers and administrators, who typically do not. They are responsible for making those decisions which are the most appropriate for their patients or clients. Exercising "permission" to act in addressing organisational problems seems to imply seeking and gaining consent or a mandate derived from some source of authority outside of an individual. However, notions of "discretion", or acting on one's own authority and judgement, and of "agency", or the capacity to act and make one's own choices, are closer to the sense of being a professional, so in such knowledge-based organisations (as healthcare organisations are) professional judgement and discretion exercised by such street-level bureaucrats are as much as likely as any managerial decision to determine successful outcomes [17].

The use of discretion rather than prescription is the key feature of the work of most healthcare professionals [10], partly because they operate in a series of complex situations which cannot easily be reduced to programmatic formats; partly because the situations which they encounter might require individualised and compassionate treatment, and partly because the exercise of such initiative in itself can inspire the trust of clients both in the individual professional themselves and in the agency which he or she represents. Professional staff have to use their personal discretion in order to become "inventive strategists" [18] by developing ways of working which seek to resolve the ever-present challenges of their excessive workload, complex cases and ambiguous performance targets.

Table 6.1   Two View of Professional Practice [14]

Technical–Rational View	*Professional–Artistry View*
Follows rules, laws, routine prescriptions	Starts where rules fade. Sees patterns and frameworks
Uses diagnosis and analysis	Uses interpretation and appreciation
Wants efficient systems	Wants creativity and room to be wrong
Sees knowledge as graspable and permanent	Sees knowledge as temporary, dynamic and problematic
Theory is applied to practice	Theory emerges from practice
Visible performance is central	There is more to it than surface features
Setting-out and testing for competence is vital	There is more to it than the sum of the parts
Technical expertise is all	Professional judgement counts
Sees professional activities as masterable	Sees mystery at the heart of professional activities
Emphasises the known	Embraces uncertainty
Standards must be fixed. They are measurable and must be controlled	That which is most easily fixed is often trivial. Professionals should be trusted.
Emphasises assessment, performance appraisal, inspection and accreditation	Emphasises investigation, reflection, and deliberation
Change must be managed from outside	Professionals can develop from inside
Quality is really about the quantity of that which is easily measurable	Quality comes from deepening insight into one's values, priorities and actions
Technical accountability	Professional answerability
Professionals should be trained for instrumental purposes	The educational development of professionals is intrinsically worldwide

However, the more recent evidence seems to suggest that, with the growth of command-and-control management in such services, such discretion has increasingly, and over time, been significantly eroded [19,20].

Emotional labour: In the UK, mental health issues in the workplace are estimated to cost the UK economy more than £15 billion each year in lost revenue and 140 million working days are calculated to be lost each year through staff sickness, much of which is stress-related [21]. Half a million people annually suffer from work-related stress [22] and staff working in healthcare experience significantly much higher work-related stress than other professional groups in society [23]. In 2014, it was estimated that stress accounted for over 30% of NHS sickness absence, costing the service £300–400 million per year [24]. The danger of staff burnout, an occupational phenomenon, rather than a medical condition and defined as "a syndrome conceptualised as resulting from chronic workplace stress which has not been successfully managed" is ever-present [25]. Burnout involves a prolonged response to chronic interpersonal stressors and manifests itself in terms of exhaustion, cynicism and a feeling of reduced personal accomplishment. In the case of the Covid-19 pandemic, there is clear and growing evidence of mental health issues, especially post-traumatic stress disorder (PTSD) among intensive care staff in hospital, especially in the case of nurses [26].

The people who work in healthcare, and especially the clinical staff, have to regularly undertake what has been termed "emotional labour". Emotional labour is a recent phrase used to describe a much older phenomenon. Revans, for example, in an early study of nursing staff morale described the hospital as an institution which was "cradled in anxiety" [27] and Menzies-Lyth [28], in an ethnographic study conducted in a teaching hospital, highlighted healthcare staff as bearing "the full, immediate and concentrated impact of distress, tragedy, death and dying which arise from patient care and which are not part of the typical working experience of most of the public".

This is because the work of healthcare clinical staff puts them in regular touch with deep-seated, largely unconscious, fears of helplessness, decay and death. The sources of such stress include close and regular contact with people undergoing suffering and death; the undertaking of "distasteful, disgusting and frightening tasks"; coping with personal feelings of pity, compassion, love, guilt, anxiety, resentment and envy and carrying the depression and fear of patients' relatives and friends. As a result, they are "cauldrons of emotion" [29]. Clinical professionals are, by training and socialisation, meant to be expert "fixers" through their clinical interventions and patients with long-term and incurable conditions or who are dying can therefore represent failure to them.

Likewise, Tallis [30] identified that:

> It is easy to forget the appalling nature of some of the jobs carried out by healthcare staff day-in, day-out – the damage, the pain, the mess they may encounter, the sheer stench of diseased human flesh and its waste products.

Tallis highlighted the imaginative and moral step involved in engaging with the realities of illness. There is a challenging process of cognitive self-overcoming on the part of humanity, not least because human beings find it much easier to assume an objective attitude towards the stars than towards their own inner organs. This self-overcoming has to be done on an individual level by healthcare staff every day as they muster the will and the necessary balance of kindness and professional detachment to perform the most intimate tasks imaginable.

Additionally, that contact with patients' and families' emotional distress and disturbance can be equally, if not more harrowing:

> Existential questions about identity, suffering, madness and death are raised and may put people in touch with extreme feelings of confusion, pain and loss. The struggle with feelings of helplessness and hopelessness in the face of suffering cannot be avoided and individuals, depending on their personality and past experience, protect themselves in different ways from the emotionally traumatic environment. [31]

These existential questions relate to issues such as health, death, freedom, isolation and meaninglessness [32–35].

Emotional labour is therefore a psychological defence mechanism – the "suppression of private feelings in order to sustain a desirable work-related outward appearance that produces in others a sense of being cared for" [36,37]. In practice it involves:

The depersonalisation and categorisation of patients.

The cultivation of a dispassionate professional detachment and self-control – a "caring but distant" demeanour which suppresses and controls emotions [38].

Ritualistic task performance to detailed and precise standardised procedures involves checking and rechecking of decisions and of form-filling used as avoidance. Paperwork becomes a way to avoid blame and manage risk. It becomes the main criterion by which work is assessed and inspected, creating a cycle of behaviour which prioritises bureaucracy over people [39].

"Responsibility-shifting" – Delegation upwards in the hierarchy to seniors in order to avoid personal responsibility.

A suspicion of change – or alternatively an obsession with regular reorganisations. It has been suggested [40] that the pendulum has now swung in the opposite direction away from a suspicion of change and towards that of the uncritical promotion of constant change which has now become the main social defence system in the UK's NHS, overloading and fragmenting the system and distracting people from the task of caring. The almost evangelical approach to such change exemplified by some politicians, healthcare leaders and managers and some consultancies can be seen as a defence mechanism itself, denying the complexity of providing healthcare to people who may suffer and die. It may also be the case that such "solutions" involving further organisational change simply overload the healthcare system and create ever more dangerous levels of anxiety. Ham et al. [41] also suggest that the pace of change within the NHS has created a very crowded policy context and, as a result, has generated confusion among staff between different programmes and their impact (or lack of impact).

Healthcare clinical professionals are thus routinely seeking to control their personal feelings and any revealing emotional expression [42] because a premium is placed on their being dispassionate and keeping their distance, so the exercising of detachment is prized. Over time, this mismatch between peoples' felt and expressed feelings leads to "emotional dissonance" [43] and eventually to emotional strain. The protection against anxiety that care-giving induces by the suppression of these personal emotions over a sustained period, especially when individuals are exposed to frequent emotional trauma, leads to a reduced ability to withstand the emotional toll of care – which, in turn, leads to either personal clinical burn-out or to an unhealthy cynicism, detachment, depersonalisation and objectification of patients, no longer noticing or acting on the distress of others, sometimes called "compassion fatigue" [44]. Defensive styles of coping then become entrenched. This is marked by the growth of a kind of personal carapace inured to reality in order to cope and to survive. An example of this was the evidence contained in the first Francis report on Mid-Staffordshire Hospital [45], which quoted examples of a lack of compassion and of callous indifference to patients by some professional staff.

While this can be true of individual healthcare workers, there is also an organisational impact. Bain [46] extended the focus from the individual clinical professional to what he termed the wider "system domain fabric", which included the organisational structures, roles, relationships and authority and accountability systems; policies and procedures and information systems; professional education and training and funding arrangements. The healthcare workplace is a "potentially explosive cauldron of, often unexpressed, emotional dynamics" [47]. These unconscious defence mechanisms permeate healthcare organisations as "emotional toxins" [48] evidenced in structures, roles and work processes and so have a major, but largely unrecognised, impact on the way they operate.

Healthcare organisations operate in society as "containers" of the emotions and anxieties of patients' relatives and friends, and a range of managerial initiatives from the 1980s onwards have served to increase and bolster the potential defence mechanisms in play to deal with the inherent anxiety of working in healthcare. Increased bureaucratisation of professional work has served to increase prescription and to decrease discretion. Prescriptive assessment and risk management procedures taken together with other bureaucratic elements of work serve a defensive purpose in allowing clinical professionals to spend less time with patients. Reassurance and relief from anxiety can be found through the performance of ritualistic tasks. Tight timescales, prescriptive "guidance", complicated recording systems and increased use of IT-based reporting all add to the workload and generate anxiety about meeting deadlines and "keeping on top" of paperwork [49,50].

Accordingly, all learning and development in healthcare organisations are powerfully marked by the nature of the day-to-day work undertaken by clinical professionals and this influence permeates the entire organisation [48]. When a public scandal in healthcare such as that at Mid-Staffordshire Hospital is eventually exposed, there is a powerful pressure on politicians and policy makers to be seen to "do something". After investigation, the default solution proposed typically involves the imposition of even more bureaucratic controls and regulations to add to the previous "initiatives", and the mandating of such requirements as compassion, better inspection, enhanced staff education and training, and the criminalising of neglect – but these initiatives alone cannot guarantee the required individual, group and organisational learning or any eventual change in everyday work practices, because they address the symptoms rather than underlying causes, which ultimately lie in the emotional labour undertaken by clinical staff [51]. The introduction of such requirements becomes another programme to add to the others, making it vulnerable to becoming yet another mechanical activity rather than keeping the purpose of healthcare in mind – compassionate caring for individuals.

Wicked problems: Healthcare organisations increasingly have to deal with "wicked" problems. Keith Grint has identified three kinds of problems which all organisations (including healthcare organisations) face and the "ideal types" associated with addressing them [52]. These are:

Critical problems: This is where it is obvious that a short-term and self-evident crisis exists, often in conditions of chaos and at an immediate tactical and operational level. There is virtually no uncertainty at all about what needs to be done; there is little or no space or time for discussion, debate or dissent and even coercion may be deemed to be ultimately permissible if the outcome is seen as being for the public good. The possibility of error is seen as a risk that simply has to be accepted in extremely testing circumstances. This is the arena of the **Commander** and the message here is "Just do what I say, it really doesn't matter what you think".

Tame problems: This is the area of "puzzles" which, just like crossword or jigsaw puzzles, ultimately do have a solution. They are "difficulties from which escapes are thought to be known" [53]. Often these are routine problems [54] where processes of logic and analysis are appropriate strategies to adopt. Such tame problems:

■ Can be described by a fairly clear and simple statement, where the root causes of the problem are either already known or are relatively easily discoverable.

■ Exist where the degree of uncertainty which is associated with the problem is limited and where the situation is stable, predictable and unambiguous. Such problems are therefore constant and do not fundamentally change with the passage of time.

■ Have broad agreement between all the interested parties or stakeholders about what success would look like.

■ Respond positively to the well-known tools of rational planning and management. In particular, they are largely amenable to project management approaches.

■ Are often subject to an organisation's standard operating procedures (SOPs).

■ Are likely to have occurred before, so are marked by the fact that previous experience and practice with the same or similar problems are useful guides towards a solution. So the "recipe" contained in the "cookbook" is essential and ensures replicability to further efforts, so that the same outcome results are guaranteed every time.

■ Have definitive and optimal solutions which would apply in any setting or context – and are therefore transferable.

■ Have a clear "stopping-point" so that it is clearly understood when a solution has finally been reached.

■ Can easily be objectively evaluated.

Tame in this context does not necessarily mean simple because a tame problem may be complicated technically. Constructing a new hospital, for example, is a tame problem as more or less correct ways of doing so already exist. Tame problems are also largely operational problems principally concerned with organisational efficiency and with looking "inwards and downwards" and focusing on issues of control and performance [55]. They are usually immediate and short term and emphasise the maintenance of consistency and the need for correction from any deviations from required targets or standards. They are thus the subject of what is known as single-loop learning [56], where the key question is "Are we doing things right?". With single-loop learning, people are not employed to modify rules but just to follow them. The aim is to ensure that everyone performs to a common standard and that any errors or deviations from the norm are detected and corrected. More complex thinking is deemed not to be necessary (others are paid for that) and the expectation is only to identify and correct any such deviations from the prescribed rules [57]. Such learning is:

Replicative: Prepared and packaged for use in situations marked by the completion of routine and repetitive tasks which call for little or no use of personal discretion.

Applicative: The emphasis is on translating learning into specific prescriptions for action in a range of different situations – with working out how something that worked in one setting can then be applied in a slightly different one [58].

An example of a tame healthcare problem would be a hospital examining its care of obstetrics patients and, through a clinical audit, finding a number of gaps between the established standards, which are derived from evidence-based guidelines, and the actual practice. A series of meetings then occur in order to discuss the guidelines, and changes are then made to working procedures and reporting and feedback on practice is enhanced. Such changes increase the number of patients receiving appropriate and timely care.

With tame problems, it is the role of the ***Manager*** to engage the appropriate process to solve the problem and the message is "I've seen this problem before and so I know what the appropriate process to apply in order to solve it is".

Wicked problems: The notion of "wicked" problems originally emerged in the 1970s in the USA in the context of social and urban planning. It became clear that problems of social policy could not be described definitively, and in a pluralistic society, there was often no undisputable public good and no objective definition of equity. Such policies cannot be meaningfully correct or false and so there are no solutions in the sense of definitive or objective answers [59], but they **can** be progressed. Sometimes described as "Saying yes to the mess" [60], wicked problems have none of the clarity of a tame problem. Instead they:

- Are problems with no definitive formulation that provides all the information needed in order to describe them, to break them down into manageable parts and to solve them.
- Are characterised by a high degree of uncertainty.
- May appear to be novel and never to have been encountered before.
- Are usually longer term and more strategic in nature.

- Relationships of cause and effect are not easily apparent, but an intervention in any part of a system is likely to have outcomes in many others, often unintended and not always desirable.
- Interact with or are "nested" within other problems and cannot simply be addressed in isolation, so it is difficult to separate the parts from the whole.
- Will appear "fuzzy", that is, unclear, incomplete, possibly contradictory and often paradoxical.
- Sit outside single professional and managerial hierarchies and exist across multiple organisational boundaries.
- Represent uncharted territory, where there is no fixed template or agreed way of doing things.
- Defy rational analysis and planning because logic-based linear approaches to problem-solving simply do not work with such highly complex systems with multiple stakeholders and often conflicting pressures and motivations.
- While expertise can help, on its own it is simply not sufficient and effective working relationships are therefore key.
- May appear to "shape-shift" as they are worked on.
- Have multiple perspectives on what exactly the problem is and what the right way forward might possibly be.
- Are strongly related to the particular context or setting in which they exist.
- Previous experience and practice appear to be of little help towards any resolution.
- Progress to be made will require both individuals and organisations to change their mind-sets and behaviour, to learn new ways of working and to choose between contradictory values.
- What exactly "success" in addressing the problem might be is difficult to define.
- Have no "stopping rule". It is impossible to say that a wicked problem has been solved, just that time, money or patience may have run out.
- Solutions to wicked problems are not true or false or right or wrong but are just better or worse alternatives, so evaluation cannot ever be objective and always requires judgement.
- Resolution of the problem may even, in turn, create further problematic issues.

Wicked problems are hard to describe and so defy the "rational" analysis which is associated with tame problems, not least because, due to multiple complex interdependencies, actions taken towards resolution often tend to lead towards unintended consequences. As a result, they are seldom completely "solved" but lead into other related problems. They often require joint working between different organisations, all of who have a different stake in the problem, so rather than the "inwards and downwards" orientation marked by tame problems, the emphasis is instead on "upwards and outwards" [55]. Logic-based and linear approaches to problem-solving are not an effective approach to such wicked problems, which are typically characterised by paradox. The biggest danger is to act on the basis of thinking that we know what to do in such cases, rather than to start from being open about not knowing and proceeding by questioning and inquiry. Rather than the single-loop learning which is typical of addressing tame problems, double-loop learning [56] is necessary in considering wicked problems and asks the question "Are we doing the right things?". Norms and standards are called into question if there is a possible better way of doing things. It involves the use of different learning modes:

Interpretative: Comprising both understanding (or ways of seeing things from a number of different perspectives) and judgement (or practical wisdom made up of an overall sense of purpose, a feel for appropriateness and a flexibility based upon a wealth of personal experience) [58].

Associative: Learning in a semi-conscious and intuitive way and often involving the use of metaphors and images [61].

Returning to the obstetrics example mentioned earlier, seeing this as a wicked problem would involve interviewing patients in some depth while reviewing such care. From this, it would emerge that the issues that concerned women were largely to do with such factors as convenience of access, the quality of information provided to them, continuity of care and the interpersonal aspects of the patient–professional relationship. As a result, obstetric care would be radically reconfigured to a system of midwife-led teams in order to give priority to these matters. The standards derived from the evidence-based guidelines would not be ignored but instead would be included in a reframed version of values and interactions.

This alternative approach also involves undertaking what has been called "bricolage" – a stitching together of a diverse range of actions and initiatives using whatever resources are at hand [62]. Bricolage involves processes of improvisation, experimentation and exploration. The term derives from the French verb "bricoler", which means to fiddle about or to tinker – the ability to make do and to use whatever is to hand or to make the most of what it is that we have. Being a "bricoleur" involves inventiveness – an ability to improvise a way forward without obvious tools or help by imagining the possibilities – for people to "act themselves into a new way of thinking" [63], what Ibarra [64] calls the "outsight principle". It may even be that intuition has a major part to play in addressing wicked problems [61]. Acting as a bricoleur requires a focus on [65]:

A sense of what has been termed "vuja de" – the complete realisation that a situation has never been encountered before and that therefore original thinking will be required to deal with it [66]. The fact that there is no written rule book of how things ought to be, so value has to be imagined and created with what we have in our reach and in our minds.

Our vulnerability and openness to not knowing or at least that what we had previously known and valued might be of limited use. It involves being comfortable with both knowing and with not knowing, asking the question "What do we not know?" and accepting that, most likely, there is much.

Engaging in a non-defensive way with change, without being overwhelmed by ever-present pressures to react, based upon resisting the urge to rush into action when anxiety and uncertainty are high.

An understanding that to address a problem, issue, challenge or question implies that simply every option has to be open.

The importance of it being a social endeavour, so a good question from one person enables the imagination and the sparking of ideas in another.

The adaption of situations, materials and what we have to hand to different purposes.

One school of thought [67] holds that healthcare issues (like many others in human service organisations) are quite distinct from physical/mechanical problems and are therefore not actually capable of being worked on by the rational-empirical scientific method of problem-definition and solution. Such issues may be intractable – that is, not permanently solvable – and such intractability may mean accepting the imperfectability of human beings and of society, deeply rooted in the human condition. No once-and-for-all solution is therefore possible. Instead, such problems have to be addressed over and over again depending upon the idiosyncratic context (time, place and historical circumstances). So any "solution" can therefore only last until the problem recurs in another form, as the problem can never be eliminated or ignored. Such problems may therefore be the inevitable consequences of human diversity and of the social structures associated with it.

This is the arena of the **Leader** who has to engage in collaborative dialogue with all the stakeholders and craft a partial, emergent or "clumsy" solution [52], that is, a "good enough for now" decision that takes the issue on a stage. The message is "I've never seen this problem before and we therefore need to get a shared view on what to do about this".

Others have previously identified the existence of wicked problems, without describing them as such. For example, as long ago as 1969, Laurence Peter asserted that:

> Some problems are so complex that you have to be highly intelligent and well-informed just to be undecided about them. [68]

Alfred Sloan, long-time president, chairman and CEO of General Motors is famous for Sloan's Dilemma which is allegedly attributed as:

"Gentlemen, I take it that we are all in complete agreement on the decision here?"

Consensus of nodding heads.

"Then I propose we postpone further discussion of this matter until our next meeting to give ourselves time to develop disagreement and perhaps gain some understanding of what the decision is all about".

And the American journalist H. L. Mencken is famed for saying:

> For every complex problem there is an answer that is clear, simple and wrong. [69]

More recently it has been proposed that:

> It is time that we stopped and stood back and looked at leadership not as a series of problems that can be solved, but as a series of contradictory, puzzling and obscure concepts that need to be managed and lived with. [70]

These warnings are important because there appears to be a strong tendency within most healthcare organisations to either assume that all the problems faced are actually tame in nature or to pretend that what are wicked problems are in fact tame and, therefore, amenable to being worked on only by rational analysis and planning. In practice, what may seem like the easy way out by applying such approaches usually leads straight back in. Such familiar solutions can not only be ineffective but can also be addictive and hence dangerous. It has been suggested that:

> Our learnt instinct is to troubleshoot and to fix things – in essence to break down the ambiguity, to resolve any paradox, to achieve more certainty and agreement and to move into the simple system zone. [71]

From a slightly different perspective, Ronald Heifetz has identified tame problems as "technical challenges" and wicked problems as "adaptive challenges" [72].

The challenges which healthcare organisations face are increasingly typified as wicked problems and require quite different approaches to be devised. Internally, healthcare organisations have to deal with the maintenance of a dynamic equilibrium or regulated pluralism [73] between multiple professions and occupations (especially between managers and clinicians), employee interests and concerns, Government priorities and those of their local communities. Examples of some of the other internal and external wicked problems faced by healthcare organisations in the UK include:

- Dealing with the continuing consequences of the Covid-19 pandemic.
- Dealing with the consequences of Brexit for healthcare in the UK.
- Addressing the emerging impact of climate change on healthcare organisations and the local communities which they serve.
- Ensuring that healthcare is just as accessible on an equitable basis to Black, Asian and Minority Ethnic (BAME) communities as it is to white people.
- Addressing the issue of the "glass ceiling" which prevents or limits the pay and career advancement of female employees.
- Likewise, addressing the continuing issue of institutional racism in healthcare organisations which inhibits the career progression for BAME employees.
- Recruiting, educating, training and retaining staff from a shrinking employment pool.
- Balancing short-term service delivery with longer-term innovation in service provision.
- Doing more for less – managing well within shrinking budgets.
- Addressing the major social and health-related problems of childhood and adult obesity, child abuse, alcoholism and drug addiction, neighbourhood crime and homelessness.
- Working jointly with local social care organisations to ensure that the patient/client is central to the redesign of services and that such services are experienced on the part of the patient/client as being "seamless". This includes the issue of communication between health and social care professionals.

Healthcare culture: The nature of the UK's NHS culture also serves to distinguish healthcare organisations from others. This culture involves:

- A number of features which are associated with all public sector organisations in the UK [74], including an aversion to failure; using failure when it does occur to score points against others rather than to learn lessons; a pressure for uniformity; a preference for command-and-control authority models; a lack of time other than to simply cope with events; secrecy being used to stifle feedback and learning; turf wars between professions and functions, despite the "joined-up" rhetoric [75]; the ubiquity of "efficiency drives" and of vested interests.
- From the 1980s, processes of slow, incremental and participative change became unfashionable and instead change had to be fast, furious and often brutal – as Peters [76] proposed, "Destruction is cool", and there is a related Polish saying "Sleep faster, we need the pillows"! Pettigrew et al. [77] described the NHS as being riven by "panics, crises, incoherence and endemic short-termism". An anti-reflexive orientation became established

that preferred fast, frequent and tangible action over any kind of reflection – a form of "sugar-rush" leap straight from instant diagnosis to rapid implementation which is redolent of Kahneman's System 1 thinking, rather than the System 2 mode – which is a slower, conscious and more thoughtful approach [78]. This is similar to Claxton's [61] distinction between the crisp, business-like thought of the "hare brain" contrasted with the more contemplative "tortoise mind".

Such an orientation – the ability to always promote decisive and directive action in the face of any uncertainty – is highly valued, indeed, some would describe it as an addiction [79]. It asks the questions "What do we know?", "How much do we know?", "How much can we get done?" and "How quickly can we arrive at a decision?" – and so encourages people to try to break down complex problems into manageable chunks [80]; to shut-out possible new ideas and feelings; to close-off what it is not intended to see or hear; to invoke prior knowledge, which may no longer even apply; to rush into action and to adopt a new certainty too quickly before any new pattern has a chance to emerge. It is what Garratt [55] described as an "action-fixated non-learning cycle". Action and decisiveness are the qualities which are most highly valued – Weisbord [81] suggested that "Managers hate to sit looking at something from all angles, they like to get on with it." In OD terms, this often involves a pace of change that is over-fast and which does not take account of the level of capacity and capability existing on the ground. Walton [47], in contrast, suggests that active listening with appropriate care and understanding gets to the core of presented issues. This is the case for both healthcare clinical professionals and for OD practitioners.

This orientation is marked by continuing feelings of urgency and so the overriding goal is to always reach out quickly for decisions – a form of "hurry sickness" [82] and therefore often to grasp at straws in order to simply make something happen [83]. This occurs when people feel chronically short of time and so tend to try to perform every task faster – and then get anxious and flustered when encountering any kind of delay.

■ An expectation is that the individual senior leaders and managers in the organisational hierarchy will automatically be the ones who will always provide or develop solutions to the challenges faced. Yet:

"Most people at the 'top' of hierarchical organisations simply do not know the innovative ways forward in addressing wicked problems which their organisations face. 'Top' people also know that they (the 'top' people) do not know but cannot say that they do not know, because there is an expectation that they should know. So they often pretend to know. People at the front line in those organisations often do know the most useful ways forward and also know that the people at the 'top' don't know what they are, but they expect the 'top' to know because it absolves those at the front line of any culpability for what may go wrong". [84]

Similarly, Argyris and Schon [85] had previously suggested that:

Organisational learning is not the same thing as individual learning. There are too many cases in which organisations know less than their members. There are even cases in which the organisation cannot seem to learn what every member knows.

Clearly, Argyris in particular became pessimistic about the capacity of organisations to engage in the kind of collective learning processes which he advocated [86].

Staff at all levels frequently do understand the nature of a problem, challenge, issue or opportunity, together with how to address it or to take advantage of it, yet they very often stay silent [87,88]. Contrast this with the aphorism attributed to Revans, that in such organisations "Doubt ascending speeds wisdom from above" [89], which undermines the hierarchical assumptions that underpin so many change models. It has, however, been suggested [90] that in many performance-driven healthcare organisations, it is more often the case that "Doubt ascending speeds retribution from above".

Any expression of doubt and resulting upwards questioning, where it is permitted at all, is really allowed only for clarification, rather than for the challenging of existing policy or strategy. Jones et al. [91], in an international study, found that any such creative dialogue was regularly inhibited by the pre-existing cultural relationships and workplace hierarchies, and in that respect the fact that, for example, following the revelations of the Mid-Staffordshire Hospital Inquiry, NHS organisations were given national policy advice to appoint Freedom To Speak Up Guardians was indicative that such candid dialogue within hierarchical systems was not something which was well valued or already "baked-in" to the system. What may be experienced by senior healthcare leaders and managers as unacceptable behaviour can then be pathologised as being a form of trouble-making dissent or even rebellion, and so it should be ignored or laughed off, through such responses as the assertion that there is little or no evidence that frontline employees have views to express, the suppression of any such views when they are expressed, facadism and defensive engagement [92].

Certainly, although there might be some degree of commitment in principle from some senior organisational leaders and managers to such listening and acting, the actual practice is very often to identify strongly with the status quo and to ignore in whole or part what emerges from the front line, rather than seeking it out, welcoming and celebrating it and working with it. Revans [53] identified a whole range of possible responses in use to "doubt ascending", and these included non-hostile scepticism, lack of interest, manipulative guidance, tactical procrastination, diagnostic inflexibility, evasion and vacillation, directive autocracy and defensive rationalisation.

It may be that the distance that such senior leaders and managers operate from the front-line and from the primary focus of their organisation acts as a form of defence mechanism and so anaesthetises them from the pervading anxiety which permeates such organisations [48]. They are perhaps "unsighted" and cannot really see what is happening in their organisations because they rely largely upon information only in the form of performance metrics. There may also be the existence of "advantage blindness" based on their job title, gender, ethnicity, age appearance and accent [93] and they may operate in an "optimism bubble" underestimating how much some issues matter to others, whilst overestimating their own ability to listen and be seen as approachable [92]. Warwick-Giles and Checkland [94] found that the activity of sense-giving to employees by senior leaders while being powerful was also problematic, as their need to project a narrative of success acted to minimise or deflect attention away from any difficulties.

As a result, there is ample scope for dissonance between what such leaders and managers believe their personal and professional values to be and those that are perceived by others within their organisation – between their espoused theory and their theory in use [95]. It has also been suggested [96] that many managers themselves feel that they in turn are being micromanaged and are compelled to adopt a short-term outlook to work. At its worst, a destructive form of hubristic leadership [97] can even be evident and the potential toxicity of the workplace due to such leadership has been extensively explored by Walton [98–102]. Ambitious senior leaders and managers are most likely to be achievement-oriented, success-driven and programmed to survive, with an acute sense of self-protection and an intensified awareness of real or imagined threats to their status, entitlement and power. They may be subject to the Dunning-Kruger effect [103] where they believe that they are more intelligent and capable than they really are. Lacking the awareness, skills and experience needed to recognise their own relative incompetence and limitations, this may lead them to overestimate their own capability and underestimate the challenges they face.

■ The discounting of what has been termed, in a study in the coal industry, as "pit sense" [104], that is, the implicit or tacit knowledge which is situated in, and derived from, the complicated reality of everyday changing work activities and practices – the day-to-day ordinary and uncodified working relationships between colleagues who just do what needs to be done and make things actually work in practice. Such effective relating is seen as "a constructive, ongoing process of meaning-making, through language" [105]. Mintzberg [106] likewise proposes that assessing many of the ongoing activities in public service organisations like healthcare requires what he calls "soft judgement", employing everyday compassion and empathy. This marginalisation of relationships and discounting of pit sense is done in favour of technical and explicit management-imposed bureaucratic procedures, rationalised on the basis of desired policy outcomes, together with a concentration on roles and job titles within the system, rather than with the relationships between individuals.

■ A preference for use of the large national or international management consultancies, often offering packaged or "pre-cooked" approaches, over the mobilisation of internal OD resources, despite the fact that research reveals that the impact of such external groups has, over time, not made any significant impact across all public services [107], and despite the perceptive insight that:

the undue intervention of experts carrying no personal responsibility for real life actions is at best, ambiguous, in general opinionative, and at worst, reactionary [53].

Bussu and Marshall [108] claim that while externally sourced and off- the-shelf OD programmes do capture the imagination of senior healthcare management, they do not work for the staff who are delivering care. Such a top-down approach to OD based on a series of ad hoc events and training activities that aim to sell senior management's vision to their staff is often perceived as disingenuous by those staff and, as a result, has limited impact. Additionally, the problematic nature of healthcare organisations contracting with such consultancies is also well documented [109,110].

■ Associated with this is the assumption that private sector organisations are always superior in the way that they are run and that all public sector organisations, including healthcare organisations, are inevitably riddled with inefficiencies and so are ineffective. This is widely known as the New Public Management (NPM) but also has been labelled as "mad management virus" [75]. Ideas and techniques drawn from the private sector were increasingly introduced into the public sector from the 1980s onwards, with the aim of supposedly making the latter more business-like and efficient [111]. The belief was that these large and expensive state bureaucracies would be brought under control through the introduction of commercial management practices, such as internal and external competition, audit, numerical targets and stringent cost controls [112]. "Hard" or quantitative skills were seen to be synonymous with enhanced managerial intelligence, precision and strength, while "soft" or interpersonal skills such as empathy and sensitivity were correspondently viewed as signs of weakness [113]. Cottam [112] notes that while NPM was presented publicly as being only a neutral theory of management and merely concerned with improving efficiency and making technical adjustments, it was actually a programme of far-reaching cultural change – an obsession with what was seen as the arms-length and transactional business of service delivery.

The viewpoint which was inherent in NPM was that leadership and management were simply generic; that all organisations possessed more similarities than differences and that performance in all organisations could be optimised by the application of a set of common management theories, skills and techniques. The idea that healthcare organisations were in any way different was rejected by the argument that they could (and therefore should) be managed in the same way as any private sector organisation, despite the fact that, for most, they did not have the reconciling function of profit [2] and that leadership within such organisations often has to be "selfless" [114].

■ Top-heavy systems of reporting upwards of organisational performance management metrics such as Key Performance Indicators (KPIs), risk management figures and other targets, which have little relation to the everyday lived experience of either front-line staff or of patients, in order to meet top-down and imposed time deadlines [115]. Targets are, by their nature, arbitrary measures [116,117] because there is no known scientific method for setting them. No matter how much in-depth analysis is undertaken to establish prevailing trajectories, parameters or average rate of prior performance, the actual adjustment to produce the target is always arbitrary. Moreover, the evidence that outcome-based performance management for social good simply makes things worse is strong [118]. The drive to continuously assess the performance of professional staff and to attempt to measure those forms of work such as compassion or empathy, which, by their very nature, are resistant to quantification, has required additional layers of management and bureaucracy [119]. Bunting [39], for example, proposes that listening comprises some nine-tenths of most health and social care jobs, and this requires the qualities of attentiveness, time, focus and trust, none of which are easily measured.

■ As a result of the spread of these performance management metrics, a movement began away from the management of people towards the measurement of performance [120], and then from the measurement of performance to a fixation with measurement itself through the instituting of multifarious permanent controlling and reporting systems. What has emerged is a fetishising of data in the mistaken belief that it makes the situation knowable and certain. It is a form of "thingification" [65] – not a direct comparison of the actual performance or output of employees but a comparison between the audited representation of that performance and output. Work thus becomes geared towards the generation and massaging of representations – of a simulacrum of reality – rather than to the goals of the work itself. As a result, senior leaders become "unsighted" and so rarely can really see what is really happening in their organisations, relying instead upon this range of generic performance metrics.

As a result, what can and does get measured is not always worth measuring, may not be what would be useful to know and may draw effort away from more important things [121,122]. This is often known as "Hitting the target but missing the point". The assumption seems to be that such measurement is a cost-free activity or one whose benefits are so obvious that no cost for undertaking them can ever be too much. Yet, as a result, so much time is devoted to recording, tracking, monitoring, assessing and cross-referencing such data. Such a culture also encourages the possibility of "gaming" results in order to exaggerate or downplay responses [123]. This danger of valuing quantitative data only and ignoring other qualitative material resembles the "McNamara Fallacy", named after the US Secretary of Defence during the Vietnam War which runs as follows:

The first step is to measure whatever can be easily measured. This is OK as far as it goes. To second step is to disregard what can't be measured easily or to give it an arbitrary value. This is artificial and misleading. The third step is to presume that whatever can't be measured easily really isn't important. This is blindness. The fourth step is to say whatever can't be measured easily really doesn't exist. This is suicide. [124]

Or as Albert Einstein is reputedly to have said, more succinctly, "Not everything that counts can be counted, and not everything that can be counted counts". Such constant and repeated measurement and evaluation also promotes an erosion of individual and group professional autonomy and discretion and fosters a growing dependence on a set of external, and often shifting, norms [125]. This growing "audit society" [126] featured:

a plethora of guidance, league tables, star-ratings, regulatory bodies and inspectorates, targets, national service frameworks, performance indicators, minimum standards, incentives, sanctions and regulations – all to cajole, coax, threaten, encourage, exhort and order public bodies to do the Government's bidding. [127]

■ There is an increasing emphasis on the identification of "good" and "bad" employees and their intrinsic personalities, rather than on the nature of the organisational culture. Instead of recognising that there can be toxic organisational cultures, the emphasis is on those individual employees who might complain too much or cause trouble – and hence job performance itself is psychologised. This focus functions as an ideological smokescreen, whereby the contextual or structural factors are ignored and the spotlight is placed on an employee's attitude instead – on their personality, enthusiasm and willingness, or their lack of it [128].

As a result, causes of public failures and scandals are labelled as individual deficits – as "bad apples" – rather than a combination of bureaucratic, professional and work-related pressures grounded in overall policy and organisational cultures [129,130]. There is thus a powerful incentive for policy makers and senior leaders and managers to scapegoat "pathological" individuals who allegedly "abuse the system" for what are often corporate and systemic failures [119]. They are portrayed as being grit thrown into the gears of what is considered to be an effective, well-oiled piece of organisational machinery [57].

■ A preference for frequent bouts of structural change – the "re-disorganisations" – and the selection and appointment of key individuals who supposedly possess the purported relevant characteristics or "right stuff" [131] – a principle which has its origins in the work of F. W. Taylor of scientific management fame [132]. The focus has been on identifying such individuals and developing their personal knowledge and skills [133] and reflects the enduring allure of so-called "heroic leadership" [134], embodying assumptions that leadership is an elite practice and a rational endeavour arising from a set of characteristics possessed by only a few special and gifted individuals [135]. The growth of "talent management" and an emphasis on identifying and developing healthcare leaders have had an "accolade effect" for those chosen for participation in such leadership development programmes, but Vince and Pedler [136] have proposed that:

those opportunities.... are likely to remain highly valued by the chosen, for whom the recognition and self-worth benefits may outweigh the inappropriateness of universal models or the need to resist undesirable shaping. In this way, those chosen for cultural assimilation collude in perpetuating development that ill-prepares them for the acknowledged complexity of leadership work.

The focus of the development of such leaders has not been on the wicked and intractable systemic problems which healthcare organisations face but rather on safer "own-job" issues. As such, it reflects the "fundamental attribution error" [137] – the tendency to over-value personality-based and individualistic explanations of behaviour, while undervaluing contextual explanations. This is exemplified by the popularity of "talent management" and the search for supposedly "hi-po" (high potential) leaders and managers.

■ Healthcare leaders and managers, just like their private sector counterparts, have increasingly, and especially from the 1980s, come to believe that they should be "free to manage", with an explicit mandate to redraw the frontiers of control between themselves and healthcare professionals. They believe increasingly that they are rational, benign and free from any vested interests and so should have the power to directly manage professionals. They believe that they represent and promote corporate objectives and "lead" in a way that transcends the limited interests of any professional group within an organisation [138]. The implication is that because leaders and managers as a group are free from professional interests, they can be seen as acting in the best interests of the public [139], despite the fact that such leaders and managers are themselves also a self-interested "caste" [140]. Doran [141] has noted that managerialism as an ideology seeks to advance and protect the interests of leaders and managers as a group.

Leaders and managers tend to become accultured by a form of "cultural doping" [142] or what Zuboff [143] has called "social amnesia" or "psychic numbing" and so accept the dominant managerial worldview. They are then mostly unwilling, unlikely and even unable to question such a perspective, perhaps due to such factors as personal career interests, preferment and patronage [144] which combine into a "cultural immune system" [145] which, by selective filtering, shuts out information that does not fit, so that seeing is not believing, rather that believing is seeing. A shared "class consciousness" serves as a unifying force among leaders and managers and seemingly places any ownership of organisational well-being squarely on their shoulders alone – and so justifies their continuing reliance on the managerial hierarchy and the control which is inherent in such bureaucratic structures. This may be an example of the "power of innocence" [146] which asserts that:

People's personal positions are arrived at and sustained by being in a group of people whose understanding of the world is similar to their own. Thus, their position is both sustained by other group members ("That's the way the world is") or even attributed to the group ("If you're a manager this is what you think"). The last thing the fish discovers is water. Innocence derives its power through being comfortably and unreflectively surrounded by others of like mind. From this stance, individuals cannot see themselves colluding with the larger flow of institutional direction and its consequences.

As Goleman [147] has suggested:

The range of what we think and do is limited by what we fail to notice, and because we fail to notice that we fail to notice, there is little we can do to change, until we notice how failing to notice shapes our thoughts and deeds.

■ An obsession with stylistic obsolescence or "neophilia" – a concentration on what is seen as being the newest and the latest, rather than being reflexive of current experience and a reliance on the accumulated wisdom acquired over time. A tendency to become bored with older things and a desire to embrace novelty for its own sake [148]. This often manifests itself as the "guru effect" – an obsession with the output of self-proclaimed management "experts" or so-called "thought leaders" without any questioning of their motivations, underlying values and starting assumptions. Some might even argue that thought leadership actually equates with thought management and thought control. A culture where the focus is always on newness leaves those people who are not associated with the latest initiative feeling insecure, undervalued and sometimes abandoned [149]. Yet, as the novelist William Faulkner astutely commented "The past is never dead. It's not even past" [150].

References

1. Pratt, J., Plamping, D. and Gordon, P. (2007) *Distinctive Characteristics of Public Sector Organisations and Implications for Leadership*, Leeds: Northern Leadership Academy.
2. Hampden-Turner, C. (1992) Foreword, in Common, R., Flynn, N. and Mellon, E. (Eds.) *Managing Public Services: Competition and Decentralisation*, Oxford: Butterworth-Heinemann, 6–8.
3. Wilkinson, D. and Appelbee, E. (1999) *Implementing Holistic Government: Joined-up Action on the Ground,* Bristol: The Policy Press.
4. Stein, H. (1981) The Concept of the Human Service Organisation: A Critique, *Administration in Social Work*, 4 (2): 1–13.
5. Hasenfield, H. (1983) *Human Service Organisations as Complex Organisations*, Thousand Oaks, CA: Sage.
6. Gouldner, A. (1957) Cosmopolitans and Locals: Toward and Analysis of Latent Social Roles, *Administrative Science Quarterly*, 2 (3): 281–306.

7. Mintzberg, H. (1979) *The Structuring of Organisations*, Englewood Cliffs, NJ: Prentice-Hall.
8. Mintzberg, H. (1983) *Structure in 5s: Designing Effective Organisations*, Englewood Cliffs, NJ: Prentice-Hall.
9. Best, G. (1999) *Managerial Hierarchies and Healthcare Reform: A Precautionary Tale for the Millenium*, London: OD Partnership Network.
10. Jaques, E. (1976) *A General Theory of Bureaucracy*, London: Heinemann.
11. Plsek, P. (2003) *Complexity and the Adoption of Innovation in Health Care*, National Institute for Health Care Management Foundation/National Committee for Quality Health Care.
12. Mannion, R. and Davies, H. (2018) Understanding Organisational Culture for Healthcare Quality Improvement, *British Medical Journal*, 363: k4907.
13. Ham, C. (2003) Improving the Performance of Health Services: The Role of Clinical Leadership, *The Lancet*, 361: 1978–1980.
14. Fish, D. and Coles, C. (1998) *Developing Professional Judgement in Health Care: Learning Through the Critical Appreciation of Practice*, Oxford: Butterworth-Heinemann.
15. Lipsky, M. (1980) *Street-Level Bureaucracy: Dilemmas of the Individual in Public Services*, New York: Russell Sage Foundation.
16. Cooper, M., Somalingam, S. and O'Donnell, C. (2015) Street-Level Bureaucracy: An Underused Theoretical Model for General Practice? *British Journal of General Practice*, 65 (636): 376–377.
17. Edmonstone, J., Lawless, A. and Pedler, M. (2019) Leadership Development, Wicked Problems and Action Learning: Provocations to a Debate, *Action Learning: Research and Practice*, 16 (1): 37–51.
18. Moore, S. (1987) The Theory of Street-Level Bureaucracy: A Positive Critique, *Journal of Health Politics, Policy and Law*, 7 (4): 968–970.
19. Wastell, D., White, S., Broadhurst, K., Peckover, S. and Pithouse, A. (2010) Children's Services in the Iron Cage of Performance Management: Street-Level Bureaucracy and the Spectre of Svejkism, *International Journal of Social Welfare*, 19 (3): 310–320.
20. Ellis, K. (2011) "Street-Level Bureaucracy" Revisited: The Changing Face of Frontline Discretion in Adult Social Care in England, *Social Policy Administration*, 45 (3): 221–244.
21. Andolo, D. (2012) Time to Talk About Workplace Stress, *Guardian*, 3rd October.
22. Health and Safety Executive (2018) *Work-Related Stress, Depression or Anxiety Statistics in Great Britain, 2018*, Bootle: HSE.
23. Health and Safety Executive (2015) *Work Related Stress, Anxiety and Depression Statistics in Great Britain 2015*, Bootle: HSE.
24. NHS Employers (2014) *Stress in the Workplace*, London: NHS Employers.
25. WHO (2019) *International Classification of Diseases*, 11th revision, Geneva: World Health Organisation.
26. Greenberg, N., Weston, D., Hall, C., Caulfield, T., Williamson, V. and Fong, K. (2021) Mental Health of Staff Working in Intensive Care During Covid-19, *Occupational Medicine*, doi:10.1093/occmed/kqaa220.

27. Revans, R. (1964) *Standards for Morale: Cause and Effect in Hospitals*, Oxford: Oxford University Press.

28. Menzies-Lyth, I. (1959) The Functioning of Social Systems as a Defence Against Anxiety: A Report on a Study of the Nursing Service of a General Hospital, in Menzies-Lyth, I. (Ed.) *Containing Anxiety in Institutions: Selected Essays: Volume 1*, London: Free Association books, 43–88.

29. Walton, M. (2021a) Leadership Constraints: Executive Behaviour When the Organisations says No! *Effective Executive*, 24 (1): 15–24.

30. Tallis, R. (2005) *Hippocratic Oaths: Medicine and its Discontents*, London: Atlantic Books.

31. Dartington, T. (2004) *Managing Vulnerability: The Underlying Dynamics of Systems of Care*, London: Karnack Books.

32. Yalom, I. (1980) *Existential Psychotherapy*, New York: Basic Books.

33. Bettelheim, B. and Rosenfeld, A. (1993) *The Art of the Obvious: Developing Insight for Psychotherapy and Everyday Life*, London: Thomas and Hudson.

34. May, R. (1983) *The Discovery of Being: Writings in Existential Psychology*, London: W. W. Norton and Company.

35. Kets de Vries, M. (2009) *Sex, Money, Happiness and Death: The Quest for Authenticity*, Basingstoke: Palgrave Macmillan.

36. Mastracci, S., Guy, M. and Newman, M. (2012) *Emotional Labour and Crisis Response: Working on the Razor's Edge*, Abingdon: Routledge.

37. Hayward, R. and Tuckey, M. (2011) Emotions in Uniform: How Nurses Regulate Emotions at Work via Emotional Boundaries, *Human Relations*, 64 (11): 1501–1523.

38. Bolton, S. (2001) Changing Faces: Nurses as Emotional Jugglers, *Sociology of Health and Illness*, 23 (1): 85–100.

39. Bunting, M (2020) *Labour of Love: The Crisis of Care*, London: Granta Books.

40. Campling, P. (2014) Reforming the Culture of Healthcare: The Case for Intelligent Kindness, *BJPsych Bulletin*, 39 (1): 1–5, February.

41. Ham, C., Baird, B., Gregory, S. and Jabbal, J. (2015) *The NHS Under the Coalition Government: Part 1: NHS Reform*, London: King's Fund.

42. Hochschild, A. (1983) *The Managed Heart: Commercialisation of Human Feeling*, Berkeley, CA: University of California Press.

43. Zapf, D. and Holz, M. (2006) On the Positive and Negative Effects of Emotion Work in Organisations, *European Journal of Work and Organisational Psychology*, 15 (1): 1–28.

44. Grandey, A. (2000) Emotion Regulation in the Workplace: A New Way to Conceptualise Emotional Labour, *Journal of Occupational Health Psychology*, 5 (1): 95–110.

45. Francis, R. (2010) *Independent Inquiry into Care Provided by Mid-Staffordshire NHS Foundation Trust, January 2005 to March 2009*, London: HMSO.

46. Bain, A. (1998) Social Defences Against Organisational Learning, *Human Relations*, 51 (3): 413–429.

47. Walton, M. (2021b) Listening with Care and Understanding: Getting to the Core of Presented Issues, *IUP Journal of Soft Skills*, 15 (1): 7–19.

48. Hinshelwood, R. and Skogstad, W. (Eds.) (2000) *Observing Organisations: Anxiety, Defence and Culture in Health Care*, London: Routledge.
49. Edmonstone, J. (2013) Healthcare Leadership: Learning from Evaluation, *Leadership in Health Services*, 26 (2): 148–158.
50. Edmonstone, J. (2013) What is Wrong with NHS Leadership Development? *British Journal of Healthcare Management*, 19 (11): 531–538.
51. Powell, M. (2019) Learning from NHS Inquiries: Comparing the Recommendations of the Ely, Bristol and Mid-Staffordshire Inquiries, *The Political Quarterly*, 90 (2): 229–237.
52. Grint, K. (2008) Wicked Problems and Clumsy Solutions: The Role of Leadership, *Clinical Leader*, 1 (2): 54–68.
53. Revans, R. (2011) *The ABC of Action Learning*, Farnham: Gower.
54. Mayer, R. (1995) The Search for Insight, in Sternberg, R. and Davidson, J. (Eds.) *The Nature of Insight*, Cambridge, MA: MIT Press, 75–88.
55. Garratt, B. (2000) *The Learning Organisation: Developing Democracy at Work*, 3rd edition, London: HarperCollins Business.
56. Argyris, C. (1976) *Increasing Leadership Effectiveness*, New York: Wiley.
57. Kuhl, S. (2019) *The Rainmaker Effect: Contradictions of the Learning Organisation*, Princeton, NJ: Organisational Dialogue Press.
58. Eraut, M. (1994) *Developing Professional Knowledge and Competence*, London: Falmer Press.
59. Rittell, H. and Webber, M. (1973) Dilemmas in a General Theory of Planning, *Policy Sciences*, 4: 155–169.
60. Stacey, R. (2002) *Strategic Management and Organisational Dynamics: The Challenge of Complexity*, Harlow: Prentice-Hall.
61. Claxton, G. (1997) *Hare Brain: Tortoise Mind: Why Intelligence Increases When You Think Less*, London: Fourth Estate.
62. Cunha, M. (2005) *Bricolage in Organisations*, FEUNL Working Paper No. 474, Nova School of Business & Economics, New University of Lisbon.
63. Pascale, R., Sternin, J. and Sternin, M. (2010) *The Power of Positive Deviance: How Unlikely Innovators Solve the World's Toughest Problems*, Boston, MA: Harvard Business School Publishing.
64. Ibarra, H. 92015) *Act Like a Leader, Think Like a Leader*, Boston, MA: Harvard Business School Publishing.
65. Traeger, J. and Warwick, R. (2020) *Artful Ways: Practice-Based Learning in Organisational Change: An Incitement to Humanity*, Hove: Mayvin Ltd.
66. Sutton, R. (2002) *Weird Ideas That Work: 11½ Practices for Promoting, Managing and Sustaining Innovation*, New York: The Free Press.
67. Sarason, S. (1978) The Nature of Problem-Solving in Social Action, *American Psychologist*, 33 (4): 370–380.
68. Peter, L. and Hull, R. (1969) *The Peter Principle: Why Things Always Go Wrong*, New York: William Morrow & Co.
69. Mencken, H. (1982) *A Mencken Chrestomathy*, New York: First Vintage Books.
70. Bolden, R., Witzel, M. and Linacre, N. (Eds.) (2016) *Leadership Paradoxes: Rethinking Leadership for an Uncertain World*, Abingdon: Routledge.

71. Plsek, P. and Greenhalgh, T. (2001) The Challenge of Complexity in Healthcare, *British Medical Journal*, 323 (7313): 625–658.

72. Heifetz, R., Grashow, A. and Linsky, M. (2009) *The Practice of Adaptive Leadership: Tools and Tactics for Changing your Organisation and the World*, Boston, MA: Harvard Business Publishing.

73. Bate, P. (2000) Changing the Culture of a Hospital: From Hierarchy to Networked Community, *Public Administration*, 78 (3): 485–512.

74. Chapman, J. (2002) *System Failure: Why Governments Must Learn to Think Differently*, London: Demos.

75. Attwood, M., Pedler, M., Pritchard, S. and Wilkinson, D. (2003) *Leading Change: A Guide to Whole Systems Working*, Bristol: The Policy Press.

76. Peters, T. (1997) *The Circle of Innovation: You Can't Shrink Your Way to Greatness*, New York: Knopf.

77. Pettigrew, A., Ferlie, E. and McKee, L. (1992) *Shaping Strategic Change in Large Organisations: The Case of the National Health Service*, London: Sage Publications.

78. Kahneman, D. (2011) *Thinking Fast and Slow*, London: Penguin.

79. Grint, K. (2010) The Cuckoo Clock Syndrome: Addicted to Command, Allergic to Leadership, *European Management Journal*, 28 (4): 306–313.

80. Edmonstone, J. (2014) On the Nature of Problems in Action Learning, *Action Learning: Research & Practice*, 11 (1): 25–41.

81. Weisbord, M. (2012) *Productive Workplaces: Dignity, Meaning and Community in the 21st Century*, San Francisco, CA: Jossey-Bass.

82. Friedman, H. and Booth-Kewley, S. (1987) Personality, Type A Behaviour and Coronary Heart Disease: The Role of Emotional Expression, *Journal of Personality and Social Psychology*, 53 (4): 783–792.

83. Gond, J-P., Cabantous, L., Harding, N. and Learmonth, M. (2016) What Do We Mean by Performativity in Organisational and Management Theory?: The Uses and Abuses of Performativity, *International Journal of Management Reviews*, 18 (4): 440–463.

84. Obolensky, N. (2014) *Complex Adaptive Leadership: Embracing Paradox and Uncertainty*, Farnham: Gower.

85. Argyris, C. and Schon, D. (1978) *Organisational Learning: A Theory of Action Perspective*, Reading, MA: Addison-Wesley.

86. Shaw, P. (2002) *Changing Conversations in Organisations: A Complexity Approach to Change*, London: Routledge.

87. Morrison, E. and Milliken, F. (2000) Organisational Silence: A Barrier to Change and Development in a Pluralistic World, *Academy of Management Review*, 25 (4): 706–725.

88. Dyne, L., Ang, S. and Botero, I. (2003) Conceptualising Employee Silence and Employee Voice as Multidimensional Constructs, *Journal of Management Studies*, 40 (6): 1111–1467.

89. Pedler, M. and Abbott, C. (2013) *Facilitating Action Learning: A Practitioner's Guide*, Maidenhead: Open University Press/McGraw-Hill.

90. Edmonstone, J. (2019) *Systems Leadership in Health and Social Care*, Abingdon: Routledge.

91. Jones, A., Blake, J., Adams, M., Kelly, D., Mannion, R. and Maben, J. (2021) Interventions Promoting Employee "Speaking-Up" Within Healthcare Workplaces: A Systematic Narrative Review of the International Literature, *Health Policy* (In press).

92. Reitz, M., Higgins, J. and Day-Duro, E. (2021) *The Do's and Don'ts of Employee Activism: How Organisations Respond to Voices of Difference*, Berkhamsted: Hult International Business School.

93. Reitz, M. and Higgins, J. (2020) Speaking Truth to Power: Why Leaders Cannot Hear What They Need to Hear, *BMJ Leader*, October.

94. Warwick-Giles, L. and Checkland, K. (2018) Integrated Care Using "Sense-making" to Understand How Organisations Are Working Together to Transform Local Health and Social Care Services, *Journal of Health Organisation and Management*, 32 (1): 85–100.

95. Argyris, C. and Schon, D. (1974) *Theory in Practice: Increasing Professional Effectiveness*, San Francisco, CA: Jossey-Bass.

96. Sherf, E., Tangirala, S. and Venkataramani, V. (2019) Why Managers Do Not Seek Voice from Employees: The Importance of Managers' Personal Control and Long-Term Orientation, *Organisation Science*, 30 (3): 447–646.

97. Sadler-Smith, E. (2019) *Hubristic Leadership*, London: Sage.

98. Walton, M. (2012) Toxicity, Hubris and Personality Dysfunctions, *Counselling at Work*, Spring: 21–25.

99. Walton, M. (2011) Derailment Themes and Personality Variables, *Counselling at Work*, Winter: 2–5.

100. Walton, M. (2008) Dealing With the Inevitability of Constraints: Toxic Sources, *Organisations and People*, 15 (3): 121–125.

101. Walton, M. (2007) Leadership Toxicity: An Inevitable Affliction of Organisations? *Organisations and People*, 14 (1): 19–27.

102. Walton, M. (2005) Leaders? Who Are They and What Do They Believe In Anyway? *International Journal of Leadership Education*, 1 (1): 23–28.

103. Dunning, D. and Kruger, J. (1999) Unskilled and Unaware of It, *Journal of Personality and Social Psychology*, 77 (6): 1121–1134.

104. Kamoche, K. and Maguire, K. (2011) Pit Sense: Appropriation of Practice-Based Knowledge in a UK Coalmine, *Human Relations*, 64 (5): 725–744.

105. Dachler, P. and Hosking, D. (2013) The Primacy of Relations in Socially Constructing Organisations' Realities, in Hosking, D., Dachler, P. and Gergen, K. (Eds.) *Management and Organisation: Relational Alternatives to Individualism*, Aldershot: Avebury Books, 93–112.

106. Mintzberg, H. (1996) Managing Government, Governing Management, *Harvard Business Review*, May-June.

107. Kirkpatrick, I., Sturdy, A., Alvarado, N., Blanco-Oliver, A. and Veronesi, G. (2018) The Impact of Management Consultants on Public Service Efficiency, *Policy and Politics*, 46 (2): 1–19.

108. Bussu, S. and Marshall, M. (2020) Organisational Development to Support Integrated Care in East London: The Perspective of Clinicians and Social Workers on the Ground, *Journal of Health Organisation and Management*, 34 (5): 603–619.

109. Edmonstone, J. and Western, J. (2002) Leadership in Healthcare: What Do We Know? *Journal of Management in Medicine*, 16 (1): 34–37.

110. Edmonstone, J. (2009) Evaluating Clinical Leadership: A Case Study, *Leadership in Health Services*, 22 (3): 210–224.

111. Ward, S. (2011) The Machinations of Managerialism: New Public Management and the Diminishing Power of Professionals, *Journal of Cultural Economy*, 4 (2): 205–215.

112. Cottam, H. (2018) *Radical Help: How We Can Remake the Relationships Between Us and Revolutionise the Welfare State*, London: Virago.

113. Williams, S. and Keep, J. (2015) Resilience Building Has a Hidden Cost, *Health Service Journal*, 125 (6460): 16–17.

114. Brooke, S. (2016) *The Selfless Leader: A Compass for Collective Leadership*, London: Palgrave.

115. Malby, B. (2008) *Organisational Performance – What Counts? Or Are Metrics the New Black?* Leeds: Centre for Innovation in Health Management, University of Leeds.

116. Seddon, J. (2016) New Public Management: Dystopian Interventions in Public Services, in Pell, C., Wilson, R. and Lowe, T. (Eds.) *Kittens Are Evil: Little Heresies in Public Policy*, Axminster: Triarchy Press, 11–17.

117. Guilfoyle, S. (2016) The Performance Management Emperor Has No Clothes, in Pell, C., Wilson, R. and Lowe, T. (Eds.) *Kittens Are Evil: Little Heresies in Public Policy*, Axminster: Triarchy Press, 83–96.

118. Lowe, T. (2016) Outcome-Based Performance Management Makes Things Worse, in Pell, C., Wilson, R. and Lowe, T. (Eds.) *Kittens Are Evil: Little Heresies in Public Policy*, Axminster: Triarchy Press, 37–52.

119. Fisher, M. (2009) *Capitalist Realism: Is There No Alternative?* Winchester: Zero Books.

120. Iles, V. (2014) How Good People Can Offer Bad Care: Understanding the Wider Factors in Society that Encourage Non-Compassionate Care, in Shea, S., Wynyard, R. and Lionis, C. (Eds.) *Providing Compassionate Healthcare: Challenges in Policy and Practice*, London: Routledge, 47–58.

121. Muller, J. (2018) *The Tyranny of Metrics*, Princeton, NJ: Princeton University Press.

122. Kleiner, A. (2002) What Are the Measures That Matter? *Organisations and People*, 25 (1): 24–27.

123. Mears, A. (2014) Gaming and Targets in the English NHS, *Universal Journal of Management*, 2 (7): 293–301.

124. Yankelovich, D. (1972) *Corporate Priorities: A Continuing Study of the New Demands on Business*, Stanford, CT: Daniel Yankelovich Inc.

125. Verhaeghe, P. (2014) Neoliberalism Has Brought Out the Worst in Us, *Guardian*, September 29.

126. Mearns, R., Richards, S. and Smith, R. (2003) *Community Care: Policy and Practice*, 3rd edition, Basingstoke: Palgrave-Macmillan.

127. Philpot, T. (2003) Planned on the Run, *Health Service Journal*, 113 (5880): 21.

128. Fleming, P. (2017) Feeling Exploited?: Unhappy With How the Boss Treats You?: Then the Problem is You, *Guardian*, August 14.

129. Flynn, M. and Mercer, D. (2013) Is Compassion Possible in a Market-Led NHS? *Nursing Times*, 109 (7): 12–14.

130. Traynor, M. (2014) Caring after Francis: Moral Failure in Nursing Reconsidered, *Journal of Research in Nursing*, 19 (7–8): 546–556.
131. Wolfe, T. (1979) *The Right Stuff*, New York: Farrar, Straus & Giroux.
132. Suzman, J. (2020) *Work: A History of How We Spend Our Time*, London: Bloomsbury Circus.
133. Jackson, B. and Parry, K. (2011) *A Very Short, Fairly Interesting and Reasonably Cheap Book about Studying Leadership*, London: Sage.
134. Bolden, R., Gulati, A., Ahmad, Y., Burgoyne, J., Chapman, N., Edwards, G., Green, E., Owen, D., Smith, I. and Spirit, M. (2015) *The Difference that Makes the Difference: Final Evaluation of the First Place-Based Programme for Systems Leadership: Local Vision*, Bristol: University of the West of England.
135. Rogers, C. (2007) *Informal Coalitions: Mastering the Hidden Dynamics of Organisational Change*, Basingstoke: Palgrave Macmillan.
136. Vince, R. and Pedler, M. (2018) Putting the Contradictions Back into Leadership Development, *Leadership and Organisation Development Journal*, 39 (7): 859–872.
137. Ross, L. (1977) The Intuitive Psychologist and his Shortcomings: Distortion in the Attribution Process, in Berkowitz, L. (Ed.) *Advances in Experimental Social Psychology*, New York: Academic Press, 98–110.
138. Edmonstone, J. (2019) Beyond Critical Action Learning?: Action Learning's Place In The World, *Action Learning: Research & Practice*, 16 (2): 136–148.
139. Traynor, M., Stone, K., Cook, H., Gould, D. and Maben, J. (2013) Disciplinary Processes and the Management of Poor Performance among UK Nurses: Bad Apple or Systemic Failure? *Nursing Inquiry*, 21 (1): 51–58.
140. Locke, R. and Spender, J. (2011) *Confronting Managerialism: How the Business Elite and their Schools Threw Our Lives Out of Balance*, London: Zed Books.
141. Doran, C. (2016) Managerialism: An Ideology and Its Evolution, *International Journal of Management, Knowledge and Learning*, 5 (1): 81–97.
142. Raelin, J. (2008) Emancipatory Discourse and Liberation, *Management Learning*, 39 (5): 519–540.
143. Zuboff, S. (2019) *The Age of Surveillance Capitalism: The Fight for a Human Future at the New Frontier of Power*, London: Profile Books.
144. Thompson, E. (1993) *Witness Against the Beast: William Blake and the Moral Law*, Cambridge: Cambridge University Press.
145. Pirsig, R. (1991) *Lila: An Inquiry into Morals*, London: Bantam Press.
146. Baddeley, J. and James, K. (1991) The Power of Innocence: From Politeness to Politics, *Management Education and Development*, 22 (2): 106–118.
147. Goleman, D. (1985) *Vital Lies, Simple Truths: The Psychology of Self-Deception*, New York: Simon and Schuster.
148. Frigotto, M. (2018) *Understanding Novelty in Organisations: A Research Path Across Agency and Consequences*, London: Palgrave Macmillan.
149. Ballatt, J. and Campling, P. (2011) *Intelligent Kindness: Reforming the Culture of Healthcare*, London: RCPsych Publications.
150. Faulkner, W. (1996) *Requiem for a Nun*, London: Vintage.

Chapter 7

The Challenges Facing Today's OD in Healthcare

This chapter considers an extensive range of challenges facing Organisation Development (OD) in healthcare, including what exactly an "organisation" is; the influential power of metaphors; the ubiquity of project management; the dangers of representational learning; the rigidity of diagnostic frameworks; the existence of "bullshit jobs"; whether OD as an activity is culture-bound; the tensions between hierarchy and democracy and between conformist and deviant innovation. It questions whether the focus should be on healthcare alone or on health and social care considered as a single system and ends by noting an emerging radical critique of OD.

From its initial emergence, the field of practice which is OD in healthcare has more recently faced a whole range of challenges. They currently include:

What exactly is an "organisation" anyway? Most people simply take healthcare organisations for granted as the places where, for citizens, healthcare is delivered or where, as employees, they spend much of their working time, but they typically underestimate their ephemeral nature. The names and abbreviations of such organisations often seem to appear, to change and disappear in a word salad of "re-disorganisation", which simply makes for continuing confusion for both the people who work in those organisations and for the users of such services.

DOI: 10.1201/9781003167310-7

At the root of this may be what is termed the "positivist" viewpoint in the behavioural or social sciences – an approach which treats organisations as entirely concrete entities with an objective existence which is quite independent of those who work within them and those who lead and manage them – so such organisations are then seen as being both easily definable and measurable [1]. This is a form of reification which occurs when entirely human creations such as work organisations are misconceived of as "facts of nature, the results of cosmic laws or manifestations of a divine will" [2]. It also reflects representationalist thinking [3] – the attempt to capture and describe a supposed external reality that seems to exist outside of the individuals that inhabit that context. Early OD completely embodied these assumptions and, as a result, was essentially rational, linear, incremental and prescriptive.

However, looked at from a quite different perspective, organisational life can be seen as something which is co-created by a combination of rational, relational, emotional and political factors, and so organisations are instead best conceived as "the temporary product of interactional processes" [4] or are a "consensual convention" [5]. They are dynamic, interpretive, discursive and meaning-making systems, the outcome of whose actions is unpredictable. This perspective is best captured by Shapiro and Carr [6] as:

> An organisation is composed of the diverse fantasies and projections of its members. Everyone who is aware of an organisation, whether a member of it or not, has a mental image of how it works. Though these diverse ideas are not often consciously negotiated or agreed upon among participants, they exist. In this sense, all institutions exist in the mind, and it is in interaction with these in-the-mind entities that we live. Of course, all organisations also consist of certain real factors, such as other people, buildings, resources and products. But the meaning of these factors derives from the context established by the institution-in-the-mind. These mental images are not static; they are the products of dynamic interchanges, chiefly projections and transferences.

Any "organisation" seen from this perspective is therefore a socially and relationally constructed phenomenon where meaning is contextual, negotiated, contested, multiple, partial and always unfinished and where public conversation is the site for the development of such meaning, holding the power to shape the ongoing social, relational and cultural reality.

The emphasis in this view is therefore more on the social process of **organising** than on organisations as concrete entities and this involves addressing such matters as competing values, paradoxes and polarities. This perspective rejects the possibility of one objective organisational "grand narrative" in favour of a reality that is socially constructed and in which context and culture influence, and are influenced by, the organisational actors. These actors, in turn, shape and are shaped by this process in which this worldview is constantly reformed and re-negotiated by coalitions and powerful players. No single final objective truth can be known because everyone is participating in or co-constructing that process. There are instead a variety of "truths" – multiple competing and often contradictory experiences. There can therefore be no single model of a right way to organise independent of the people who make up a particular "organisation".

There is thus a danger of ignoring those vital dynamics which relate to organisational politics and emotions as these are "complex, difficult to understand and at times overwhelming" [7]. Armstrong [8] has noted that:

> Every organisation is an emotional place. It is an emotional place because it is a human invention, serving human purposes and dependent on human beings to function. And human beings are emotional animals; subject to anger, fear surprise, disgust, happiness or joy, ease and unease. By the same token, organisations are interpersonal places and so necessarily arouse those more complex emotional constellations that shadow all interpersonal relations; love and hate, envy and gratitude, shame and guilt, contempt and pride.

This perspective is clearly derived from the third "post-modern" modernity highlighted in Chapter 3, and here healthcare organisations are seen as being far from rational and stable entities. Organisational reality is considered to be shaped by those conversations and dialogues that take place between the people within these settings, and these conversations and dialogues are constantly shifting. "Organisations" are rather communities of meaning, sustained and perpetuated by communication and interaction patterns and shaped by individuals' power relations and emotions. Hence, organisational development and learning is seen as the process of creating, retaining and transferring knowledge and understanding within an "organisation" and between "organisations". It can be seen as a means of encouraging "systemic eloquence" – the ability of the parts of a healthcare system to talk well to each other [9,10].

The power of metaphors: Metaphors are compressed interpretations of the world characterised by simplification and the discarding of certain disconfirming information. The particular metaphorical language which is used regularly in order to describe organisations and what they do always tells us something important. Morgan [11] suggested that the continuing use of metaphorical language was a useful means of identifying the underlying assumptions which were in operation about organisations and the people who work in them. Morgan identified eight such metaphors – machines, organisms, brains, cultures, political systems, psychic prisons, flux and transformation and instruments of domination. Edmonstone [12] identified four major metaphors which he found in use in UK healthcare organisations, the first three of which were:

Military: Terms like "Advance", "Arrows to fire", "Bite the bullet", "Boots on the ground", "Brush-fire problems", "Circular firing-squad", "Cold conflict", "Combat", "Draw a line in the sand", "Firefighting", "Flagship", "Helicopter view", "Holding the line", "Keeping your powder dry", "Line of sight", "Magic bullet", "Parachute in", "Spearhead" and "Target". Previously many healthcare managers were also called "Officers".

Sporting and Games: Such words and phrases as "Aces in their places", "Ahead of the game", "Back of the net", "Balls in the air", "Batting average", "Big hitter", "Cards on the table", "Close of play", "Domino effect", "Drop the ball", "Game plan", "Hardball", "Level playing-field", "Moving the goalposts", "Step up to the plate", "Swim-lane", "Tackle" and "It's a marathon, not a sprint".

Finance: The use of "Accountability", "Ballpark figure", "Bang for the buck", "Baseline", "Benefits", "Bottom-line", "Buy-in" and "Run the numbers". Additionally, we "spend" time, "earn" our living, "pay" attention or compliments and are regarded as "resources" or "assets". We engage in "trade-offs" which we hope will have a "pay-off". Sometimes it takes a "toll" on us and we "pay the price".

The machine metaphor: Despite the frequent use of these military, sporting and financial metaphors, the most powerful metaphor constantly in use to describe all organisations (and specifically healthcare organisations) remains that of the machine, where the emphasis is on a set of predetermined goals and objectives and where the organisation is expected to work in a systematic, efficient and predictable manner. For over 150 years, economic theory has reinforced such a bias towards such mechanistic models and metaphors [13]. The machine metaphor embodies a number of assumptions:

■ That every observed effect has a previous observable cause.
■ That even the most complicated things can be understood by breaking down the whole into its component parts and then analysing those parts.
■ That the focus should be on the particular characteristics of the parts.
■ That a change in one part affects only those other parts which are immediately close to it – the "knock-on" or billiard ball effect.

- That if we analyse past events sufficiently, then this will help us to both predict and control future events.
- That the intelligence of organisations resides in the minds of those who design and redesign them.

So the language most frequently used reflects this machine orientation – terms like "Structure", "Design", Tools", "Techniques", "Standardisation", "Routines", "Specifications", "Step up a gear", "Run like clockwork", "Like a well-oiled machine", "Levers to pull", "Buttons to press", "Policy instruments", "Fine-tune", "Quantifying", "Human resources", "Human capital" and "Re-engineering".

This indicates the great extent to which those describing and working in organisations have been seduced by this machine metaphor and so have internalised both the language itself and the related way of thinking. Yet organisation charts, for example, are not machine blueprints onto which organisational reality maps directly, as "The map is not the territory it represents" [14]. As such, organograms only reveal what senior leaders and managers wish their organisational world would look like or perhaps even imagine that what is described there is both real and accurate.

The machine metaphor encourages the adoption of linear change management models predicated entirely upon analysis and logic, to the extent that the term "clockwork manager" has been coined to describe those pursuing change in this manner [15]. This metaphor (as with all such metaphors) is a fiction which gives an illusion of control to senior people in organisational hierarchies who can then regard the individuals and groups within "their" organisation as being interchangeable (and so replaceable) elements of the overall machine – and so can be controlled and manipulated accordingly.

However, such a view bypasses the complex human dynamics and ignores the feelings of anxiety which any change engenders [16]. This is because the way that people at work feel about any specific changes may be influenced as much by their own attitudes towards change in general, rather than by the merits or otherwise of the specific changes themselves, yet the latter are typically expressed only in rational and logical terms [17]. Organisations are made up of informal structures, rules and norms, as well as the formal structures, policies, practices and procedures. These informal rules, patterns of behaviour and communication, norms and friendships are created by people to meet their own emotional needs, where each person has their own personal history and a unique web of relationships [18]. Stacey [19] refers to this as the shadow side of an organisation.

As a result, people in organisations do not necessarily simply obey the instructions that are given to them in a machine-like manner. Instead they think, react and interpret such instructions. As someone once said, "With every pair of hands you also get a brain". People often have different ways of making sense of the world, based on their different personal and professional assumptions and experiences, and so may have completely conflicting views and perspectives on the same thing.

The language which is used to describe organisations most likely sustains the ways in which we see them and the people who work in them. It has been suggested [20] that "If people change their words they change their perception of reality. As they change their reality, their behaviour changes automatically". Ballatt and Campling [21] suggest that there is a need to break away from such hidebound and conventional language and to move towards those language forms that are more life-affirming and that reflect the "intelligent kindness" which they maintain is the underlying basic assumption of healthcare. They quote the late historian Tony Judt [22] about the need for a language that binds us all together:

> We need to discover a language of dissent. It can't be an economic language since part of the problem is that we have for too long spoken in an economic language where everything has been about growth, efficiency, productivity and wealth, and not enough has been about collective ideals around which we can gather, around which we can get angry together, around which we can be motivated collectively, whether on the issue of justice, inequality, cruelty or unethical behaviour. We have thrown away the language with which to do that. And until we rediscover that language how can we possibly bind ourselves together?

The living system metaphor: Instead of the machine metaphor, there is an emerging alternative based on the idea of organisations as living systems. This maintains that human (or social) systems simply cannot be controlled, measured or fixed as if they were machines; that such systems are complex, unpredictable and constantly evolving and adapting and that the different parts of a system are connected and are interdependent, so that the relationships and connections between the parts are paramount. If a healthcare organisation is conceived of as a complex adaptive system, then a relevant description is that of:

> A dynamic network of agents acting in parallel, constantly reacting to what the other agents are doing, which in turn influences behaviour and the network as a whole. Control tends to be dispersed and decentralised and the overall behaviour of the system is the result of many decisions made constantly by individual agents. Order emerges rather than being predetermined. It is not possible to reverse the system's history and the future is often unpredictable. [23]

The characteristics of such complex adaptive systems include:

- A large number of different elements which interact together dynamically and continually in a nonlinear way and which affect each other over time, creating higher and higher levels of complexity. As a result, the focus is on the relationships between the parts, rather than the parts themselves. They are "messy" webs that are constantly shifting and involve both tangible things (like people) interwoven with intangible things (like context and culture).
- A history where the past has helped to shape present behaviour, so that today's problems often have their origins in yesterday's solutions.
- Openness, so it is often difficult to define exactly where the system boundaries are located. Where to draw the system boundary depends upon the discussion or the question being asked [24].
- Interactions are nonlinear and their effects are distant in time and space, with that element of a system which generates a problem often being quite distant from the area showing the symptoms of the problem.
- There is no central controlling mechanism. The different parts of the system are not aware of the behaviour of the system as a whole and respond only to what little information is available to them or that which is known locally. Everyone who is part of the system inevitably holds a different perspective on its nature, purpose and boundaries. No one can see the whole picture about how to make changes happen because the system looks quite different depending on where you are situated within it. So to understand the system as a whole, multiple perspectives from different angles by multiple stakeholders are needed, because no one person or group holds the whole truth.
- Everything and everyone in the system exists in relationships, and relationships involve emotions.
- Even small changes can have large effects, but the areas of highest leverage are often the least obvious.
- The system is constantly learning to adapt to changing circumstances.
- Order emerges "for free" – the system does exactly what it is (consciously or unconsciously) designed to do.

The living systems metaphor has increasingly seemed a useful analogy for describing and working with healthcare organisations [15,24–28].

The ubiquity of project management: Most OD activity has been programmatic in nature. That is, it has been episodic, project management based and with a distinct beginning, middle and end [29] – effectively "bracketed-off", separate and distinct from the ongoing and everyday mainstream processes of professional and managerial practice. Project management in healthcare in the UK is typically grounded in the principles of the PRINCE 2 structured framework [30] and embodies the principle of linearity – a forward movement scheduled and controlled through time from the present towards a desired future state. Each successive step supposedly moves the organisation closer to the eventual endpoint and so at each step objectives and targets ("milestones") can be monitored and evaluated against the overall project management plan. It is based on a seven-step approach [31]:

- **Set the goal:** Being clear about the actual purpose of change. The idea is that the more concrete, tangible and specific the purpose is, the better the change project will run.
- **Set a final deadline:** At an early stage, a final end date for the change project completion needs to be set.
- **Identify the sub-tasks:** The overall purpose is broken down into a series of sub-tasks, which helps to define the particular steps which are required to meet the change project's overall purpose.
- **Order the sub-tasks:** The sub-tasks are organised into the order in which they will be performed. The starting point is decided, then what comes next, then next, and so on. Progression depends upon both the nature of the sub-task and the appropriate time sequence.
- **Set targets:** Target dates are set so that a deadline exists for each sub-task. Extra time is built in to cover any delays or problems. "Milestone" points are established – review dates for evaluating progress and modifying the course of the change project where this is necessary.
- **Assign sub-tasks:** All possible sub-tasks are assigned among a change project team's members, with everyone knowing their own responsibilities and target dates.
- **Monitor progress**

The ubiquity of project management in particular as a means of managing change has increasingly been criticised as a "cookbook" or "recipe" approach which denies the messy real-world complexity, the dependence upon local circumstances and the overriding centrality of working relationships [32]. The study which made these criticisms also concluded that the National Health Service (NHS) "needs to think beyond projects and towards more systemic shifts in processes and attitudinal and behavioural change".

The author of this book has also been jointly guilty of previously making this fundamental error [33]. When a piece of change work is defined as a project and is externally funded then there is also usually a significant degree of bureaucracy which is associated with managing the project and with regularly reporting the results to the external funders.

The underlying assumptions behind this project management approach to OD are that it is entirely possible to agree on all the pre-planned objectives at the outset of a particular change activity; that it is likewise possible to agree on all the different means by which those objectives can be assured, and, finally, that it is possible to accurately measure and assess the outcome of such a project [34]. The belief is that change can be completely planned in advance and is linear in nature, and so it is therefore obvious that this belief is grounded in the assumptions of the machine metaphor.

The danger of representational learning: Representational learning is the surface and superficial acquisition of the latest organisational, leadership and management jargon and acronyms, so that people simply learn to "talk a good game" [12] and to reframe the language they use without reframing any of their professional or managerial practice [35]. It is also profoundly related to the gap between their espoused theory (or what people at work say that they do) and their theory in use (what it is that they actually do in practice) [36].

Could it even be the case that there is just such a gap between what OD practitioners profess and what they are perceived by others as doing in practice in their day-to-day work? Vince [7] has pointed to the "jargon-soaked" language of OD itself, suggesting that OD interventions even have to be constantly reinvented as new packages – "a whole wardrobe of new clothes for the emperor". The ever-expanding OD litany encompasses (or has previously encompassed) such contributions as appreciative inquiry, the balanced scorecard, benchmarking, business process re-engineering, dialogic OD, force-field analysis, future-proofing, future search, holacracy, large group events, lean, open space, PEST, SWOT, talent management, theory U, thought leadership, world café and the learning organisation [37]. For many front-line healthcare employees, this flowering of OD jargon can only be experienced as a form of mystification, as too abstract, jargon-laden and wordy – even woolly, when surely the real requirement is to "only connect" [38] – the moral importance of making connection between individuals across all the barriers of class, status, race, and religion. Kernick [27] notes that there is a bewildering array of such ideas promulgated by organisational "gurus" who are only intent on promoting their own perspective and suggests that:

> The history of Organisation Development has been characterised by an overwhelming volume of literature that means nothing to those who actually get on and do the work.

This danger of neophilia highlighted in Chapter 6 is associated with such OD fads and fashions and has been highlighted by Abrahamson [39] with the suggestion that such fashion demand is ultimately based upon senior leaders' and managers' collective aesthetic tastes, with the attraction of their being seen, in the eyes of their peers, to be both modern and progressive.

The rigidity of diagnostic frameworks: OD practitioners often feel bound to offer diagnostic frameworks (or more accurately frames of reference) and models such as the six-box model [40] or the 7-S model [41] on which they are able to "hang" the data they have collected but which often embody a set of undeclared assumptions. A framework is, by definition, only a simplified and incomplete version of that which it describes. Of course, the deployment of the term diagnostic also implies the use of a medical metaphor, with the associated implication that such diagnosis is necessary in order to ensure that organisational "health" is achieved. Yet there are no correct or absolute frames of reference and what is observed is dependent, at least in part, on the OD practitioner's role as an observer. It has been noted that:

> To some extent we are all prisoners trapped within the perceptual frameworks that determine how we view our experiences. [42]

and likewise that:

> At any moment we are prisoners caught in the framework of our theories; our expectations; our past experiences; our language. But we are only prisoners in a sense. If we try we can break out of our framework at any time. Admittedly, we shall find ourselves again in a framework; but it will be a better and roomier one, and we can, at any moment, break out of it again. [43]

Such "mind-forged manacles" [44] are frameworks and models clearly deployed with the intention of seeking to help OD practitioners' clients, but they also over-simplify the complex and dynamic nature of particular local situations [45] and so impose upon the client certain pre-packaged ways of viewing their experience and, therefore, may exclude the opportunity for people in the client system to declare exactly what it is that is particular, unusual and exceptional about their local setting. The focus instead is on de-contextualised templates, one-dimensional aggregation and the search for, and delineation of, particular patterns. Such frameworks and models also encourage and support a top-down approach to change [15]. The prevalence of boxes and connecting arrows in such frameworks reveals that, in addition to the medical metaphor, the other metaphor upon which they are based is ultimately the machine one. Bushe and Nagaishi [46] claim that OD "lost its way" when such prescriptive diagnostic models took over the field.

The need to address anxiety: Anxiety is the distress or uneasiness caused by fear of danger or misfortune. Such danger or misfortune may be real or imagined, clear and present or vague and anticipated and threatening physically, emotionally or psychologically.

It has a "Goldilocks" relationship with change [47]. If a person or group experiences too little anxiety, there is no motivation to change. If they experience too much anxiety, there will be destructive or self-limiting effects. They will deny, deflect, distort, defend or be otherwise too fearful to change. They will be wary in trusting others and most likely avoid any experimentation. Only when there is enough anxiety to motivate a search for new thoughts and behaviours, but not so much as to lead to fearful debilitation, can anxiety enable change [48]. It can provide the energy needed in order to risk being honest, direct, challenging and different.

Change makes most people anxious and their reactions to change are not solely rational or intellectual processes but also emotional, not least because people will have previously experienced both positive and negative reactions to change which they view through the template of their own emotional and psychological history. Such experiences will have been shaped and conditioned through family, work, professional, organisational and social groupings and have been influenced by other broader economic, social and political forces operating in their employing organisations and across the wider society. As a result, people deploy a range of emotional and perceptual filters as a means of anxiety reduction, including denial, avoidance, and oversimplification.

Anxiety is ever-present in all healthcare organisations yet seems to be missing from most accounts of OD in such organisations. As such, it is the elephant in the room, which needs to be properly addressed. The backdrop to anxiety in healthcare organisations relates to the VUCA/RUPT context within which all organisations operate, to the extent that the current era has even been termed the "age of anxiety" [49]; to the emotional labour which is an everyday reality for most healthcare clinical professionals and more recently and specifically to the incidence of post-traumatic stress disorder, severe depression and heightened anxiety demonstrated by many staff as a result of the Covid-19 pandemic [50] and recently described as a form of "moral injury" [51,52] – the distress that arises in response to actions or inactions that violate personal moral codes, the set of individual beliefs about what is right or wrong.

Anxiety-induced individual behaviour includes [25]:

- **A reluctance to join in:** An unwillingness to be creative in terms of personal behaviour and ideas and to ask the "What if…?" questions, resulting in highly "serious" behaviour.
- **A narrow self-view:** A low self-assessment of personal abilities and resources with a resulting "resource myopia" – an inability or unwillingness to recognise the valuable personal contribution that might be made.

- **Fear of losing face:** Worry about being perceived as having admitted to personal or professional incompetence or as having backed down.
- **Fear of recrimination:** An assumption that colleagues might misunderstand changed behaviour and get angry or resentful.
- **Fear of losing control:** Making matters worse than they might already seem to be.
- **Fear of failure:** In the eyes of colleagues in the employing and other organisations. Fearing the possibility of failure promotes difficulty in taking even calculated risks.
- **Fear of ambiguity:** An avoidance of those matters which lack clarity over where possible outcomes are unknown or unpredictable. A reluctance to try something out, to see whether it works or not and an overemphasis on the known at the expense of the unknown.
- **Fear of disorder:** A dislike of complexity (often labelled as "confusion") and a preference for order, structure and balance, often expressed in terms of opposites, such as good versus bad or right versus wrong, with a corresponding failure to appreciate and integrate the best from such seemingly polarised viewpoints.
- **Fear of looking foolish:** Attracting negative comments from colleagues as having acted "out of character".
- **Fear of being vulnerable:** Of not really knowing what might happen as a result of trying an alternative approach.
- **Fear of letting someone else make a big mistake:** Feeling responsible for what another person or persons do.
- **Fear of influencing others:** A concern not to appear aggressive or "pushy" and hence a hesitation in identifying with emerging views.

These in-built reactions often lead to patterned avoidance behaviours or "defensive routines" [53] – unconscious strategies for self-protection which inhibit the potential to learn. These will have been acquired over time and through personal experience because it will be believed that they maintain personal safety. They have also been described as examples of "dynamic conservatism" – the tendency (consciously or unconsciously) to fight hard in order to remain the same [54] and include:

- **Spending time on inconclusive deliberations:** These are endless, unproductive and unsatisfactory meetings where decisions are regularly not reached or where the same issues permanently reoccur. It is the arena of the "definite maybe" and the "waver game" where a group cycles back and forth between two or more alternative decisions without ever coming to a final conclusion. When they almost get there, they immediately flip back to the opposite possibility and so the game begins again.

■ **Surface skimming:** It is not possible to fit the complexities and unpredictability of organisational life into an idealised and rational model as they are, by their very nature "messy". The messiness of such situations can feel highly disturbing, especially by those who have a need to feel always in control and who, as a result, miss the opportunities for deeper learning about underlying concepts and assumptions. Attempts are usually made to minimise such discomfort by reducing complexity through ever-tighter controls and an even greater focus on desired outcomes. This then misses opportunities for deeper learning that can actually create greater clarity about the possible choices available. It can also lead to misunderstandings, as there is insufficient space to inquire into the underlying concepts and assumptions. Deeper reflection is avoided because it would mean exposing and then experiencing situations as being much more complex than originally envisaged, thereby increasing people's frustration and anxiety.

■ **Believing that everything is urgent:** This relates to the "hurry sickness" characterised by a preference for non-reflexive urgent action which is a feature of NHS culture, as outlined in Chapter 6. Time spent in meetings with tight agendas, where decisions are avoided tends to acerbate this.

One way of dealing with anxiety is to seek sanctuary in the views of "experts". Such people seem to provide anxiety-reducing answers and to offer what can seem like safety and security. This is often the realm of national and international management consultants who superficially appear to offer "magic bullets" to resolve challenges. Lawrence [55] contrasts what he calls the "politics of salvation" with the "politics of "revelation". The former involves seeking to rescue people by giving them solutions and not letting them take the authority to make decisions for themselves. As such, it is conceived as a regressive approach – a move away from facing uncertainty and anxiety by creating an illusion of certainty. It is a false prospectus because ultimately there is no real alternative to people owning, focusing on and working on their own challenges, often with facilitative help, with all the messiness, confusion and uncertainty which that entails. The latter involves creating the conditions for people and systems to discover and transform situations for themselves.

Menzies-Lyth [56] identified resistance to change as a social defence mechanism operating in healthcare as a means of distracting from the existential anxieties associated with the uncertainties of sickness, pain and death and the enormity of the task of dealing with them. Ballatt and Campling [21] suggest that, paradoxically, rather than resistance to change, an uncritical acceptance of constant and inexorable organisational change in the NHS has now taken its place. Research has highlighted the psychological costs of such change on employees. For instance:

■ Reorganisations have been shown to have detrimental effects on staff health and psychological well-being, especially when those affected feel that they have limited control over events [57–59].

■ Repeated or multiple experiences of organisational change appear to have detrimental consequences for employees' mental health [60].

■ When such changes involve a reduction in the numbers of staff, those who remain experience "survivor syndrome" – a form of trauma involving guilt, anger, anxiety, fear and apprehension [61,62].

Confronting anxiety may involve individuals relinquishing their earlier roles, ideas and practices in order to create, find or discover new and more adaptable ideas, ways of thinking and acting, and to cope with the instability of changing conditions and the insecurity which change provokes. This is the process of "unlearning" whereby well-established patterns of thinking and behaviour are interrupted and breached and redundant mind-sets are re-evaluated, re-positioned and embodied within a wider repertoire of possible responses. It is not simply about forgetting, but paradoxically is concerned with advancing by slowing down, stepping back and letting go from prior understanding that may limit the future [63,64]. It involves the cultivation of what the poet John Keats described as "negative capability", a state in which a person "is capable of being in uncertainties, mysteries, doubts, without any irritable reaching after facts and reason" [65]. Handy [66] conceived this as an attitude of openness of mind:

> which learners need to cultivate, to help them to write-off their mistakes as experience. We change by exploration, not by treading well-known paths. We start our learning with uncertainties and doubts, with questions to be resolved. We grow old wondering who we will be and what we will do. If we cannot live with these uncertainties, we will not learn and change will always be an unpleasant surprise.

Similarly, the psychoanalyst Wilfred Bion saw negative capability as the ability to tolerate the pain and confusion of not knowing, rather than imposing ready-made or omnipotent certainties upon an ambiguous situation or an emotional challenge [67]. Negative capability involves reflecting on and re-ordering half-formed ideas in a state of potential and deferred judgement in which more complex transformations can occur [68].

Such confrontation of anxiety requires the creation and use of what has been called a "container", which is a metaphor based on the alchemical notion that thoughts and feelings have to be held safely for any positive change to occur. It implies a holding environment, a safe psychological space and an enabling framework which acts as a transitional arena for feelings and emotions as well as for rational calculations to be expressed, in order to enable what may potentially be unique to emerge, rather than slipping into well-meaning but premature understandings and solutions that avoid discomfort and effort [69].

Containment is the hard work of facing up to, understanding and managing the emotions that are aroused by change, rather than simply engaging in defensive routines. It is a benign process of both support and challenge. Support (or emotional warmth) helps people to feel confident and encourages them. Challenge opposes conventional ways of doing things and seeks alternatives. Support cannot simply be engineered but takes time to build. An appropriate degree of support is often needed before any real challenge can be acceptable. The latter is likely itself to generate anxiety, which can potentially have destructive or self-limiting effects, but can also provide the energy which is needed to risk being honest, direct, challenging and different.

Learning in this way involves vulnerability and risk-taking as people admit to the limits of their understanding or even to a lack of understanding. It is the capacity to receive unprocessed emotions and transform them into some understanding of what is being experienced so that the feelings and emotions can be thought about and understood [70]. This can be facilitated by an atmosphere of trust, such that people may feel psychologically safe to both unlearn and learn [71], and of empathy – "the ability to identify with what someone else is thinking or feeling, and to respond to their thought and feelings with an appropriate emotion" [72]. The engendering of such trust and empathy can be achieved by a range of activities, including action learning sets [9], Schwartz rounds [73], coaching [74] and mentoring [75].

People can come to manage their anxiety in such a way that enables courageous and creative thinking and action without minimising the scale of the challenges faced. Acknowledging, and then managing, such fear is an important task. It is also inevitable that there will be "failures", but it is possible to learn as much by failing as by succeeding. As the playwright Samuel Beckett said "Ever tried. Ever failed. No matter. Try again. Fail again. Fail better" [76]. A culture which can embrace failure as a way to encourage a continuous learning cycle, with people at all levels sharing responsibilities would be such a desirable outcome.

The growth and prevalence of "bullshit jobs". The anthropologist David Graeber suggested that "bullshit jobs" were a form of paid employment that was so completely pointless, unnecessary or pernicious that even the employee undertaking such a job could not justify its existence, even though, as part of the conditions of employment the employee felt obliged to pretend that this was not the case [77]; while by contrast Sennett [78] had made the powerful case that good work must include at least a degree of autonomy, the chance to develop and refine individual skills and an opportunity to exercise a degree of personal judgement. Graeber describes such bullshit jobs as psychologically destructive when paired with the work ethic that associates work itself with self-worth. The growth of white-collar managerial jobs in the NHS, especially in the areas of auditing and inspecting the work of others, what Graeber called "box-tickers", or people who create the appearance that something useful is being done, when it is not, is an aspect of the reporting upwards culture and of measurement for its own sake mentioned in Chapter 6. To what extent might OD challenge this phenomenon as deflecting attention away from the purposes of healthcare organisations? Even more challenging, to what extent also might some health-care employees even perceive the role of OD practitioner as being a bullshit job?

Is OD culture-bound? The roots of OD lie in the USA and the UK, although it would now claim to be an international phenomenon. It is considered to be the major approach to organisational change across the Western world and increasingly also globally [79]. If culture is simply considered to be the set of shared symbols and practices – the customs, traditions and values of a society or community, such as a nation or ethnic group, which ties people together and which are acquired over time and transmitted through social learning, from one generation to the next, then addressing the issue of culture is important because:

> culture expresses the systems of power, property relations, religious institutions, etc, inattention to which merely flattens phenomenon and trivialises analysis. [80]

Everyone is subject to the processes of acculturation and socialisation, which induce us to internalise existing institutional frameworks and the dominant systems of beliefs, ideas and values. So everyone is inevitably embedded in their own local culture and that culture is also embedded in everyone [81]. Using the analogy of a riverbed Baggini [82] has suggested that:

> Just as a riverbed builds up sediment comprised of that which washes through it, values and beliefs begin to sediment in the minds of people who inhabit those cultures from birth, so that we mistake the build-up for an immutable riverbed. Through these channels of the mind our thoughts and experiences flow, not noticing how they are being directed.

So we are channelled by the flow of the water but also channel that flow by our own existence,
    while the same sentiments were expressed earlier by Keynes [83]:

> The difficulty lies not in the new ideas but in escaping from the old, which ramify, for those brought up as most of us have been, into every corner of the mind.

and in an even more poetic sense:

> Ah, my friends from the prison, they ask unto me
> How good, how good does it feel to be free?
> And I answer them most mysteriously
> Are birds free from the chains of the skyway? [84]

OD quite clearly emerged from a predominantly Anglo-American value-set from the late 1940s onwards, but increasingly, and not least due to globalisation, most societies are now increasingly multicultural in nature, and this raises important questions as to whether those Anglo-American values mesh wholly or partly with those of people who originate from different ethnic origins and religious orientations. Boyacigillo and Adler [85] point out that the totality of organisational and management thinking is based on a normative Western model significantly derived from (white) American bureaucratic organisations, so is sourced from a culturally specific and non-representative example. They suggest that this focus is both self-fulfilling and self-perpetuating.

Lent [86] describes this as both cultural essentialism and cultural imperialism because it implicitly assumes a set of human universals – distinctive values and beliefs about human nature that form the bedrock of Western thought and are silently assumed to be those that drive people all over the world and throughout all history. A post-modern perspective asserts that each culture develops its own version of reality that arises from its specific physical and environmental context. It would propose that trying to "essentialise" a culture's reality and compare it with that of another culture risks de-contextualising it and therefore invalidating its unique attributes.

In one example of cross-cultural challenges, Mughal et al. [87], in considering the behaviour of MBA students in business schools in Pakistan, noted the reluctance of male Moslem students to engage directly with female students, associated with a local cultural upbringing which legitimised the predominance of men within a segregated society. Likewise, in the creation of a Master's programme in Human Resources for Health in Bosnia-Herzegovina [88], an employer asserted that "It is good to have knowledge, but dangerous to always show it".

There is also a related issue that while would-be OD practitioners in non-Western societies may adopt the methodologies of OD, in terms of intervention approaches, the original underlying humanistic ethos of OD may be either ignored or discounted because it runs counter to local practitioners' cultural upbringing and is therefore a challenge to their deeply rooted beliefs. In other words, it has become an espoused theory rather than a theory-in-use [89] and a form of representational learning [90,91].

An emerging anthropological and ethnographic view [92,93] emphasises the existence of multiple personal identities, because local cultural contexts are obviously not uniform or homogenous, and such a view is also power-sensitive, focusing on the continuing impact of such historical circumstances as slavery, colonialism and imperialism. As a result, a more realistic, dynamic and pluralistic perspective on cultural differences (and similarities) is needed, where working relationships in healthcare organisations are perceived as being potentially underpinned by a set of historical and current power dynamics and where all the parties to cultural interactions do not necessarily consider themselves to be equal. All this points to the need for OD practitioners to be highly sensitive to those cultures which do not simply reflect the founding Anglo-American values and to recognise that even within and across UK and US organisations there may well now be a diverse range of values.

Hierarchy or democracy? Hierarchy is a central belief in almost all organisations, including healthcare organisations. It is the notion that in organisations a single person has the most power and authority and that each subsequent organisational level represents a lower degree of power and authority. It is crystallised in grades and job titles and people in such hierarchies supposedly relate to each other in "superior-subordinate relationships" [94]. Hierarchy has established itself not only objectively, in the real workaday world, but also subjectively, in individual consciousness. Percolating into virtually every realm of experience, it has assimilated the syntax of everyday discourse, with a claim that it represents the "logic of history" [95]. It forms the backcloth against which most people working in organisations view their role, power and the formal channels of communication – a kind of circuitry by which ideas, energy and influence get transmitted. It provides clarity about who does what and the set lines of accountability and control appear to offer a strong comfort blanket. Despite more recent suggestions of the "death of hierarchy" and its replacement by such reputed forms as laterarchy or heterarchy, it appears to remain the dominant mode in most healthcare organisations.

Yet healthcare does not represent a pure hierarchical form. As Chapter 6 has indicated, it is marked by the disconnected hierarchy between those who deliver healthcare to patients and local communities and those working in managerial roles. A further complication has historically been the separate domains discussed in Chapter 2 and the subsequent creation, from the 1980s, of a hierarchy of domains running Policy → Management → Service/Professional.

Raelin [96] confronts the suggestion, which early OD embodied, that hierarchy and democracy in organisations are compatible and so can peacefully coexist. While it is often argued that hierarchical leaders are increasingly sharing their leadership roles with others in the organisation and are taking advantage of the resulting shared expertise as a way of enhancing organisational performance, Raelin maintains that, when such democratic leadership occurs, it does so, only with the conditional permission of those in control. "Empowerment", in other words, does not occur without the empowering of employees by those at the top of the hierarchical organisational pyramid. Examples of this include the introduction of Shared Governance in nursing and allied health professions in both the UK and USA [97,98]. In this, Raelin's views align with the Radical OD viewpoint (see below). Using an analogy, hierarchy colonises power, but empowerment allows for a modicum of self-government.

It has often been argued that hierarchy is a natural order, but Raelin claims that this is ontologically based on a priori reasoning – it is true because it exists as such – and has therefore become institutionalised and "encrusted" within organisational discourse. Evidence across civilisation and time, through accounts of a variety of egalitarian, communitarian, utopian, social movement, self-management, and network communities all point to the ability of people to self-organise with limited hierarchical structures [95,99–104]. Meadows [24] points out that systems often have the property of self-organisation – the ability to structure themselves, to create new structure, to learn, diversify and complexify.

Raelin proposes that OD practitioners who specifically dedicate themselves to producing a self-renewing organisation; who assert that any party affected by a change should be involved in the change process and who encourage the endorsement of a learning culture within the organisation should maintain that it is acceptable to dialogue quite openly about such hierarchy-based "undiscussables" as unpopular views, defensive routines [53], conflicts of interest and personality clashes. They should attempt to shape those more democratic structures and systems that tolerate dissent and encourage open communication, all constructed to encourage mutual and free inquiry, a challenge to dominant narratives and an openness to learning and discovery.

Conformist or deviant innovation? The useful distinction made by Legge [105] between conformist and deviant innovation still remains a highly relevant observation for OD, as it has increasingly become associated with the Human Resource function. Conformist innovation meant buying completely into the prevailing organisational value system, pursuing the associated incremental change within well-prescribed boundaries and using expertise as a source of power in order to improve the position of the function in an organisational pecking order. Deviant innovation meant questioning those prior assumptions upon which that value system was based, seeking to reframe the status quo, attempting to gain acceptance for alternative success criteria and where necessary, "speaking truth to power".

Over forty years ago, Legge saw the Human Resource function as representing an un-reflexive and un-problematical compliance with a bounded economic and social agenda when considering all matters of organisational change. This was driven by Human Resource professionals only doing what they believed was necessary in order to enhance both their intra-organisational and inter-organisational image and career prospects, and consequently failing to take into account the broader interests of other stakeholders in the wider society. As a result, over time, senior Human Resource professionals have been increasingly rewarded for helping to achieve quite narrow definitions of organisational performance [106,107]. More recently, Martin et al. [108] have confirmed that this traditional picture of conformist innovation on the part of the Human Resource function has changed very little in the intervening years since Legge's original analysis.

As a result, the continuing association of OD with the Human Resource function seems to confine it to conformist innovation only, and by definition to then addressing only "tame" organisational problems, while largely ignoring "wicked" ones [109]. It remains focused on single-loop learning ("Are we doing things right?") rather than double-loop learning. ("Are we doing the right thing?") [89]

Healthcare only or health and social care? People working in healthcare often tend to have a self-referential habit of mind and to focus only on healthcare within well-defined boundaries. Yet it has become more and more obvious that healthcare is intimately bound up with, and needs to be integrated with, social care and so it makes sense to consider health and social care as a single local system. There are many barriers to this view, however, including:

- The NHS being largely perceived in the wider society as being solely a healthcare service provider, while social care falls within the ambit of local government, which has increasingly come to see its role as an enabling "place shaper" and a commissioner of services from a wide range of public, private, social enterprise, voluntary and charitable entities.
- The need to pay attention to the electoral cycle and to mobilise political support for change has historically has been seen as something countercultural by the NHS, which has viewed local government as being short-termist and driven by prevailing political moods; while local government in turn has seen the NHS as something of a leviathan lacking any form of proper democratic accountability (the "democratic deficit");

as demonstrating political naivety and as being out of touch with the changing attitudes and preferences within local communities.

- A mismatch and lack of alignment with regard to the geographical areas covered between healthcare and social care organisations.
- Separate budgets and different financial regimes, with different orders of priority. Different sources of revenue, involving national and local taxation regimes.
- Different performance management regimes and cultures, both in terms of organisational performance metrics and individual performance appraisal.
- Different and often confusing inspectorial and regulatory frameworks and regimes and a resultant difficulty in being open and honest in the face of failures. As a result, a tendency to blame scapegoats or "bad apples", rather than to address systemic issues.
- Separate education, training and development (and hence socialisation) arrangements with regard to the major professions involved, often leading to stereotyping of the "other".
- Different employee remuneration structures and terms and conditions of employment.
- Variable decision-making processes, especially in terms of the levels of delegated authority in place within managerial and professional hierarchies. In local government, the role of elected councillors in decision-making is different in nature from that of appointed healthcare board non-executives.

Yet it has become increasingly clear that single health and social care organisations can no longer respond effectively to the shared wicked issues that they face unless they work collectively and across the whole local system. Single organisations have neither the people nor the finance needed to respond effectively to the current and anticipated future levels of public expectation, nor do they singly possess the sufficient know-how required in order to address such complex and multidimensional problems, unless they pool their intelligence, skills, finance and information. Where currently every professional is held responsible for the outcomes of their own particular agency and for addressing questions of care in isolation ("silo-working"); where there is a need to prove successful outcomes from current work in order to apply for the next round of funding or to bid for the next piece of work, there is a strong tendency to tune-out the absolute scale of the challenges faced. So it instead calls for an entirely new way of thinking, a shift in mind-set, culture and behaviour and a recognition that the previous traditional organisational approaches are irrelevant to such challenges. This was originally described as "leadership of place" [110] – a coordinated vision and collaborative working that cuts across boundaries between institutions. Such boundaries included organisational, territorial, professional and those timescales associated with budgetary or political arrangements. More recently it has been termed "systems leadership" [25], that is:

> leadership within and across organisational and geopolitical bound-aries, beyond individual professional disciplines, involving a range of organisational and stakeholder cultures, often without direct managerial control of resources and working on issues of mutual concern that cannot be addressed by any one person or agency.

However, faced with this need to work in a radically different manner, most OD practitioners in healthcare (together with their counterparts in local government-based social care and those operating in or across the private, voluntary and chari-table sectors) simply do not yet seem to have demonstrated the vision, willingness and bravery necessary to operate across existing organisational boundaries in such a countercultural manner and to place improved outcomes for service users and local communities before such internal matters as the elegance of single organisa-tion structural design or the permeability or otherwise of well-defended profes-sional boundaries [111,112].

The radical OD critique: In a powerful critique of current OD practice, Cole [113] suggests that the progressivist accounts of its evolution are, in fact, quite naïve. Workplaces are not seen to be ever-improving examples of a linear process of betterment but rather to demonstrate how human relation theories which pro-mote "voice" and "engagement" actually feign inclusion. While employees may even believe that they are being empowered, the power balance between capital and labour is ultimately unequal and exploitative, concealed behind a veil of faux humanism. It is asserted that all organisations, whether private or public, operate within a wholly neoliberal context so that, at worst, OD is a means of "cosmetic shrouding" or veiling over the worst excesses of modern work and the organisa-tional settings in which it takes place, while fostering illusions of involvement and partnership. Although it espouses empowerment, voice, engagement and the inclusion of employees in decision-making, in reality it leaves power relations, which are unequal and exploitative, untouched and so nothing fundamental really changes. This is what Mintzberg [114] called the "empty gift of the bosses". It acts as the velvet glove within which operates the iron hand of hierarchy and power. At best, it simply seeks to ameliorate those excesses – but wholly from within that overall neoliberal context – and so does not seriously challenge any of the underlying organisational and social premises, and by that omission, it serves unwittingly to reinforce them. Historically, power has reinforced itself by shaping and controlling organisational and social knowledge, which is always produced within the context of power structures [115].

Similarly, Fisher [116] points to the widespread sense that not only is the current social and organisational system seen as the only viable one but also that it is impossible to even imagine a coherent alternative to it, not least because it has become a plastic entity, capable of metabolising and absorbing anything with which it comes into contact. He points out that for anyone under twenty years old in Europe and North America such a lack of an alternative is no longer even an issue. It is like a pervasive atmosphere, conditioning the regulation of all work and education and acting as a kind of invisible barrier constraining more novel thought and action.

This radical critique points towards the gaping hole at the heart of OD practice – the overriding role of power in the workplace – and so reveals the significant limitations and negative impacts of current OD practice. By ignoring, denying or wishing away any power issues, OD practitioners have become "blind watchmakers" condemned to senselessly (and perhaps unconsciously) reproduce the current situation – a case of "If you always do what you have always done, you will always get what you have always got".

Such doubts are not new – Carnevale (2003) [117] had previously suggested that OD was:

> a device to manipulate workers by giving them the illusion that they are empowered when they are caught up in the same old game of let's pretend what you say matters as long as it doesn't really threaten our control in this organisation.

It implies that OD needs to develop a more sophisticated understanding of power in organisational life that recognises that organisations and employees do not exist in a vacuum and realises that power moves through and between "senior" and "junior" people to constitute a day-to-day reality and to entrench wider social and material inequalities. This understanding should include how and what power is located in the identity of OD as a field of practice and of the activities of OD practitioners.

Summing up these multiple challenges it seems that:

- Rather than seeing healthcare organisations as being fixed entities which early OD, being grounded in a positivist world view did, organisations are now increasingly seen as being co-created communities of meaning.
- That meaning is, at least in part, created by the language used to describe organisations which reflects a set of underlying metaphors, and especially reflects the dominance of the machine metaphor. An emerging alternative metaphor is to view healthcare organisations as living entities – as complex adaptive systems.

- The project management approach to dealing with organisational change is grounded in the machine metaphor and ignores the major importance of everyday working relationships.
- There is a danger of OD as a field of practice promoting only espoused views in organisational life (what people at work say they do, rather than what they actually do) through the continuing use of management jargon and acronyms.
- Unfortunately, the diagnostic frameworks and models which many OD practitioners employ as part of their work typically ignore and exclude the everyday lived experience of people at work.
- Many existing managerial jobs in healthcare may actually be "bullshit" jobs and some people might even see being an OD practitioner as an example of just such a job.
- There are real questions about whether OD as a field of practice is culture-bound, given its Anglo-American origins, and so does not necessarily mesh well with other ethnic and religious cultures and ignores important historical power dynamics.
- Conflictful tension exists in all organisations between hierarchy on the one hand and democracy on the other, and healthcare is no exception to this. OD seems to ignore this but needs to take a view on such matters.
- The association of OD with the Human Resource function has located it, for now, firmly within the conformist innovation camp.
- Increasingly there is a need to consider health and social care as a single system and to do so challenges many of the historical assumptions and working practices of OD practitioners.
- OD tends to ignore the issue of power in organisations and so may serve to mask, and excuse, the power imbalance between the people in healthcare who directly provide care and the senior leaders and managers. It is also unquestioning of the neoliberal assumptions which permeate organisational life.

References

1. Francis, H. (2002) HRM and the Beginnings of Organisational Change, *Journal of Organisational Change*, 16 (3): 309–327.
2. Berger, P. and Luckmann, T. (1966) *The Social Construction of Reality: A Treatise in the Sociology of Knowledge*, New York: Anchor/Doubleday.
3. Chia, R. (1996) *Organisational Analysis as Deconstructive Practice*, Berlin: De Gruyter.

4. Rigg, C. (2008) Action Learning for Organisational and Systemic Development: Towards a "Both/And" Understanding of "I" and "We", *Action Learning: Research and Practice*, 5 (2): 105–116.
5. Harari, Y. (2019) *Twenty-One Lessons for the 21st Century*, London: Vintage.
6. Shapiro, E. and Carr, A. (1991) *Lost in Familiar Places: Creating New Connections Between the Individual and Society*, New Haven, CT: Yale University Press.
7. Vince, R. (2004) *Rethinking Strategic Learning*, London: Routledge.
8. Armstrong, D. (2004) Emotions in Organisations: Disturbance or Intelligence? In Huffington, C., Halton, W., Armstrong, D. and Pooley, J. (Eds.) *Working Below the Surface: The Emotional Life of Contemporary Organisations*, London: Karnac Books.
9. Edmonstone, J. (2011) *Action Learning in Healthcare: A Practical Handbook*, London: Radcliffe Publishing.
10. Oliver, C. (1996) Systemic Eloquence, *Human Systems: Journal of Therapy, Consultation and Training*, 7 (4): 247–264.
11. Morgan, G. (1986) *Images of Organisations*, London: Sage.
12. Edmonstone, J. (2016) Leadership Metaphors, *Leadership in Health Services*, 29 (2): 118–121.
13. Raworth, K. (2017) *Doughnut Economics: Seven Ways to Think Like a 21st Century Economist*, London: Random House Business Books.
14. Korzbski, A. (1959) *Science and Sanity: An Introduction to Non-Aristotelian Systems and General Semantics*, Forest Hills, NY: Institute of General Semantics.
15. McMillan, E. (2008) *Complexity, Management and the Dynamics of Change*, Abingdon: Routledge.
16. Carter, A. and Varney, S. (2018) *Change Capability in the Agile Organisation*, Brighton: Institute for Employment Studies, University of Sussex.
17. Marshak, R. (2006) *Covert Processes at Work: Managing the Five Hidden Dimensions of Organisational Change*, San Francisco, CA: Berrett-Koehler.
18. Burnes, B. (2009) Reflections: Ethics and Organisational Change: Time for a Return to Lewinian Values, *Journal of Change Management*, 9 (4): 359–381.
19. Stacey, R. (1996) *Complexity and Creativity in Organisations*, San Francisco, CA: Berrett-Koehler.
20. Logan, D., King, J. and Fischer-Wright, H. (2008) *Tribal Leadership: Leveraging Natural Groups to Build a Thriving Organisation*, New York: Harper-Collins.
21. Ballatt, J. and Campling, P. (2011) *Intelligent Kindness: Reforming the Culture of Healthcare*, London: RCPsch Publications.
22. Judt, T. (2010) Interviewed in *London Review of Books*, 25 March.
23. Holland, J. (1999) *Emergence: From Chaos to Order*, Reading, Mass: Perseus Books.
24. Meadows, D. (2008) *Thinking in Systems: A Primer*, White River Junction, VT: Chelsea Green Publishing.
25. Edmonstone, J. (2019) *Systems Leadership in Health and Social Care*, Abingdon: Routledge.
26. Malby, B. and Fischer, M. (2006) *Tools for Change: An Invitation to Dance*, Chichester, Kingsham Press.

27. Kernick, D. (2004) Complexity and the Development of Organisational Theory, in Kernick, D. (Ed.) *Complexity and Healthcare Organisation: A View from the Street*, Abingdon: Radcliffe Medical Press, 83–91.

28. Sherwood, D. (2002) *Seeing the Forest for the Trees: A Manager's Guide to Applying Systems Thinking*, London: Nicholas Brealey Publishing.

29. Beer, M., Einsenstadt, R. and Spector, B. (1990) Why Change Programs Don't Produce Change, *Harvard Business Review*, 68 (6): 158–166.

30. Hinde, D. (2012) *PRINCE 2 Study Guide*, Oxford: John Wiley and Sons.

31. Edmonstone, J. (2010) A New Approach to Project Managing Change, *British Journal of Healthcare Management*, 16 (5): 114–119.

32. Ham, C., Parker, H., Singh, D. and Wade, E. (2007) *Beyond Projects: Case Studies from the Care Closer to Home/Making the Shift Programme*, Birmingham: NHS Institute for Innovation & Improvement/Health Services Management Centre, University of Birmingham.

33. Havergal, M. and Edmonstone, J. (2003) *The Facilitator's Toolkit*, Aldershot: Gower Publishing.

34. Edmonstone, J. (1988) A False God?: How Relevant is Competency-based Education and Training to the NHS?, *Health Services Management*, 84 (6): 156–160.

35. Haggis, T. (2003) Constructing Images of Ourselves?: A Critical Investigation into "Approaches to Learning" Research in Higher Education, *British Educational Research Journal*, 29 (1): 89–104.

36. Argyris, C. and Schon, D. (1974) *Theory in Practice: Increasing Professional Effectiveness*, San Francisco, CA: Jossey-Bass.

37. Bunker, B., Alban, B. and Lewicki, R. (2004) Ideas in Currency and Organisation Development Practice: Has the Well Gone Dry? *Journal of Applied Behavioural Science*, 40 (4): 403–422.

38. Forster, E. (2012) *Howards End*, London: Penguin Classics.

39. Abrahamson, E. (1991) Managerial Fads and Fashions: The Diffusion and Rejection of Innovations, *Academy of Management Review*, 16 (3): 586–612.

40. Weisbord, M. (1976) Organisational Diagnosis: Six Places to Look for Trouble With or Without a Theory, *Group and Organisation Management*, 1 (4): 430–447.

41. Waterman, R. Peters, T. and Phillips, J. (1980) Structure is not Organisation, *Business Horizons*, 23 (3): 14–26.

42. Brookfield, S. (1995) *Becoming a Critically Reflective Teacher*, San Francisco, CA: Jossey-Bass.

43. Koestler, A. (2005) *Darkness At Noon*, London: Vintage.

44. Blake, W. (1972) *London, Complete Writings*, Oxford: Oxford University Press.

45. Davidson, D. (2004) The Organisational Development Cycle: Putting the Approaches into a Process, in Peck, E. (Ed.) *Organisational Develop,ment in Healthcare: Approaches, Innovations, Achievements*, Abingdon: Radcliffe Publishing, 63–75.

46. Bushe, G. and Nagaishi, M. (2018) Imagining the Future through the Past: Organisation Development isn't (just) about Change, *Organisation Development Journal*, Fall: 23–36.

47. Briere, F., Pascale, S., Dupere, V., Castellanos-Ryan, N., Allard, F., Yale-Souliere, G. and Janosz, M. (2017) Depressive and Anxious Symptoms and the Risk of Secondary School Non-Completion, *British Journal of Psychiatry*, 211 (3): 163–168.

48. Marshak, R. (2016) Anxiety and Change in Contemporary Organisation Development, *OD Practitioner*, 48 (1): 11–19.

49. Day, A. (2020) *Disruption, Change and Transformation in Organisations: A Human Relations Perspective*, Abingdon: Routledge.

50. Greenberg, N., Weston, D., Hall, C., Caulfield, T., Williamson, V. and Fong, K. (2021) Mental Health of Staff Working in Intensive Care During Covid-19, *Occupational Health*, doi:10.1093/occmed/kqaa220.

51. Slade, S. (2021) Moral Injury and the Covid-19 Pandemic: Reframing What It Is, Who It Affects and How Care Leaders Can Manage It, *BMJ Leader*, 4 (4): 224–227.

52. Alexander, M. (2021) NHS Staff Are Suffering From "Moral Injury", A Distress Usually Associated With War Zones, *Guardian*, 12th April.

53. Argyris, C. (1985) *Strategy, Change and Defensive Routines*, London: Pitman Publishing.

54. Schon, D. (1973) *Beyond the Stable State: Public and Private Learning in a Changing Society*, Harmondsworth: Penguin.

55. Lawrence, G. (2000) *Tongued with Fire: Groups in Experience*, London: Karnac Books.

56. Menzies-Lyth, I. (1959) The Functioning of Social Systems as a Defence Against Anxiety: A Report on a Study of the Nursing Service of a General Hospital, in Menzies-Lyth, I. (Ed.) *Containing Anxiety in Institutions: Selected Essays: Volume 1*, London: Free Association Books, 43–88.

57. Bamberger, S., Vinding, A., Larsen, A., Nielsen, P., Fonager, K. and Nielsen, R. (2012) Impact of Organisational Change on Mental Health: A Systematic Review, *Occupational and Environmental Medicine*, 69 (8): 592–598.

58. Oreg, S., Vakola, M. and Armenakis, A. (2011) Change Recipients' Reactions to Organisational Change: A 60-Year Review of Quantitative Studies, *Journal of Applied Behavioural Science*, 47 (4): 461–524.

59. Vahtera, J., Kivimaki, M. and Pentti, J. (1997) Effects of Organisational Downsizing on Health of Employees, *The Lancet*, 359: 913–930.

60. Flovik, L., Knardahl, S. and Christensen, J. (2018) Organisational Change and Employee Mental Health: A Prospective Multilevel Study of the Association between Organisational Changes and Clinically Relevant Mental Distress, *Scandinavian Journal of Work and Environmental Health*, 45 (2): 1–12.

61. Applebaum, S., Delage, C. Labib, N. and Gault, G. (1997) The Survivor Syndrome: The Aftermath of Downsizing, *Career Development International*, 2 (6): 278–286.

62. Wolfe, H. (2004) *Survivor Syndrome: Key Considerations and Practical Steps*, Brighton: Institute for Employment Studies.

63. Brook, C., Pedler, M., Abbott, C. and Burgoyne, J. (2016) On Stopping Doing Those Things that Are Not Getting Us to Where We Want to Be: Unlearning and Critical Action Learning, *Human Relations*, 69 (2): 369–389.

64. Chokr, N. (2009) *Unlearning or How Not to be Governed*, Exeter, Societas Imprint Academic.
65. Keats, J. (1899) *The Complete Poetical Works and Letters of John Keats*, Cambridge: Houghton Mifflin.
66. Handy, C. (1989) *The Age of Unreason: New Thinking for a New World*, London: Business Books.
67. Symington, J. and Symington, N. (1996) *The Clinical Thinking of Wilfred Bion*, London: Routledge.
68. McAra-McWilliam, I. (2007) *Impossible Things?: Negative Capability and the Creative Imagination*, Paper presented at conference on Creativity or Conformity?: Building Cultures of Creativity in Higher Education, Cardiff: University of Wales Institute.
69. French, R. (2001) Negative Capability: Managing the Confusing Uncertainties of Change, *Journal of Organisational Change Management*, 14 (5): 480–492.
70. Bion, W. (1967) Notes on Memory and Desire, *The Psychoanalytic Forum*, 2 (3): 272–273.
71. Coghlan, D. and Rigg, C. (2012) Action Learning as Praxis in Learning and Changing, *Research in Organisational Change and Development*, 8: 59–89.
72. Baron-Cohen, S. (2012) *Zero Degrees of Empathy: A New Theory of Human Cruelty and Kindness*, London: Penguin Books.
73. Maben, J., Taylor, C., Dawson, J., Leamy, M., McCarthy, I., Reynolds, E., Ross, S., Shuldham, C., Bennett, L. and Foot, C. (2018) A Realist Informed Mixed Methods Evaluation of Schwartz Center Rounds® in England, *Health Services and Delivery Research*, 6 (37): 127.
74. De Haan, E. and Burger, Y. (2014) *Coaching With Colleagues: An Action Guide for One-To-One Learning*, Basingstoke: Palgrave Macmillan.
75. Connor, M. and Pokora, J. (2007) *Coaching and Mentoring at Work: Developing Effective Practice*, Maidenhead: McGraw-Hill/Open University Press.
76. Beckett, S. (1995) *Nohow On*, London: Grove Press.
77. Graeber, D. (2018) *Bullshit Jobs: A Theory*, London: Simon and Schuster.
78. Sennett, R. (2009) *The Craftsman*, London: Penguin.
79. Burnes, B. and Cooke, B. (2012) The Past, Present and Future of Organisation Development: Taking the Long View, *Human Relations*, 65 (11): 1395–1429.
80. Thompson, E. (1991) Time, Work-Discipline and Industrial Capitalism, in Thompson, E. (Ed.) *Customs in Common*, London: Penguin, 352−403.
81. Ryde, J. (2019) *White Privilege Unmasked: How to be Part of the Solution*, London: Jessica Kingsley.
82. Baggini, J. (2018) *How The World Thinks: A Global History of Philosophy*, London: Granta Publications.
83. Keynes, J. (1936) *Preface in The General Theory of Employment, Interest and Money*, Cambridge: Macmillan Cambridge University Press.
84. Dylan, B. (2018) *Ballad in Plain D, Bob Dylan: The Lyrics 1961–2012*, New York: Simon and Schuster.
85. Boyacigillo, N. and Adler, N. (1991) The Parochial Dinosaur: Organisational Science in a Global Context, *Academy of Management Review*, 16 (2): 262–290.
86. Lent, J. (2017) *The Patterning Instinct: A Cultural History of Humanity's Search for Meaning*, Amherst, NY: Prometheus Books.

87. Mughal, F., Gatrell, C. and Stead, V. (2018) Cultural Politics and the Role of the Action Learning Facilitator: Analysing the Negotiation of Critical Action Learning in the Pakistani MBA Through a Bourdieusian Lens, *Management Learning*, 49 (1): 69–85.

88. Edmonstone, J. and Robson, J. (2014) Action Learning on the Edge: Contributing to a Master's Programme in Human Resources for Health, *Action Learning: Research and Practice*, 11 (3): 361–374.

89. Argyris, C.(1976) *Increasing Leadership Effectiveness*, New York: Wiley.

90. Edmonstone, J. and Robson, J. (2013) Blending-In: The Contribution of Action Learning to a Masters Programme in Human Resources in Health, *International Journal of Human Resource Development and Management*, 13 (1): 61–75.

91. Bong, H-C. and Cho, Y. (2017) Defining Success in Action Learning: An International Comparison, *European Journal of Training and Development*, 41 (2): 160–176.

92. Mahadevan, J. (2017) *A Very Short, Fairly Interesting and Reasonably Cheap Book About Cross-Cultural Management*, London: Sage.

93. Patel, T. (2014) *Cross-Cultural Management: A Transactional Approach*, Abingdon: Routledge.

94. Jaques, E. (1976) *A General Theory of Bureaucracy*, London: Heinemann.

95. Bookchin, M. (2005) *The Ecology of Freedom: The Emergence and Dissolution of Hierarchy*, Oakland, CA: AK Press.

96. Raelin, J. (2020) Hierarchy's Subordination of Democracy and How to Outrank It, *Management Learning*, 51 (5): 620–633.

97. Porter-O'Grady, T. (Ed.) (1992) *Implementing Shared Governance: Creating a Professional Organisation*, St. Louis: Mosby.

98. Edmonstone, J. (2003) *Shared Governance: Making It Happen*, Chichester: Kingsham Press.

99. Kanter, R. (1972) *Commitment and Community*, Cambridge, MA: Harvard University Press.

100. Woodburn, J. (1982) Egalitarian Societies, *Man: New Series*, 7 (1): 3–26.

101. Delanty, G. (2002) Communitarianism and Citizenship, in Isin, E. and Turner, G. (Eds.) *Handbook of Citizenship Studies*, London: Sage, 121–132.

102. Girard, M. and Stark, D. (2002) Distributing Intelligence and Organising Diversity in New Media Projects, *Environment & Planning A: Economy and Space*, 34: 1927–1949.

103. Osterman, P. (2006) Overcoming Oligarchy: Culture and Agency in Social Movement Organisations, *Administrative Science Quarterly*, 51: 622–649.

104. Suzman, J. (2020) *Work: A History of How We Spend our Time*, London: Bloomsbury Circus.

105. Legge, K. (1978) *Power, Innovation and Problem-Solving in Personnel Management*, Maidenhead: McGraw-Hill.

106. Guest, D. and King, Z. (2004) Power, Innovation and Problem-Solving: Personnel Managers' Three Steps to Heaven, *Journal of Management Studies*, 41 (3): 401–423.

107. Marchington, M. (2015) Human Resource Management (HRM): Too Busy Looking Up to See Where It Is Going Longer Term, *Human Resource Management Review*, 25 (2): 176–187.

108. Martin, G., Siebert, S. and Robson, I. (2018) Conformist Innovation: An Institutional Logics Perspective on how Human Resource Executives Construct Business School Reputations, *International Journal of Human Resource Management*, 29 (13): 2027–2053.

109. Edmonstone, J., Lawless, A. and Pedler, M. (2019) Leadership Development, Wicked Problems and Action Learning: Provocations to a Debate, *Action Learning: Research and Practice*, 16 (1): 37–51.

110. Gibney, J. and Murie, A. (Eds.) (2008) *Towards a "New" Strategic Leadership of Place for the Knowledge-Based Economy*, Birmingham: University of Birmingham, School of Public Policy for Academy for Sustainable Communities.

111. Perkins, N., Hunter, D., Visram, S., Finn, R., Gosling, J., Adams, L. and Forrest, A. (2020) Partnership or Insanity?: Why Do Health Partnerships Do the Same Things Over and Over Again and Expect a Different Result?, *Journal of Health Services Research and Policy*, 25 (1): 41–48.

112. Nancarrow, S. and Borthwick, A. (2005) Dynamic Professional Boundaries in the Healthcare Workforce, *Sociology of Health and Illness*, 27 (7): 897–919.

113. Cole, M. (2020) *Radical Organisation Development*, Abingdon: Routledge.

114. Mintzberg, H. (1996) Managing Government; Governing Management, *Harvard Business Review*, May/June.

115. Foucault, M. (1980) *Power/Knowledge: Selected Interviews and Other Writings, 1972–1977*, New York: Pantheon Books.

116. Fisher, M. (2009) *Capitalist Realism: Is There No Alternative?* Winchester: Zero Books.

117. Carnevale, D. (2003) *Organisational Development in the Public Sector*, Cambridge, MA: Westview Press.

Chapter 8

Into the Future – The Possible Next Stages in Healthcare OD

The next stages in the development of Organisation Development (OD) in healthcare will be enacted by OD practitioners, by the "organisations" that they work both for and with and by the emerging social and economic context within which they take place. The purpose of this chapter is to set out some of the key influences and choices in that process, so it is not intended to be any kind of blueprint, recipe or even grand narrative for OD. It is rather an exploration of some of the factors that will be in play. Inevitably, there will also be others which are presently unknown or currently not recognised. It begins with a reprise of what the major messages are from this review of healthcare OD to date. It then considers the overwhelming influence of managerialism on OD, before using the "Lyotard Triangle" to identify the tension between the drive towards organisational performance and the possibilities of personal and social emancipation. It examines the centrality of values in OD and OD as a moral and ethical practice.

Faced with the transition from the second modernity to a post-modern state of affairs, meta-modernism is posited as a potential exit from this polarised dilemma. It is suggested that the need is to start small, and the subsequent widening of the circles of learning is proposed as a useful way forward. The need to be open to new approaches to both thinking and action by OD practitioners is addressed, as is the need for a fresh approach to change project management.

DOI: 10.1201/9781003167310-8

The question of the most appropriate base or location for OD is considered, and the possibility of resistance to this development route is also examined. The chapter concludes by returning to the original values of early OD and notes that the future lies significantly in the hands of OD practitioners themselves.

Where are we now? In seeking to sum-up where OD in healthcare presently stands, it is helpful to tease out the lessons which emerge from the journey so far, especially since this book proposes that, to understand OD's development, it is important to always consider the political, social and economic contexts within which it has previously developed and continues to develop. At its simplest, OD has been, and is, about attempts to plan and implement organisational change using the insights and methods of the behavioural sciences.

At the outset, when OD emerged in a post-World War II setting in the USA and the UK as an outgrowth of the second modernity, it had an obvious human-istic value-base which emphasised:

- Individual human dignity at work.
- The agency of human beings, both individually and collectively.
- That organisations should be shaped for people, rather than vice versa.
- That organisations were pluralistic entities where both consensus and con-flict existed.
- That power differentials should be reduced and all voices should be heard equally.
- That collaborative ways of working should be fostered.
- That change should be driven by data collected, analysed and fed back.

It saw organisational change as a progressive activity which was rational, orderly, top-down, linear and data-driven, and it was assumed that the values mentioned above were widely shared, both within individual organisations and across soci-ety as a whole.

The 1980s saw a fundamental change in the context within which OD was operating. A third modernity grounded in post-modernism and embodying a dominant neoliberal ideology saw organisations reject the possibilities of operat-ing in a pluralist manner and opt instead for a unitary command-and-control model of working. The focus turned to the short, rather than to the long term, and OD came increasingly to deal only with "tame" issues, to adopt a conform-ist innovation way of working and to see itself as simply an instrumental means towards predefined ends.

The establishment of OD in the UK's National Health Service (NHS) began in the mid-1970s, and the evolving experience there has produced a range of conclusions, not least that OD was initially seen as something which was quite countercultural to the mainstream managerial and professional ways of working in existence at that time. It became clear from the early experience of doing OD that many of the problems which OD encountered were "wicked" in nature and that OD in healthcare was different in many ways from that which had been employed in the Anglo-American industrial and commercial enterprises where it had been initially adopted. These differences included the centrality of emotional labour for healthcare clinical professional staff, who also had a degree of autonomy and a loyalty to their profession, as opposed simply to their employer and, as a result, there were different views in existence of what professional practice was between healthcare managers and clinical professionals.

It gradually became clear from this experience that organisational support for OD from senior levels was important but that front-line employees needed to be central to OD activity; that an equal emphasis on feelings, motivation and learning as well as quantification and the taking of action was necessary; that time, space and legitimacy were vital to enable such reflexive learning to take place and that steering arrangements were necessary for such learning to be identified and shared. It also became clear that OD activity was increasingly colonised from the 1990s by the Human Resource function.

OD in healthcare in the UK's NHS existed in a culture which was hierarchical in nature and which assumed that the private sector was always superior to the public sector. This viewpoint was highly action-oriented, rather than reflexive and accepted and welcomed the primacy of quantitative performance metrics. As a result, it largely discounted the importance of the implicit ongoing working relationships between healthcare employees that ensured that services were delivered. The NHS frequently used outsourced OD expertise and, over time, psychologised job performance, largely ignoring more systemic matters.

OD now faces a range of challenges, not least the sense that "organisations" are increasingly seen as socially constructed communities of meaning, rather than fixed and stable entities. The latter understanding was based upon the potency of the machine metaphor, but an alternative metaphor which saw organisations as living systems was increasingly gaining acceptance. There was a recognition that the choice of language in organisational life was important and that there was a danger of representational learning only taking place, and that this danger included the field of OD itself. Further important recognitions included the concern that OD diagnostic frameworks imposed a set of preexisting assumptions and the possibility that, in an increasingly global environment, OD was culture-bound as a result of its Anglo-American antecedents. The permeability and mutual dependence of healthcare with social care raised the question of whether a healthcare-only focus was still relevant and the emergence of the Radical OD critique raised the issue of power in organisational life and the compatibility, or otherwise, of hierarchy and democracy.

The tyranny of managerialism: Healthcare, in common with many other sectors of society, is dominated by the ideology of managerialism – an interlocking set of beliefs, attitudes and values that support the viewpoint that healthcare leaders and managers alone are the most essential, important and desirable elements for both the good administration and governance of healthcare organisations and for the delivery of healthcare itself [1]. Such a view has been propagated by university business schools [2] espousing somewhat grandiose organisational strategies and visions. Business schools have often advanced a mechanistic formula for management of knowledge and skills grounded in an "identikit" of how-things-ought-to-be competences and based on a preference for universality and standardisation.

The origins of managerialism may well lie with the early management theorists who tried to establish their legitimacy by transposing ideas, principles and language from the natural sciences, as if people at work behaved exactly like the controlled variables in scientific experiments. There is a case made that managerialism is not just an extension and manifestation of neoliberal thinking but has a different historical lineage, growing out of the post-World War II work of the RAND corporation think-tank in the USA and embodied in such activities as operational research, cost–benefit analysis and programme budgeting [3], but that it has since become inextricably intertwined with the neoliberal agenda. Boltanski and Chiapello [4] claim that recent management theory has acted as a transmitter of neoliberal ideas into the workplace, with the injunction to work flexibly, within flatter hierarchies and emphasising the dominance of targets. Similarly, Styhre [5] has identified the impact of neoliberalism on management thinking and practice, suggesting that managerial practices such as auditing and boundary-less careers have been inextricably entangled with the neoliberal political agenda.

Sennett [6] observed that the leaders of transmission in this respect were the global tech companies, such as Apple and Google, a viewpoint which later Zuboff [7], citing also Amazon and Facebook, certainly shared. The increase in employees working from home during the Covid-19 pandemic has even led to the increased potential use by employers of employee surveillance tools which enable the employer to see all of an employee's emails and the documents which they read or create; to learn of all appointments – who the employee talks to and when; to listen in to or read transcriptions of an employee's telephone calls; to monitor an employee's internet usage – the sites visited and the duration, even to turn on the camera and watch the employee at work [8]. Such developments indicate the arrival in tangible terms of the "surveillance society" [7,9], although it has also been argued that it has long been preceded by previous more nuanced personal restraints [10,11].

The spread of managerialism in the UK public sector probably began with the 1964 Wilson Government, as noted in Chapter 3, and includes the civil service Fulton reforms of the 1960s, the introduction of chief executives into local government from the 1970s and the spread of general management in the NHS from the 1980s. The managerial viewpoint has been endorsed by the evolving history of competence-based leadership approaches in the NHS over the last twenty years [12].

This growth of managerialism may also lie in the way that public sector leadership and management has been defined in the UK. Van Wart [13] has suggested that it can be almost totally typified as being ends-driven, focusing only on specific performance targets – that it is "a bureaucracy of specifications, monitoring and reporting" [14]. The worldview of politicians may be the driving force underlying this [15], although there is also a strong case that the problem extends far beyond politicians and into UK society as a whole, as this particular form of leadership and management has become romanticised [16] – think of the television programme "The Apprentice" as an example of this. It has been described as embodying "performativity" – the subordination of knowledge and truth to the production of efficiency in order to meet the demands of key stakeholders, such that the active and the technical tend to dominate over the reflective and humane [17].

Managerialism asserts that dissension, conflict and argument are largely unnecessary for the solving of organisational problems. It is a reflection of the essentially unitary view of organisations [18] which emphasises a single source and locus of organisational control (senior healthcare leaders and managers), a single identity and loyalty focus (the employing healthcare organisation) and adherence to a single set of common organisational objectives (goals, targets, performance indicators). Conflict within this approach is seen as a rare and transient phenomenon, typically attributed to the activities of organisational troublemakers and deviants. The managerial prerogative is emphasised, reflecting the command-and-control model where senior leaders and managers make key decisions and employees simply do the work [19]. The assumption is that in a hierarchy, all knowledge is a function of "seniority", and the "lower" you are in the hierarchy, then the less you know or are even capable of knowing. These beliefs appear to offer a spurious certainty to senior healthcare leaders and managers in the unstable and uncertain world of "liquid modernity" [20] and are "unthinkingly accepted by many politicians and their civil servants and policy advisers" [21] as it serves to reinforce their belief in, and perceptions of, control.

The underlying assumptions which lie behind managerialism have also been identified by Edwards [22] and Mintzberg [23]. They are:

■ That the primary value in organisational life is solely economic efficiency or the pursuit of the maximum output with the minimum input.
■ That all aspects of organisational performance can be properly evaluated by objective measures in quantitative terms, via a form of cost–benefit analysis.

■ An abiding faith in the tools and techniques of management science, together with the ability of leaders and managers to use those tools and techniques to solve problems.
■ That all activities should be entrusted to professional leaders and managers who are responsible for performance. If they are successful, they should be rewarded and/or promoted. If they are unsuccessful, they should be quickly replaced.

From this viewpoint, all that is needed for organisational success is a rational assessment of problems (essentially an orderly and linear top-down process) and that this simply involves gathering and collating the requisite information, listing the options, calculating the cost–benefit of each, evaluating the consequences and choosing the best course of action. The logic therefore goes:

■ Understand the problem – this involves gathering information to specify exactly what the problem is.
■ Analyse the data gathered.
■ Formulate a solution.
■ Implement that solution.

The more complex the problem, the more important it was seen to follow this orderly flow. There is an underlying assumption that all the facts pertaining to a particular situation can be defined, collected, analysed and that a single solution can be found in this sequential manner, not least because previous solutions have been found to this or similar difficulties. It is assumed that there is an existing knowledge base of tried and tested solutions which it is possible to exploit, and thus, it can be predicted with ease and in advance exactly what success would look like. It is a picture of already knowing – a problem and its domain are known, as are the right processes and techniques needed to solve it.

Such a view is entirely rooted in the machine metaphor and values short termism for the benefit of stakeholders through the evolved hierarchy of domains (Policy → Management → Service) which Chapter 1 outlined. It emphasises a separation between the "leaders" who direct work without executing anything and the "followers" or producers who execute the work without directing it, with the latter being implicit in the linguistic ontology of the former. Increasingly the former seem to have little meaningful connection with the day-to-day work of the organisations which they "lead". As a result, OD in healthcare has become "boxed-in" by the senior managerial perceptions of organisational reality and what senior leaders and managers deem to be the problems that OD is directed towards and so is required to "fix".

It has become solely the instrument of sustaining an organisation's managerial imperative and its directive agenda and has developed a focus solely on macro- or organisation-wide issues. As a result, it seems to have moved far away from the original ethical values which OD embodied. The more it has done so the less it has been able to keep in touch with and involve all the people who actually deliver healthcare services and who were affected by top-down-driven change programmes, with their ongoing concerns and priorities – and therefore has been less able to promote and advance the original humanistic and democratic values. An OD which was detached from such managerial control and direction would be free to work in a pluralist manner and at the behest of all kinds of individuals, groups, teams, professions, organisations, service users and trade unions, as well as senior leaders and managers and would not be constrained by a managerial-only agenda. There is also a larger question – whether "organisations" are now even the most relevant focus? People at work are increasingly interconnected and interdependent, being embedded in a series of overlapping personal and professional networks and fields of practice as well as the more conventional organisational forms, so rather than "organisation", "context" might even be a better description.

The Lyotard Triangle: Pedler et al. [24] developed a framework or cognitive map, originally for the consideration of action learning, but with great relevance to OD. The so-called "Lyotard Triangle [25] proposes three positions with regard to the application of knowledge, as shown in Figure 8.1.

They are:

Speculative: Learning and development which is pursued for its own sake, unconcerned with any application to practice and concerned only with theoretical rigour.

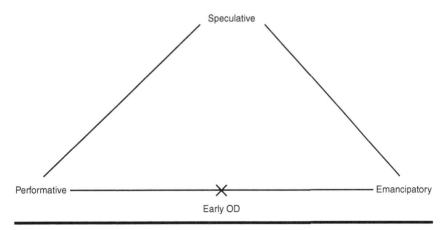

Figure 8.1　The Lyotard triangle.

Emancipatory: Learning and development which helps to overcome oppression and attain the highest human potential – the holistic development of the person in the world. As such, it is intended to "break the spell" or "unshackle" people from the established, pre-packaged or orthodox ways of thinking, being and doing [26]. It has been suggested that:

> Emancipation is always a matter of ongoing resistance to the culture that claims us: more a case of escapology – an obscure grappling with social chains and restraints in an underwater sack. [27]

Performative: Learning and development that helps action in the world, resolves practical problems and produces improved goods and services – and so is solely concerned with improving and modernising management and performance. Performativity has been defined as:

> a technology, a culture and a mode of regulation that employs judgements, comparisons and displays as means of incentive, control, attrition and change – based on rewards and sanctions (both material and symbolic). The performance of individuals and of organisations serve as measures of productivity or output, or displays of "quality" or instances of promotion or inspection. As such they stand for, encapsulate or represent the worth, quality or value of an individual or organisation. [28]

Complex social processes and events are translated into simple figures or categories of judgement and thus appear as misleadingly objective and hyperrational. The annual review, the performance appraisal meeting, inspections and peer reviews, site visits and the regular collection, recording and publication of results are the mechanics of performativity. Performance measures have become increasingly "hard", quantitative and demanding [29] and individuals are subjectively judged against them. Summing up the total performance of an individual with a single rating is a gross oversimplification of a complex set of factors that influence that performance and which may well lie beyond the ability of any individual alone to influence [30]. It is a fallacy that an individual's contribution to overall productivity can be accurately measured – labour economists have been attempting to do this for many years with little success because organisational performance is always more than the sum total of its individual parts [31]. Even the softer aspects of work performance are judged against what employers deem as specified and quantified competences. There is a deflection of attention away from those aspects of social or emotional development that appear to have not only immediate measurable performative value but also a focus on "soft" control, through approaches such as positive psychology and emotional intelligence.

Early OD had originally sought to position itself at a midpoint between the Emancipatory and Performative positions and saw no contradiction between striving for the improvement of organisational performance and the personal development and enhancement of individuals within a work setting. However, the advent of the neoliberal worldview as a fundamental aspect of the third modernity and the concentration on short-term "business"-related matters has led to an over-concentration on the Performative position – which has led inexorably in turn to an instrumental view of OD as merely a technique or means towards predetermined ends [32]. This manifests itself as an unwillingness to have any underlying assumptions challenged in the face of a "bias for action" [33] and a "continuous stream of work-related activities" [34]. The emancipatory potential of OD is therefore blunted, because personal and organisational learning and development is not just about enhancing performance but is also potentially liberating – a process of self-discovery, self-knowledge and creativity, leading to possibilities of organisational (and social) action. It can be seen as a step towards greater self-insight and greater awareness of the political and cultural dimensions of organisational life [35]. Such emancipatory learning has been described as:

> that which frees people from personal, institutional or environmental forces that prevent them from seeing new directions, from gaining control of their lives, their society and their world. [36]

It helps to:

> create new understandings by making conscious the social, political, professional, economic and ethical assumptions constraining or supporting individual and collective action in a specific context. [37]

The UK's social and economic system (as with that of most other nations) is built on the assumption of degrees of inequality and of there being economic and social winners and losers, and the interests of these groups do very much diverge. Picking a side on this divide is, or should be, very much a lived reality for OD practitioners who might well need to retreat from the supposedly detached neutrality and professional "validity" offered by natural science evidence bases, as much of psychology has done. Otherwise, OD only engages in circular conversations that privilege the processes of inquiry over the act of advocacy in organisational life. What exactly is the point of a spirit of curiosity that endlessly enquires but take no view of the world? It is not even a neutral position, it is relativism, and relativism just re-cycles the status quo.

OD and values: The term "values" has many meanings in different contexts, and there are numerous definitions. A useful one is that of Rokeach [38]:

> A value is an enduring belief that a specific mode of conduct or end-state of existence is personally or socially preferable to an opposite or converse mode of conduct or end-state of existence.

The emphasis here is on the values that people (including OD practitioners) have, rather than those that inhere in objects. Gillon [39] suggests that OD values are the principal reason that many individuals choose to enter OD as a career. Values are seen as having an enduring quality. That is, while they do not represent "eternal verities", the definition allows for the emotional component of a value – that one feels good or bad about it. It also encompasses a motivational aspect – the striving towards value attainment. The terms "mode of conduct" and "end-state of existence" refer to what Rokeach terms instrumental and terminal values. Instrumental values can refer either to morality and ethics (such as behaving honestly) or to competence (such as behaving rationally). Some terminal values may be intrapersonal in their focus (such as peace of mind) while others may be interpersonal (such as authentic relationships). The degree and extent of "oughtness" of values is partly a function of society's preference with regard to the values.

Values serve two important functions. One is that of standards which guide personal and professional conduct and help the evaluation and judgement of self and others, while the other is motivational – concerned with striving towards value attainment. So if values occupy a central place in personal and professional lives, this need to achieve standards of excellence becomes conceptually tied to the need to maintain and enhance self-esteem, both through self-evaluation and the evaluation of others. This is shown diagrammatically in Figure 8.2.

Rokeach's orientation implies that people can act as well as react, that they are agents rather than patients and that therefore the concept of values is of central importance to any study of human beings.

The turn away from the early "love/trust" model of OD marked by the work of Goodge [40] and Tranfield [41] seemed to imply the development of a value-free OD with the practitioner becoming simply a pragmatic "social engineer" continually adapting to progressively changing realities, rather than striving for what these proponents would regard as unattainable visions of an ideal organisation.

Early OD quite clearly had an explicit humanistic value base as Chapter 1 illustrates. It is also obvious that this value base emerged from a particular context – that of the second modernity, and that the context in which OD currently

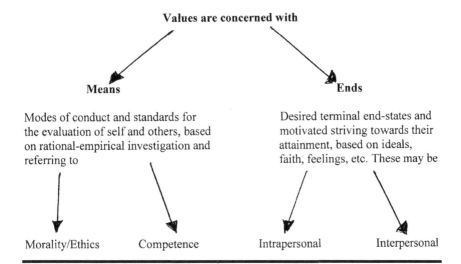

Values are concerned with

Means

Modes of conduct and standards for the evaluation of self and others, based on rational-empirical investigation and referring to

Ends

Desired terminal end-states and motivated striving towards their attainment, based on ideals, faith, feelings, etc. These may be

Morality/Ethics   Competence   Intrapersonal   Interpersonal

Figure 8.2   A model for understanding values in OD.

operates has changed significantly. This raises important questions for current OD practitioners, such as:

■ To what extent do you believe that the original OD values were ever realistic and achievable?
■ Do these OD values still hold true many years later as ends to still be pursued?
■ If the context for OD work changes, to what extent can or should OD values change in turn?
■ Is a value-free OD a possibility or not?

OD as a moral and ethical practice: If ethics are the moral principles that govern the behaviour of OD practitioners and the way that they conduct their activity, then they are clearly related to the underlying values of OD and to those of OD practitioners themselves. They are beliefs about what is right or wrong and provide a basis for judging the appropriateness or otherwise of behaviour. They guide people in their dealings with other individuals, groups and organisations [42]. The original humanistic values of early OD were:

■ Individual human dignity at work.
■ The agency of human beings being recognised, both individually and collectively.
■ That organisations should be shaped for people, rather than vice versa.

- That organisations were pluralistic entities where both consensus and conflict existed.
- That power differentials should be reduced and all voices should be heard equally.
- That collaborative ways of working should be fostered.
- That change should be driven by data collected, analysed and fed back.

The credo of the third and post-modern modernity would claim that all values are historically contingent, so would therefore imply that these humanistic values related only to the period from the late 1940s to around 1980, as that was their historical context. It would also suggest that OD was a grand theory or meta-narrative which should therefore be distrusted. Yet meta-modernism (see below) asserts that such a grand narrative is just as necessary as it is problematic; that the cultivation of ironic detachment should be balanced with practical engagement and that it is entirely feasible to place an emphasis on OD's humanistic values, while still retaining a degree of scepticism. Indeed, Day [43] has maintained that turbulence and uncertainty, as features of a VUCA/RUPT world, call for organisations to adopt just such a humanistic philosophy that values human dignity and believes in the capacity of people to grow and take responsibility for their lives.

An ethical orientation would seem to be constructed upon two key elements:

A commitment to reflexivity – a reflective practice that acknowledges the active presence of the OD practitioner as a reflector as an integral part of that upon which they seek to reflect.

An adherence to critical thinking, in such areas as strategies, policies, publicity, communication, protocol, position papers, thought leadership, research, pictures and practices that coalesce around people in corporate life and then necessarily require people in corporate life to turn their close attention to everything that surrounds them.

Wheatley and Kellner-Rogers [44] suggest that "organisation is always an expression of identity", and in this respect, Traeger and Warwick [45] suggest three question areas for practitioners that they claim sit at the heart of ethical OD practice:

How are we planning for the future?

- How do I ensure that I ask the right questions before I decide on a course of action?
- How do I know when I have involved the right people and information in planning a course of action?

■ How do I know if I have hurt or harmed?
■ How will I know if I have done any good?
■ How will I account for myself to others – what will I say in planning my course of action?

How do we make the next step as we interact with others?

■ How will I develop awareness of the wider influences and contexts of what I am experiencing?
■ How will I act in the network relationships in which some people are more powerful and others less powerful?
■ How can I ask questions that will enable me to get more insightful views of conversation?
■ How will I know that I have been "conditioned" to act or think in a certain way?

How are we influenced and how are we being influenced?

■ How can we stop ourselves sleepwalking into poor and unethical decision-making?
■ How do we keep alive enough difference so that we can see our world with "new eyes"?
■ How do we keep aware of the changing contexts and how this affects our stakeholders?
■ How can we keep asking difficult questions of ourselves?

In a speech in Washington DC on 6 February 1968, Dr Martin Luther King said:

> On some positions cowardice asks the question "Is it safe?". Expediency asks the question "Is it politic?". Vanity asks the question "Is it popular?" But conscience asks the question "Is it right?". There comes a time when one must take a position that is neither safe, nor politic, nor popular, but it must be done because conscience says it is right. [46]

This may well involve speaking truth to power, regardless of personal risk, yet the reality is that to do so may be potentially career-threatening for the OD practitioner leading to loss of work and even to loss of employment. These are dilemmas that OD practitioners must inevitably face, and this suggests that they must also recognise that they are personally and professionally located within existing power structures; that they need to consistently demonstrate exemplary conduct, with little or no gap between their espoused values and their values in use [47] and that they need to display humility and respect for others. As a result, they need to pay close attention to personal reflexivity and to self-care [48]. In engaging with organisational power issues Cole [49] offers the following questions when approaching OD work:

- Do those who commission OD work appreciate the significance of power in this context, and are they genuinely willing to allow a conversation about it to take place as a major facet of the work?
- Do the senior leaders recognise this and show a willingness to allow people to speak openly about their work lives?
- In assessing the system in which you are to start work, what is your personal understanding of the power in that space?
- In starting work, are you really giving adequate space, time and freedom for people to speak openly and without fear of retribution about their experience of power?
- Are you content to carry the messages of power through the work and to its conclusion, to see meaningful outputs and outcomes?

while Edmonstone [50] posed related questions for OD practitioners:

- Are you content to work in, with or for an organisation that regards OD as simply an instrumental set of techniques towards predetermined ends?
- How might you ensure that the emancipatory potential of OD is not subverted?
- Does your OD work challenge the taken-for-granted assumptions and potential passivity of the people you work with and promote unlearning as well as learning?

An emerging new OD? Early OD, being grounded in the second modernity, assumed that objective reality was something which was quite capable of being studied, measured and planned for – that there was an objective and knowable truth about the nature of organisations that could be uncovered through the application of a set of tools and techniques that generated useful data. However, the third, or post-modern, modernity asserts that all interpretations of what constitutes reality are open to negotiation and are never fully shared by everyone – that there are instead multiple subjective realities [51]. There are important questions, of course, about whether this latter approach actually engages with the important issues originally addressed by OD such as the place of democracy in the workplace, healthy and fulfilling work and working environments and

Table 8.1   Traditional OD and New OD [52]

Conventional OD Approach	Post-Lewinian OD Approach
Single, discoverable, objective reality	Multiple, socially constructed, subjective realities
Reality is discovered by using rational and analytic processes	Reality is negotiated and involves power and political processes
Change results from collecting and applying valid data using objective problem-solving methods	Change results from creating new social agreements through explicit or implicit negotiation
Change can be planned, is episodic and linear	Change can be self-organising, is continuous and/or cyclical
Emphasis is on changing behaviour and what one does	Emphasis is on changing mind-sets and how one thinks
Action research by change agents	Discourse, narratives and meaning

ethical organisational practices. Nevertheless, a "post-Lewinian" OD approach has been contrasted with early or traditional OD as shown in Table 8.1 [52].

This emergent OD is based upon some key premises [53]:

■ Reality and relationships are socially constructed.
■ Organisations are meaning-making systems.
■ Language – broadly defined – matters.
■ Groups and organisations are continuously self-organising.
■ Creating change requires changing conversations.
■ There is a need to structure participative inquiry and engagement to increase differentiation before seeking coherence.
■ Transformational change is far more emergent than planned change.
■ OD practitioners are part of the process and not apart from the process.

There is perhaps a real danger of engaging in dichotomous thinking here – of regarding the choices as either an adherence to the tenets of early OD or to post-Lewinian OD. This is based on Cartesian dualism where A is always pitted against B. Perennial debates over such polarities as objective versus subjective, rationalism versus empiricism and scientific management versus human relations all reflect this intellectual tradition [54].

An alternative which embraces a both/and orientation, rather than an either/or one, has been described as "meta-modernism", a phenomenon originally derived from arts and culture studies [55]. This suggests that there is, or needs to be, a continuing movement or oscillation between the poles of early OD and post-Lewinian OD, as a means of moving beyond them. It involves embracing the doubt and scepticism that post-modernism entails, as well as the hope and sincerity which marked early OD. It asserts that grand narratives (such as a belief in, and the promotion of, organisational progression) are just as necessary as they are problematic and that a sense of ironic detachment can be balanced with sincere engagement and hope. In other words, it is quite possible to search for and emphasise values and meaning, while continuing to be sceptical. In a phrase attributed to Maria Popova [56] "Critical thinking without hope is cynicism and hope without critical thinking is naivete". Meta-modernism is not a philosophy as it does not define a closed system of thought. It is descriptive, rather than prescriptive.

The prefix "meta" is conceived as a means of transcending the burdens of modernism's and post-modernism's polarised intellectual heritage. Oswick [57] suggests that the two forms of engagement can coexist and be used in a complimentary fashion, and Gilpin-Jackson [58] proposes that the action research/consultancy model outlined in Chapter 1 is ultimately an iterative process which enables a whole range of different intervention approaches to be used. It is therefore possible to blend both approaches, not least because early OD generally reflects the objectivity and data-oriented perspectives dominant in most organisations. The focus, however, is less on diagnosis in order to present a prescriptive solution and more on gaining greater understanding of the situation in order to take action – and then reflecting on the impact of that action in order to act again [59].

In this respect, even some post-modern writers do also argue that a more open and democratic approach to change is both preferable and achievable [60], proposing that it is possible to:

> create a democracy of enactment in which the process is made open and available to all, such that we create opportunities for freedom and innovation, rather than simply for further domination.

Likewise, Wooten and White [61] assert that core OD values, such as equality, empowerment, consensus-building and horizontal relationships, are ones which are particularly relevant to organisations.

Ripples in the organisational pond: Cole [11] asserts that every individual in a given context has within their gift, through their reflexive awareness and ability to act differently, both individually and collectively, the capacity to shape and reshape the culture in which they automatically find themselves. He contrasts these "minute actions and inter-relationships" with grand top-down and "cascaded" OD programmes. Stacey [62] claims that this is where potentially transforming conversations are started and Pedler [63] concurs, noting that it is:

> through the questioning and awareness-raising processes that can produce changes of heart and mind where the near-invisible processes of change can begin.

In a participatory evaluation study of an OD intervention to support integrated care in three London Boroughs, Bussu and Marshall [64] noted the limited reach and scope of the top-down OD approach which was adopted, based on coaching and staff engagement events, often delivered by external consultancies and mostly focused at the senior management level. OD initiatives were designed to get staff to buy-in to a given vision entirely based on senior leaders' and managers' experience, instead of helping to develop new understandings based on the experience of the professional staff who delivered care. There was great frustration on the part of front-line staff at the lack of any genuine bottom-up involvement in shaping a change agenda and a lack of follow-up on their suggestions. Bussu and Marshall concluded that a more bottom-up OD would have had greater potential. Such small-scale initiatives needed to be rolled-out systematically, otherwise they would tend to have limited sustainable impact on everyday working routines on the ground. The original research upon which this was based [65] concluded that:

> Front-line staff often feel change imposed on them and there is a general perception that changes to services are introduced to mimic other organisations without enough understanding of the local context.

If the complex adaptive system perspective is correct, then no one within a system (including senior leaders and managers) can even see the system as a whole, so to impose frameworks, competences or mindsets on others are really no more than a form of indoctrination.

Stacey [62] makes a useful distinction between what he calls the "legitimate" side of an organisation and what he terms the "shadow" side. The former consists of the linkages that are either formally and intentionally established by the most powerful organisational members or established by well-understood and implicit principles that are widely accepted by people in the organisation – a shared culture or accepted ideology. The shadow side, which is inherently adaptive and nonlinear, is made up of the linkages spontaneously and informally established by individuals among themselves during the course of interacting within the legitimate system. The result is another network, a kind of shadow of the legitimate system consisting of informal social and political links, in which people develop their own rules for interacting with each other in the course of their interaction.

This suggests that the role of OD may well be to help people in the shadow system at work to map the current reality of the "terrain" in which they operate (in other words, with how things are) and how they wish to respond to the "adjacent possibilities", rather than how things "ought" to be. It involves helping people to become their own map-makers and not just the readers and interpreters of others' maps. Internal OD practitioners in particular are located within the interstices of an organisation and so are well able to influence others by providing sufficient time and space for individuals and groups to examine what they do in the present, how they currently work together to do it and how they might do so differently and better in future. It implies OD practitioners ending all attempts to specify how people should think and act or to seek to engineer a particular kind of idealised future end-state such as a "can-do" or "transformational" organisational culture and avoiding becoming embroiled in reductive perceptions that bear no resemblance to the complex reality of peoples' working lives [66].

Instead it involves posing helpful questions [67] and a focus on helping people to make some sense of what is happening in their local interactions; by questioning the extent to which what work that is done together is useful; by creating connections and relationships through a concentration on those micro-decisions and small actions which are capable of being taken forward in the present in order to creatively shape the future and by extending the scope and scale of such work beyond the current bounds. The focus is therefore on people's lived experience and day-to-day realities, with how people organise themselves, rather than on an "organisation"; less on individual motivations and actions and more towards relational and contextual views of power in the workplace. It also quite clearly acknowledges the existence of uncertainty, ambiguity and contradiction.

This role may involve beginning reflexive and candid conversations that scrutinise, question and challenge the default assumptions and choices of individuals and groups; identifying so-called "common-sense" or commonplace assumptions; exploring multiple perspectives and identifying existing conversational patterns and interdependencies in order to help people to make greater sense of their experience. It involves the cultivation of "reflective curiosity" [66], "reflective activism" [68] and "practical authoring" [69]. This is a stance that encourages the ownership of the processes by which the organisational world is constructed and sustained. It encourages an engagement in reflective practice, including the application of relevant knowledge within the workplace in order to inform and enhance action. It requires active engagement in continual review and repositioning of assumptions, values and practices. Such an approach values insight and intuition and may raise such questions as:

■ Who are we and what are we doing together?
■ How have we come to think and behave as we do?
■ Who or what are we becoming and how useful is this to ourselves and others?

It is therefore less about any form of one-dimensional "diagnosis" and assumes instead the existence of a series of complex and non-linear relationships, and therefore is more about enabling individual and shared learning, based on a reflection on lived experience. It is rather more about organising than organisations – the processes of improvising, experimenting, learning and adapting together. In this respect, it has much in common with jazz improvisation [70]. The knowledge created by such engagement is entirely relevant to the particular contexts within which people live and work and to the specific individuals with whom they work. It is a form of "artistry in practice" in which people become "knowledgeable doers" [71]. In this respect, there is no such thing as a neutral learning process. Learning either functions as an instrument which is used to facilitate the integration of people into the logic of the existing system and its underlying values and bring about conformity to it or it becomes the means by which people deal critically and creatively with their reality and discover how to participate in the transformation of their world.

Such small-scale, "below the radar" initiatives, where people in networks of micro-relationships are able to carve out some "permission space" in order to try something different, recognises that individuals and groups (and OD practitioners) have to start where they are and do useful things at a smaller level, but can then show other people the differences that are being made and then invite them to join in. It assumes that such sense-making and the co-creation of meaning through the building of emotional and personal commitment comes before the creation of any solutions. There is growing agreement among some practitioners and scholars that such a bottom-up approach is desirable, whereby the purpose and benefits of change should not only be understood and embraced by front-line staff but also co-produced with them, through incremental changes and by fostering a form of distributed leadership [72,73]. This approach, which Raelin [74] has termed "leaderful practice", has an excellent pedigree. Friere [75] proposed that:

> The starting-point must be the present, existential, concrete situation, reflecting the aspirations of the people. We must pose this to the people as a problem which challenges them and requires a response – not just at an intellectual level, but at a level of action.

Similarly, Wadsworth [76] asks:

> How can we build in routine times, spaces and sacrosanct places for observing and speaking (especially at cross-purposes), far, far sooner? – before too much damage is done and before too many unwanted ways become "the ways we do things round here (or else)."

and Revans [77] maintained that:

> A man may well learn to talk about taking action simply by talking about taking action (as in classes at a business school), but to learn to take action (as something distinct from learning to talk about action), then he needs to take action (rather than talking about taking action) and to see the effect, not of talking about taking action (at which he may appear competent), but of taking the action itself (at which he may fall somewhere short of competent).

For such ripples in the organisational (or organising) pond to spread outwards from these conversations, it certainly requires encouragement, which is not always guaranteed, not least because the predominant managerial ideology often sees the questioning of management policies and decisions as being inappropriate, potentially career-limiting and therefore something to be attempted only by the foolish or the brave [78]. Without a considered approach to developing and harnessing such learning, it will be limited to isolated pockets or "cultural islands" blocked by numerous barriers and boundaries to transmission and exchange. What is required are means of avoiding ad hoc and short-term initiatives with limited reach and scope and widening the circles of inclusivity [21]. Nicolini [79] describes this as a "rhizomatic" approach – a rhizome being a form of bulb that extends its roots in different directions – a variety of relationships and associations that extend in both space and time to form a gigantic, intricate and evolving texture of dependencies and references. This enables relationships and dialogue to continue and develop beyond the level of the individual or group, and the term "learning architecture" [80,81] has been coined to describe this. It denotes "the way an organisation promotes and structures learning, both individual and organisational". The means of permeating other groups, functions and professions are many and varied [82] and include:

> Action learning [83]
> Attachments [84]
> Buddy pairs [85]
> Coaching [86,87]

Communities of practice [88]
Conversational conferences [89,90]
Exchanges [84]
Future search [91]
Mentoring [92,93]
Open space [94]
Reverse mentoring [95]
Secondments [84]
Schwartz rounds [96]
Shadowing [84]
Workshops
World café [97]

The underlying cultural values for a learning architecture include [98]:

Celebration of success: If excellence is to be pursued with commitment, then its attainment must be valued across the organisational or system culture.

Absence of complacency: The old adage "If it ain't broke, don't fix it" does not apply. Instead, innovation and change are valued across the system and also involve identifying current good practice and encouraging it being carried forward.

Tolerance of mistakes: Learning from failure is a prerequisite for development, and this means accepting the positive spin-offs from errors, rather than seeking to blame and to scapegoat.

Belief in human potential: People are valued for their creativity, energy and innovation, so their personal and professional development are both cherished and fostered.

Recognition of tacit knowledge: Those front-line people closest to the action have the best and most intimate knowledge concerning both potential and flaws. Their tacit knowledge is therefore valued and there is a systematic enlargement of their discretion, responsibility and capability.

Openness: The sharing of knowledge emphasises informal channels and personal contacts over any written reporting procedures. So cross-professional groupings and the planned rotation of staff are essential ingredients.

Trust: For people to give of their best, to take appropriate risks and develop their capacity, they must trust that such activities will be appreciated and valued. In particular, they must be confident that should they err, then they will be supported and not castigated.

Such learning typically is associated with the activities of "tempered radicals" – "People who want to succeed in their organisations, yet want to live by their values or identities, even if they are somehow at odds with the dominant culture of their organisations." [99]. The dangers which tempered radicals need to guard against include [100]:

■ A developing feeling of "lost innocence" as they increasingly come to question their own taken-for-granted assumptions.
■ A possible sense of despair at the implications of them adopting what may appear to their peers as a radical analysis with respect to their professional or organisational context.
■ A growing feeling of "impostership" as they may doubt their own worthiness to question their own organisation or profession – or even both.
■ Experiencing a feeling of "cultural suicide" as they encounter the disbelief and possible hostility of their colleagues when they question or challenge the accepted professional and/or organisational practices.

Tempered radicals will therefore require continuing support, and this may well be a role for OD practitioners.

This focus on improving working relationships is increasingly important as health and social care systems become more complex and less bounded. All these means potentially foster more open and public dialogue which inevitably demands an equality of voice and the right to be heard, so "normal" hierarchical procedures and norms need to be suspended in order for such an exchange to take place. This can possibly occur spontaneously, but it is much more likely that these exchanges will have to be designed and sequenced. While islands of dialogic excellence will exist, where some locations do learn and innovate, other locations will not (or cannot?) do so, so there will need to be a conscious aim to widen the circles of learning or ripples in the organisational (and system) pond, as shown in Figure 8.3.

This retreat from OD grand narratives and from "scripted" top-down and programmed interventions also demands a significant degree of humility from OD practitioners, for whom such activities may appear highly seductive in both prestige and career terms. Gillon [38] has noted that the more OD has focused on such organisation-wide issues, the more loosely connected it has become to individual and group issues and so has departed from its original democratic and humanistic values. Similarly, it has been noted that senior leaders and managers prefer large-scale "bottom-line"-oriented OD interventions, which are less collaborative and stray further and further from those original OD values [101]. While many studies suggest that 75% of change processes have "failed" [102–104], Bushe and Nagaishi [105] assert that this quoted figure only represents such top-down and prescriptive OD interventions. Critten [106], building on Stacey [62], suggests that the evolution of such networked conversations represents the gradual

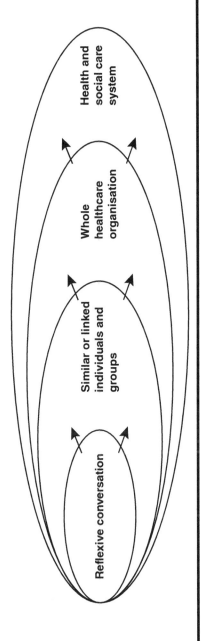

Figure 8.3 Widening the circles of organisational learning.

emergence of a new form of organising out of the old. He proposes that this need not, in the short-term, affect the day-to-day affairs happening on the legitimate side. One form of organising is not immediately going to replace another, but their coexistence does offer future options.

Schon [107] maintained that for what he termed "learning agents" (for which read OD practitioners), it implied an open-endedness which was incompatible with traditional notions of expertise or professionalism, since both carried with them the concept of cumulative bodies of theory which could be applied predictably to particular situations. Instead the learning agent must be able to synthesise theory out of experience of the situation, while being in the situation, while also expecting it to explode or decay, not least because it is merely a point of view of the situation. Such an individual must be able to confront multiple and conflicting perspectives on a situation and be able to work in the here-and-now, willing and able to use themselves as an informational instrument by listening rather than asserting, confronting anxiety and suspending commitment until the last possible moment. Schon describes such behaviour as an ethic for existential knowing.

Openness to new approaches to thinking and action: While there has been no shortage of innovation within the OD field of practice, so much of this has been at the level of so-called "tools and techniques" and largely reflective of the machine metaphor and of a managerial agenda. One alternative approach is to apply the principles of design to the crafting of OD activity [108]. Buchanan [109] has noted that effective design is grounded in the principle of the quality of experience of the users of services.

As an example of this, Cottam [110] has noted that healthcare and associated social care are both based upon what she calls an industrial system of hierarchy, rules and transactional relationships. All the multifarious approaches adopted for reform, restructuring and reorganisation have centred upon management and control and have severely limited the possibilities for human connection within the existing systems. In this, she is close to the arguments of Illich [111] and Illich et al. [112] that institutionalisation serves to undermine people, diminishes their capacity to resolve problems and kills conviviality, as healthcare (and related social care) organisations can end up working in ways that reverse their original purpose.

She identifies the very human tendency to take new things and attempt to fit them into existing ways of thinking and doing, not least because of a sense of impatience for change. When something that works is discovered, the first instinct is not to create new conditions and arrangements but to attempt to push new solutions through old frameworks, so anyone who is concerned with change is thus faced with a conceptual challenge. One example of this is the UK Government's Improving Access to Psychological Therapies (IAPT) programme which relies on an economic model of treatment, featuring psychiatric diagnosis, fast through-put and quick-win outcomes recorded in performance data, betraying a set of underpinning neoliberal assumptions [113]. Similarly, the vast expansion of digital therapy via online platforms [114] also reveals how human need is channelled through pre-existing information technology and economic calculations.

Cottam suggests that there is a profound need to help many people working in health and social care to unlearn – to strip away their learned institutional behaviours [26,115] and to provide support to these front-line professional workers both emotionally and practically as they do so.

Cottam also directs attention to the useful distinction between bonding and bridging behaviour and relationships [116]. The former relates to the frequent and intense relationships developed between people of a similar background but which excludes others. Bonding relationships are obvious within the healthcare and social care professions and lead towards "silo" working and the stereotyping of those others who are not from the same profession. Bridging relationships connect individuals to those people and experiences in professions and situations which are different from what they have previously known. The clear implication for Cottam is that bridging relationships need to be strongly fostered.

Rooted in descriptions of a series of practical experiments in the areas of family life, health, work and aging, she offers an alternative collaborative bridging process for working with service users, professionals and volunteers, based on a process of:

- Setting up
- Framing the problem/finding the opportunity
- Idea generation
- Prototyping
- Going live/replication

Cottam's work, which she calls "social design" or design for social good, provides a challenge to OD practitioners to break away from a solely managerial agenda and to work directly with local communities, volunteers, service users and front-line professionals to create or recreate new or existing services which span organisational boundaries and are increasingly relevant to the entire health and social care system. In this, Cottam's argument is close to Seddon's [117] view that the principal need is to understand value from the point of view of the patient or service user, and that this can only be done when demand – that is, the things that patients and service users want – is thoroughly understood. Social design fuses a range of insights from anthropology, psychoanalysis, business tools and the design process.

Bushe [118] has identified how most of what is called OD focuses on intra-organisational issues only. How open are healthcare OD practitioners to such new ways of thinking and action and how concerned, free and willing are they to engage in such work? This is work which would involve policymakers working directly with front-line staff and service users, ditching the lanyards and the name tags, and putting the lived experience of service users at the heart of the process. Early approaches embodying such approaches are already slowly emerging [119]. Cottam's work also has parallels with that of Costello [120] on the potential of "sympathy groups" to effect change in human services.

Alternatives to current project management: The ubiquity of project management-based approaches to the management of change has already been described in Chapter 7. Pritchard [121] has identified why most change projects fail. The reasons were:

- The solution to the issue in question is "sold" in the organisation before there is any shared agreement about what the issue actually is.
- One-way communication is the norm, in place of any real engagement. What consultation takes place is therefore tokenistic.
- What has gone before is rubbished.
- Projects are not integrated with the whole wider organisational activity but are fragmented.
- "Delivery" of the project itself overtakes delivering the intended purpose of the change. The ticking of milestone boxes dominates.

There will inevitably always be a need for some means of steering OD work and this is likely to be based upon the following [122]:

- A starting assumption that organisational reality is "messy" and that the wicked problems that healthcare systems face cannot be addressed by using those methods which were devised to work on tame problems.
- An assumption that real (as opposed to short-term and cosmetic) change will take much longer than most people will anticipate – it is a marathon rather than a sprint.
- A belief that transformational change is far more emergent than planned change.
- Persistent and consistent support and challenge is needed from senior influential people in existing hierarchical arrangements.
- An awareness of the wider context within which people are working, including national policies and initiatives.
- An acceptance of "variable geometry" – a recognition that there are diverse approaches to the same destination, and of "variable speed" or different

rates of progress in different places, rather than "one best way". Such acceptance of equal paths and speeds to the same place has been termed "equifinality" [123].

■ A shielding of local change activity from national "initiative-itis". That is, a non-participation in those diversionary schemes which mean little or nothing to key front-line staff.

■ The dropping of any generic, a-cultural and packaged approaches to change for approaches that are specific and wholly sensitive to the local context and culture.

■ An expectation that there will be unexpected surprises and that new questions will arise along the way, which were certainly not envisaged at the outset.

■ Rather than a multitude of stand-along OD interventions, the development of a "learning architecture" [80] or suite of mutually supportive activities which have a multiplier effect by feeding off and reinforcing each other through feedback loops [124].

■ Managing the expectations of the key stakeholders so that their expectations do not either move too far ahead of, or fall behind, the capability of the system to change.

■ The building of relationships and rapport between key stakeholders needs to be much more important that any rigid adherence to deadlines. Change ultimately happens at the speed of trust.

■ Amplifying success by offering emergent good practices as models from which others might learn, with the caveat that local circumstances may differ.

So, project management, rather than following a rigid methodology, needs to become much more exploratory, tentative and incremental. Steering arrangements need to be "a little bit more than not enough" – that is, just robust and sufficient enough to allow adequate exploration of the unknown and not to constrain initiative. Rather than a predetermined aim or purpose, the emphasis might well be placed on simply getting started on a change initiative without fully agreeing on any ultimate aims, by establishing a "working path" [125], because it may not be possible to get complete agreement on such matters at the outset. The guiding image is that of a compass, rather than a route map. Sufficient attention would need to be given to processes of review, evaluation and learning, so as well as any pre-set and agreed milestones, there would always be emergent milestones – key activities which could only be recognised and identified retrospectively by such a review process.

This reflects a learn-as-we-go approach, which embodies the flexibility to change as events unfold and as learning about what does and does not work becomes available. It allows the overall strategy to increasingly emerge from successful actions and activities by building from the ground up and being opportunistic and incremental with a strong focus on action, experimentation and innovation, which encourages people to "act themselves into a new way of thinking", rather than think themselves into a new way of acting [126]. In this way, particular change projects will arise from the dialogue and sense-making across the whole system, rather than through a single sponsor, a single project manager and a small and select project team [127].

Location, location, location: Where exactly should OD "fit" in relation to existing organisational structures and systems? As Chapter 3 has illustrated, the incorporation of OD into the Human Resource function has ensured that it has adopted a conformist innovation mode of operating which has largely concentrated on a set of tame organisational issues. A review of the Human Resource function some twenty-five years after Legge's original paper confirmed the widespread adoption of the conformist innovator role and evidenced little sign of any desire on the part of the function to act as deviant innovators [128]. There was a clear-cut alignment with a managerial viewpoint and a perceived part for Human Resources to play in "managing the employee contribution". It is also noticeable that OD seldom features in Human Resource literature [39]. The transactional, regulatory and legalistic orientation of the Human Resource function, largely concerned with recruiting, promoting, retaining and rewarding people, is at odds with the developmental outlook of OD. Indeed, it has been suggested [129] that there is a fundamental conflict between the purpose and mission of the two functions. At its core, the Human Resource function exists to manage compliance, to avoid risks and to reduce expenditure on staff costs to the lowest possible level commensurate with getting essential work done. By contrast, OD is about enabling an organisation to expand capacity and capability, experiment where appropriate, explore ideas, take calculated risks and improve the work and working lives of people at work. Ultimately, Human Resources is concerned with regulation – with the emphasis on unity and cohesiveness, while OD is concerned with revelation – with a concern for the emancipation of people from the structures and systems which limit and stunt their potential for development [130]. So what are the potential alternative options for OD's location?

The first distinction to make is between internal and external OD practitioners, and the possibilities for the latter would seem to lie with either an academic base or with a consultancy agency. With regard to the academic location, while this can offer a degree of detachment and neutrality from internal healthcare organisational politics plus an analytic and potentially critical perspective, Dovey and Rembach [131] highlight the likely associated inhibiting difficulties, including internal structural inertia (such as routinised academic processes and procedures); personal politics (violation of hierarchical academic authority and bureaucratic protocols); fear of creating a precedent (too risky); reified mental models; fear of loss of control and inappropriate assumptions, such as "this is the way the world works". The consultancy agency option suffers from the tendency for such consultancies to often concentrate their offer on "chunked" data collection and diagnosis within prescribed boundaries only; the seduction of adopting off-the-peg standardised or generic approaches based upon previous assignments and the ever-present commercial requirement to concentrate on profit margins.

For internal OD practitioners a key question relates to the extent to which senior organisational leaders have well worked-out motives for "doing OD" in the first place [132] and the extent to which they are willing to support the exploration and tackling of wicked issues. Are such organisational leaders willing to sponsor OD work and experiment with new ways of working on intractable problems? Or are they more likely to avoid these in favour of interpretations that can be addressed by the adoption of tame approaches and a focus on what seems technically resolvable? Certainly, they will be under various internal and external pressures to produce performance results and to avoid corporate and personal reputational damage and so might well choose to direct OD resources towards simpler and tamer questions. Even where OD is well supported, there remain many cultural processes that encourage the discounting of such wicked issues and promote "learning inaction" [133] – a series of activities which feature the avoidance of conflicts and challenges [134]. The danger for internal OD practitioners is that they buy-in completely to a managerial agenda only and hence themselves become simply instruments of that agenda. The possibility of OD practitioners being sponsored and promoted (and where necessary protected) directly by Chief Executives, for example, remains an option but one which clearly runs the risk of capture by such a solely managerial agenda. Gillon [39] suggests that:

> Few leaders have the persistence or personality to stick with involving others to achieve long-term change, especially when under pressure within the organisational cultural context or dealing with the tension of competing goals.

and that:

> Only leaders and organisations with a strong moral compass are likely to be able to resist the siren call of short-term expediency in order to promote long-term sustainability.

Similarly, Gilpin-Jackson [59] asserts that:

> Leaders must be willing to give up control of the change process and outcomes because any attempt to control these will undermine the process and erode trust.

Another possibility might lie with a location within a separate "development agency" funded by a consortium of healthcare employing organisations but managerially independent of them. A hybrid arrangement, combining both internal and external ways of working, is a further possibility.

Engaging with the "dry husks": Cole [11] refers to existing formal organisational structures and systems as "dry husks" which he implies are increasingly irrelevant in a VUCA/RUPT world and comprise what Stacey [62] called the legitimate element of organisations. Antonio Gramsci famously asked "How do we proceed with optimism of the will and pessimism of the intellect?" [135]. If evolving OD represents the optimism of the will, then the pessimism of the intellect inevitably asks what are such dry husks likely to make of OD as it challenges many of their taken-for-granted assumptions and may even serve to undermine aspects of their hierarchical status? Not least because it most likely poses a potential existential threat to the livelihood and careers of many individuals who are located within, and benefit from, existing hierarchical structures. However, if it is accepted that all organisations are simply not ever totally rational, planned and stable entities and that organisational life is continually being shaped by the conversations and dialogues that take place between the people within them, and so is constantly shifting [136], then the discursive (but also risky) process described above represents a way for organisational members to gradually enact new ways of organising as they reflect, conceptualise and act. Most likely, this will be the subject of an elongated process, where the eventual impact will most likely be hard-won, but can also be substantive and lasting, as opposed to being cosmetic and transitory.

Evaluating OD: The Introduction suggested that the OD literature revealed a preference for only demonstrating success stories and so the continuing absence of evaluation of OD activity may be seen as an Achilles heel for healthcare OD. Yet the Hospital Internal Communications (HIC) project, an early OD intervention in the UK's NHS which was described in Chapter 3, did feature comprehensive external evaluations ten years apart [137,138] as well as a parallel internal exercise [139]. This preference for success stories may also relate to the positive publication bias [140,141] mentioned in the Introduction. While there is almost universal agreement on the importance and value of evaluation activity, the evidence suggests that many OD interventions continue to follow, one after the other, with little evaluation of their impact before a rapid transition on to the next initiative. There may be several reasons for this, including the existence of the neophilia mentioned in Chapter 6, with its preference for what is seen as the newest or latest managerial trend. In the public sector, where many national initiatives are inspired by politicians and are then cascaded in a hierarchical manner down into local settings, there is the ever-present possibility that any evaluation of such initiatives being undertaken may result in an unacceptable finding, which might be career-limiting for those associated with the study, and so might best be avoided.

There are many challenges associated with evaluation, including:

Time: How to evaluate OD interventions conducted over the short term that are intended to have much longer-term impacts?

Complexity: In any OD intervention, there are likely to be multiple factors at play, so how can the effect of one activity be disentangled from the others, particularly when they may overlap?

Value: What counts as "success"? What is valued and by whom? Involving all the diverse stakeholders in the evaluation process is clearly helpful, provided it seeks to identify and surface their assumptions – what exactly were the stakeholders seeking to achieve through the OD intervention?

Horses for courses: The size and complexity of an evaluation needs to be in proportion to the activity being evaluated and the form the evaluation takes should, in turn, reflect the values of the activity itself

Cost: To conduct evaluation is not cost-free. While clients of OD work will be concerned with the outcomes of such work, evaluation activity will require additional work, with its inherent costs in both time and money, whether it is sourced internally or externally. Ideally, evaluation (and the associated costs) would be planned into any OD activity at the outset, although in practice this has seldom happened and, where evaluation does take place, it is most often conducted as an afterthought.

Politics: Evaluation is a complex and highly political process. The underlying assumptions behind evaluation are discovering "What works?" and "For whom does it work?" as a means of identifying what future evidence-based action might be needed. However, policy decisions regarding OD activity can be, and often have been, made despite evidence of what does or does not work well in practice. As has been pointed out in Chapter 1, evaluation can even be designed to gather data that support a particular policy direction. Even when evaluation is conducted, if the results are politically sensitive then they may never even see the light of day publicly and hence may be ignored. Decisions are made based on much more than evaluation evidence – values, interests, personalities, timing, circumstances and happenstance all also play their part.

It is also worth recalling that:

Evaluation can only ever provide good quality information to improve decision-making. It is unlikely to supply ready-made answers because the results will need to be interpreted as part of a process of discussion and judgement with the views of different stakeholders and the intended outcomes of the activity being taken into account. [142]

There are two common models adopted in consideration of evaluating OD work. The first is the Return on Investment (ROI) approach, which was examined in Chapter 1, where it was identified that the mental model behind it was too narrow and the time-horizon too short, not least because the model had its origins in the machine metaphor for organisations. The other is the four-level Kirkpatrick model [143] which emerged from the need to evaluate training activity. The levels in this model are:

Reactions: To an intervention or activity in the form of individual thoughts and feelings. It is the level of the "happy sheet" administered to a captive audience and is the most common form of assessment used.

Learning: Or to what degree people acquire or change their knowledge, skills or attitudes.

Behaviour: Or to what degree people apply what they have learned and demonstrate this in their changed behaviour.

Outcomes/results: Or what is the impact of such changed behaviour on individual, group and organisational performance.

The model is very individual-centred and training-based but does recognise that the journey from reactions to outcomes features significant numbers of intervening variables which make it difficult to ascribe simple cause-and-effect relationships. Moreover, the correlation between the levels is weak – a positive result at one level does not necessarily lead to a positive result at the next. By a concentration on easy–to-assess individual reactions, the tendency is to side-line all the other contextual factors.

Both approaches are, in their different ways, highly quantitative-based. Quantitative measurement may not just be undesirable for evaluating certain activity but perhaps may be impossible. To measure anything an objective yardstick is needed, such as centimetres for length, kilometres for weight and litres for volume. Human activity at work involves a range of complex tasks that are highly context-dependent, and it may well be a fallacy to believe that such activity can be measured objectively using a yardstick and resulting in "hard" figures. Verhaeghe [144] notes that measurement of this kind tends to use bipolar Likert scales, which involve people rating statements by selecting from a range of possible responses, such as Poor, Adequate, Good and Very Good, often expressed as −2, −1, 0, +1 and +2. These are intuitive approximations based upon subjective criteria and so any translation of results into figures serves to create a false impression of objective quantifiability, which Verhaeghe describes as methodologically specious.

Both models are examples of summative (or judgemental) evaluation [145] which is concerned with assessing the measurable impact or contribution of an intervention. The key word here is "measureable" because they rely upon "hard" quantitative data, claim objectivity, offer quick answers and are most usually valued by budget holders. The alternative approach is formative evaluation which is essentially developmental; is concerned with improving the intervention and contributing to the overall learning from the process. It provides rich information which includes the impact of the setting or context on changed learning and performance. Formative evaluation is important because OD works much more through generative causation (or creating the conditions where things can change and move on to destinations as yet unknown) than through successionist causation (or the achieving of predictable and pre-known outcomes) [146]. Thorpe et al. [147] identify three varieties of evaluation – simple, learning and holistic. It is the latter (a formative approach) which is most relevant to evaluating OD activity because it acknowledges that cause, effect and learning are all important, but that any intervention operates within a system and there is therefore a need to understand how the system impacts on the intervention and vice versa. This involves asking some "why" questions about the design and delivery of the intervention and some "how" questions about the overall impact on change.

It is worth recalling that the original values of OD were humanistic and democratic, and this book makes the case that these remain valid, albeit in a different political, economic and social context. So, it is worth posing a series of macro-level evaluative questions for the evaluation of any OD activity in healthcare. These are not listed in any particular order.

- Does it address wicked problems in organisations and not just tame ones, by promoting bricolage?
- Does it encourage reflection on any gap which exists between espoused theory and theory in use?
- Does it pursue double-loop rather than single-loop learning?
- Does it foster real, rather than representational learning?
- Does it reflect a move away from the machine metaphor of organisations and towards a living system metaphor?
- Does it promote deviant innovation and not just conformist innovation?
- Does it recognise and embrace both tacit and explicit knowledge?
- Does it recognise the ubiquity of power in the workplace and promote greater power equalisation for individuals and groups?
- Does it recognise that there is a tension between performance and empowerment in organisational life which needs to be balanced?

- Does it recognise the cultural diversity within and across organisations?
- Does it promote capability, rather than competence?
- Does it help to create meaningful and stimulating work?
- Does it help people to work well together?
- Does it enhance self-worth and choice at work and respect dignity?
- Does it help people to realise their potential?
- Does it support sustainable change and lessen dependency on external help?
- Does it address anxiety and emotional labour at both individual and organisational levels?
- Does it feature a steering approach which is exploratory, tentative and incremental?
- Does it contribute towards an overall learning architecture?
- Does it support individual and group unlearning, as well as learning?
- Does it reflect the local idiosyncratic context?
- Does it recognise the interdependence of health and social care and promote integration between them?
- Does it do all this as ends, rather than as means?

In our hands: The future development of OD in healthcare will lie, to a great extent, with the emerging intentions and ensuing activities of healthcare OD practitioners, operating within the social, economic and political context within which they find themselves. That assertion indicates that this book rejects the third modernity or post-modern view that involves being condemned to a perpetual present without any hope for a future which is different from what currently exists. It involves engaging with both academic rigour and practical relevance in further developing OD theory and practice [148] and also engaging with the big questions of the day, including such overarching issues as the provision of healthcare for social good, the impact of climate change, the diminution of natural resources, economic and social inequality, institutional racism, religious intolerance, misogyny, industrial conflict, work/life balance, unethical, immoral and illegal organisational and social behaviour. This implies a rewidening of ambition towards the original concerns addressed by Lewin, because OD has narrowed its ambitions to such an extent that it has been in danger of sacrificing the goals of the individuals within the organisation [149] in order to enable organisations to become effective [150] and hence has led to accusations that it is merely a vehicle for managerial co-optation [151]. Burnes and Cooke [148] suggest that such a re-engagement and recovery of OD as a progressive social movement has the power to motivate OD practitioners and related academics alike. For some OD practitioners, this will entail major personal change in relation to the nature of their work and career path. Bridges [152] highlighted that:

Transition always starts with an ending. To become something else you have to develop a new attitude or outlook, you have to let go of the old.

Thompson [153] has suggested that a more robust consciousness on such matters can be nourished by a degree of "occupational independence" in certain social roles – such as that of OD practitioner? Certainly OD practitioners do display a high degree of that marginality which is associated with open-mindedness and flexibility [154].

One possible option available to OD practitioners would be simply to adopt the "blind watchmaker" role [155] and accept that OD works without any purpose or foresight and has now become only an instrumental behavioural science technology – a set of means which will enable healthcare organisations to pursue a series of ends which are ultimately determined by a predominantly neoliberal worldview. This would certainly be a case of "If you always do what you've always done, you always get what you've always got".

Alternatively, the original humanistic values of early OD may be seen as still being highly relevant and therefore worth pursuing, albeit in a different political, economic and social setting, so it is not about walking into the future with eyes set firmly on a rear-view mirror perception of the past but rather combining a reaffirmation of those original values with the healthy scepticism which a meta-modernist orientation proposes. As Schon [107] has remarked, old questions are not answered – they only go out of fashion. In Gramsci's terms (see above), it means not an either/or choice between them but rather a combining of an optimism of the will with a degree of pessimism of the intellect. Graeber [156] has maintained that:

> The ultimate hidden truth of the world is that it is something we make. And could just as easily make differently.

The Victorian critic John Ruskin [157] asserted that:

> The fact is, we are all and always, asleep through our lives, and it is only by pinching ourselves very hard that we ever come to see or understand anything.

As the Spanish poet Antonio Machado [158] has suggested:

> Life is the path you beat while you walk it.
> It is the walking that beats the path.
> It is not the path that makes the walk.

References

1. Enteman, W. (1993) *Managerialism: The Emergence of a New Ideology*, Madison, WI: University of Wisconsin Press.
2. Shenhav, Y. (1999) *Manufacturing Rationality: The Engineering Foundations of the Managerial Revolution*, Oxford: Oxford University Press.
3. Knafo, S., Dutta, S., Lane, R. and Wyn-Jones, S. (2019) The Managerial Lineage of Neoliberalism, *New Political Economy*, 24 (2): 235–251.
4. Boltanski, L. and Chiapello, E. (2005) *The New Spirit of Capitalism*, London: Verso.
5. Styhre, A. (2014) *Management and Neoliberalism: Connecting Policies and Practices*, Abingdon: Routledge.
6. Sennett, R. (1998) *The Corrosion of Character: The Personal Consequences of Work in the New Capitalism*, New York: W W Norton.
7. Zuboff, S. (2019) *The Age of Surveillance Capitalism: The Fight for a Human Future at the New Frontier of Power*, London: Profile Books.
8. Finnegan, M. (2020) The New Normal: When Work-From-Home Means the Boss is Watching, *ComputerWorld*, 29th October.
9. Amoore, L., Ball, K., Graham, S., Green, N., Lyon, D., Wood, D., Norris, C., Pridmore, J., Raab, C. and Saetnan, A. (2006) *A Report on the Surveillance Society for the Information Commissioner*, Kingston, ON: Canada Surveillance Studies Network.
10. Foucault, M. (1991) *Discipline and Punish: The Birth of the Prison*, London: Penguin.
11. Cole, M. (2020) *Radical Organisation Development*, Abingdon: Routledge.
12. Edmonstone, J. (2011) The Challenge of Capability in Leadership Development, *British Journal of Healthcare Management*, 17 (12): 541–547.
13. Van Wart, M. (2003) Public Sector Leadership Theory: An Assessment, *Public Administration Review*, 63 (2): 214–228.
14. Seddon, J. (2003) *Freedom From Command And Control: A Better Way to Make the Work Work*, Buckingham: Vanguard Education.
15. Russell, J. (2006) The Public Feels Patronised, Bullied and Betrayed, *Guardian*, 23 June.
16. Meindl, J., Ehrlich, S. and Dukerich, J. (1985) The Romance of Leadership, *Administrative Science Quarterly*, 30 (1): 78–103.
17. Edmonstone, J. (2016) Action Learning, Performativity and Negative Capability, *Action Learning: Research and Practice*, 13 (2): 139–147.
18. Fox, A. (1985) *Man Mismanagement*, London: Hutchinson.
19. Storey, J. and Holt, R. (2013) *Towards a New Model of Leadership for the NHS*, London: NHS Leadership Academy.
20. Baumann, Z. (2000) *Liquid Modernity*, Bristol, MA: Polity Press.
21. Attwood, M., Pedler, M., Pritchard, S. and Wilkinson, D. (2003) *Leading Change: A Guide to Whole Systems Working*, Bristol, MA: Polity Press.
22. Edwards, J. (1998) Managerial Influences in Public Administration, *International Journal of Organisation Theory and Behaviour*, 1 (4): 1–5.
23. Mintzberg, H. (1996) Managing Government; Governing Management, *Harvard Business Review*, May-June.
24. Pedler, M., Burgoyne, J. and Brook, C. (2005) What Has Action Learned to Become? *Action Learning: Research and Practice*, 2 (1): 49–68.

25. Lyotard, J. (1984) *The Postmodern Condition: A Report on Knowledge*, Manchester: Manchester University Press.
26. Chokr, N. (2009) *Unlearning or How Not to be Governed*, Exeter: Societas Imprint Academic.
27. Jones, T. (2019) *Bob Dylan and the British Sixties: A Cultural History*, Abingdon: Routledge.
28. Ball, S. (2003) The Teacher's Soul and the Terrors of Performativity, *Journal of Educational Policy*, 18 (2): 215–228.
29. Taylor, P. (2013) *Performance Management and the New Workforce Tyranny: A Report for the Scottish Trade Union Congress*, Glasgow: University of Strathclyde.
30. Armstrong, M. (2009) The Process of Performance Management, in Armstrong, M. (Ed.) *A Handbook of Human Resource Management Practice*, 11th edition, London: Kogan Page.
31. Fleming, P. (2017) Feel Exploited?: Unhappy With How The Boss Treats You?: Then the Problem is You, *Guardian*, August 14.
32. Furedi, F. (2004) *Where Have All the Intellectuals Gone?: Confronting Twenty-First Century Philistinism*, London: Continuum Press.
33. Harrison, R. (1995) Choosing the Depth of Organisational Intervention, in Harrison, R. (Ed.) *The Collected Papers of Roger Harrison*, New York: McGraw-Hill.
34. Oliver, J. (2008) Reflections on a Failed Action Learning Intervention, *Action Learning: Research and Practice*, 5 (1): 79–83.
35. Rigg, C. (2006) Understanding the Organisational Potential of Action Learning, in Rigg, C. and Richards, S. (Eds.) *Action Learning, Leadership and Organisational Development in Public Services*, Abingdon: Routledge.
36. Apps, J. (1985) *Improving Practice in Continuing Education: Modern Approaches for Understanding the Field and Determining Priorities*, San Francisco, CA: Jossey-Bass.
37. Trehan, K. (2011) Critical Action Learning, in Pedler, M. (Ed.) *Action Learning in Practice*, 4th edition, Aldershot: Gower Publishing.
38. Rokeach, M. (1973) *The Nature of Human Values*, New York: Free Press.
39. Gillon, A. (2016) Conceptualising Organisation Development: Practitioner and Academic Perspectives: A UK Study, PhD thesis, Nottingham Trent University.
40. Goodge, P. (1975) The Love/Trust Model and Progress in OD, *Journal of European Training*, 4 (3): 179–184.
41. Tranfield, D. (1978) *Some Characteristics of Organisation Development Consultants*, Doctoral thesis, Sheffield Hallam University.
42. Jones, G., George, J. and Hill, C. (2000) *Contemporary Management*, 2nd edition, Boston, MA: McGraw-Hill.
43. Day, A. (2020) *Disruption, Change and Transformation in Organisations: A Human Relations Perspective*, Abingdon: Routledge.
44. Wheatley, M. and Kellner-Rogers, M. (1996) *A Simpler Way*, San Francisco, CA: Berrett-Koehler.
45. Traeger, J. and Warwick, R. (2020) Purpose and Ethics of Organisation Development: Moral Practice of the Moment, Mayvin: https://mayvin.co.uk/purpose-ethics-of-organisation-development-moral-practice/.
46. Carson, C. (2001) *A Call to Conscience: The Landmark Speeches of Dr Martin Luther King Jr*, New York: Warner Books.

47. Argyris, C. and Schon, D. (1974) *Theory in Practice: Increasing Personal Effectiveness*, San Francisco, CA: Jossey-Bass.
48. Keep, J. (2013) *Developing Self-Care at Work*, PhD thesis, Bristol: University of the West of England.
49. Cole, M. (2020b) *The Role of Power in Organisation Development*, CIPD: https://cipd.co.uk/knowledge/strategy/organisational-development/thought-pieces/role-power.
50. Edmonstone, J. (2020) A Tale of Two Ethoses: Neoliberalism and Action Learning, *Action Learning: Research and Practice*, 17 (3): 259–272.
51. Dawson, P. and Andriopoulos, C. (2017) *Managing Change, Creativity and Innovation*, London: Sage Publications.
52. Marshak, R. (2006) Emerging Directions: Is There a New OD? In Gallos, J. (Ed.) *Organisational Development: A Jossey-Bass Reader*, San Francisco, CA: Jossey-Bass.
53. Bushe, G. and Marshak, R. (2014) The Dialogic Mindset in Organisation Development, *Research in Organisational Change and Development*, 22: 54–97.
54. Nonaka, I. and Takeuchi, H. (1995) *The Knowledge-Creating Company: How Japanese Companies Create the Dynamics of Innovation*, Oxford: Oxford University Press.
55. Vermeulen, T. and van den Akker, R. (2010) Notes on Meta-Modernism, *Journal of Aesthetics and Culture*, 2 (1): 56–77.
56. Popova, M. (2019) *Figuring*, Edinburgh: Canongate Books.
57. Oswick, C. (2009) Re-Visioning or Re-Versionising? A Commentary on Diagnostic and Dialogic Forms of Organisation Development, *Journal of Applied Behavioural Science*, 45 (3): 369–374.
58. Gilpin-Jackson, Y. (2013) Practicing in the Grey Area between Dialogic and Diagnostic Organisation Development, *OD Practitioner*, 45 (1): 60–66.
59. Wolf, J., Hanson, H. and Moir, M. (Eds.) (2011) *Organisation Development in Healthcare: High Impact Practices for a Complex and Changing Environment*, Charlotte, NC: Information Age Publishing.
60. Hatch, M. (1997) *Organisation Theory: Modern, Symbolic and Postmodern Perspectives*, Oxford: Oxford University Press.
61. Wooten, K. and White, L. (1999) Linking OD's Philosophy with Justice Theory: Postmodern Implications, *Journal of Organisational Change Management*, 12 (1): 7–20.
62. Stacey, R. (1996) *Complexity and Creativity in Organisations*, San Francisco, CA: Berrett-Koehler.
63. Pedler, M. (2020) On Social Action, *Action Learning: Research and Practice*, 17 (1): 1–9.
64. Bussu, S. and Marshall, M. (2020) Organisational Development to Support Integrated Care in East London: The Perspectives of Clinicians and Social Workers on the Ground, *Journal of Health Organisation and Management*, 34 (5): 603–619.
65. Bussu, S. and Marshall, M. (2018) *Organisational Development Towards Integrated Care: A Comparative Study of Admission Avoidance, Discharge from Hospital and End of Life Care Pathways in Waltham Forest, Newham and Tower Hamlets*, London: University College London.
66. Flinn, K. (2018) *Leadership Development: A Complexity Approach*, Abingdon: Routledge.

67. Vogt, E., Brown, J. and Isaacs, D. (2003) *The Art of Powerful Questions: Catalysing Insight, Innovation and Action*, Mill Valley, CA: Whole Systems Associates.
68. Morgan, G. and Ramirez, R. (1984) Action Learning: A Holographic Metaphor for Guiding Social Change, *Human Relations*, 37 (1): 1–27.
69. Shotter, J. (1993) *Conversational Realities: Constructing Life Through Language*, Thousand Oaks, CA: Sage.
70. Newton, P. (2004) Leadership Lessons from Jazz Improvisation, *International Journal of Leadership in Education*, 7 (1): 83–99.
71. Thompson, N. and Pascal, J. (2012) Developing Critically Reflective Practice, *Reflective Practice*, 13 (2): 1–15.
72. Erlingsdottir, G., Ersson, A., Boreel, J. and Rydenfalt, C. (2018) Driving for Successful Change Processes in Healthcare by Putting Staff at the Wheel, *Journal of Health Organisation and Management*, 32 (1): 69–84.
73. Willis, C., Saul, J., Bevan, H., Scheirer, M., Best, A., Greenhalgh, T., Mannion, R., Cornelissen, E., Howland, D., Jenkins, E. and Bitz, J. (2016) Sustaining Organisational Culture Change in Health Systems, *Journal of Health Organisation and Management*, 30 (1): 2–30.
74. Raelin, J. (Ed.) (2016) *Leadership-as-Practice: Theory and Application*, New York: Routledge.
75. Friere, P. (1972) *Pedagogy of the Oppressed*, London: Penguin.
76. Wadsworth, Y. (2011) *Building in Research and Evaluation: Human Inquiry in Living Systems*, Sydney: Allen & Unwin.
77. Revans, R. (1971) *Developing Effective Managers: A New Approach to Business Education*, London: Longman.
78. Pedler, M. and Abbott, C. (2013) *Facilitating Action Learning: A Practitioner's Guide*, Maidenhead: McGraw-Hill.
79. Nicolini, D. (2013) *Practice Theory, Work and Organisation*, Oxford: Oxford University Press.
80. Wilhelm, W. (2005) *Learning Architectures: Building Individual and Organisational Learning*, New Mexico: GCA Press.
81. Pedler, M., Warburton, D. and Wilkinson, D. (2007) *Improving Poor Environments: The Role of Learning Architectures in Developing and Spreading Good Practice*, Bristol, MA: Environment Agency.
82. Edmonstone, J. (2019) *Systems Leadership in Health and Social Care*, Abingdon: Routledge.
83. Edmonstone, J. (2018) *Action Learning in Health, Social and Community Care: Principles, Practices, Resources*, Boca Raton, FL: CRC Press.
84. Edmonstone, J. (2013) *Personal Resilience for Healthcare Staff: When the Going Gets Tough*, London: Radcliffe Publishing.
85. Fo, W. and O'Donnell, C. (1974) The Buddy System: Relationship and Contingency Conditions in a Community Intervention Program for Youth with Non-Professionals as Behavior Change Agents, *Journal of Consulting and Clinical Psychology*, 42 (2): 163–169.
86. De Haan, E. and Burger, Y. (2014) *Coaching With Colleagues: An Action Guide for One-to-One Learning*, 2nd edition, Basingstoke: Palgrave Macmillan.

87. Parsloe, E. and Wray, M. (2000) *Coaching and Mentoring: Practical Methods to Improve Learning*, London: Kogan Page.
88. Wenger. E. and Snyder, W. (2000) Communities of Practice: The Organisational Frontier, *Harvard Business Review*, January-February.
89. Zuber-Skerritt, O. (Ed.) (2017) *Conferences as Sites of Learning and Development: Using Participatory Action Learning and Action Research Approaches*, Abingdon: Routledge.
90. Pratt, J., Plamping, D. and Gordon, P. (2003) Conversational Conferences, *British Journal of Healthcare Management*, 9 (3): 98–103.
91. Weisbord, M. and Janoff, S. (1995) *Future Search: An Action Guide to Finding Common Ground in Organisations and Communities*, San Francisco, CA: Berrett-Koehler.
92. Connor, M. and Pokora, J. (2007) *Coaching and Mentoring at Work: Developing Effective Practice*, Maidenhead: McGraw-Hill/Open University Press.
93. Garvey, R., Stokes, P. and Megginson, D. (2009) *Coaching and Mentoring: Theory and Practice*, London: Sage.
94. Owen, H. (1997) *Open Space Technology: A User's Guide*, 2nd edition, San Francisco, CA: Berrett-Koehler.
95. De Vita, E. (2019) Reverse Mentoring: What Young Women Can Teach the Old Guard, *Financial Times*, 7 March.
96. Maben, J., Taylor, C., Dawson, J., Leamy, M., McCarthy, I., Reynolds, E., Ross, S., Shuldham, C., Bennett, L. and Foot, C. (2018) *A Realist Informed Mixed Methods Evaluation of Schwartz Center Rounds® in England*, London: National Institute for Health Research.
97. Brown, J. and Isaacs, D. (2005) *The World Café: Shaping our Futures through Conversation*, San Francisco, CA: Berrett-Koehler.
98. Davies, H. and Nutley, S. (2004) Organisations as Learning Systems, in Kernick, D. (Ed.) *Complexity and Healthcare Organisation: A View from the Street*, Abingdon: Radcliffe Medical Press, 59–68.
99. Myerson, D. and Scully, M. (1995) Tempered Radicals and the Politics of Radicalism and Change, *Organisational Science*, 6 (5): 585–600.
100. Brookfield, S. (1994) Tales from the Darkside: A Phenomenology of Adult Critical Reflection, *International Journal of Lifelong Education*, 13 (3): 203–216.
101. Bradford, D. and Burke, W. (2004) Introduction: Is OD in Crisis? *Journal of Applied Behavioural Science*, 40 (4): 369–373.
102. Towers Watson (2013) Towers Watson Change and Communication ROI Survey, Retrieved from https://www.towerswatson.com/en/Press/2013/08/Only-One-Quarter-of-Employers-Are-Sustaining-Gains-From-Change-Management.
103. Eaton, M. (2010) Why Change Programmes Fail, *Human Resource International Digest*, 18 (2): 37–42.
104. Balogun, J. and Hope Hailey, V. (2004) *Exploring Strategic Change*, 2nd edition, London: Prentice-Hall.
105. Bushe, G. and Nagaishi, M. (2018) Imagining the Future Through the Past: Organisation Development isn't (just) about Change, *Organisation Development Journal*, Fall: 23–36.

106. Critten, P. (2016) A Radical Agenda for Enabling Organisational Transformation Through Work-Applied Learning, *Journal of Work-Applied Management*, 8 (1): 65–78.

107. Schon, D. (1973) *Beyond the Stable State: Public and Private Learning in a Changing Society*, London: Pelican.

108. Brown, T. (2008) Design Thinking, *Harvard Business Review*, June: 84–92.

109. Buchanan, R. (2015) Worlds in the Making: Design, Management and the Reform of Organisational Culture, *She Ji: The Journal of Design, Economics and Innovation*, 1 (1): 5–21.

110. Cottam, H. (2018) *Radical Help: How We Can Remake the Relationships Between Us and Revolutionise the Welfare State*, London: Virago Press.

111. Illich, I. (1975) *Limits to Medicine: Medical Nemesis: The Expropriation of Health*, London: Marion Boyars.

112. Illich, I., Zola, I., McKnight, J., Caplan, J. and Shaiken, H. (1977) *Disabling Professions*, London: Marion Boyars.

113. Jackson, C. and Rizq, R. (2019) *The Industrialisation of Care: Counselling, Psychotherapy and the Impact of IAPT*, Monmouth: PCCS.

114. Rizq, R. (2020) What Have We Lost? *Psychodynamic Practice: Individuals, Groups and Organisations*, 26 (4): 336–344.

115. Pedler, M. and Hsu, S. (2014) Unlearning, Critical Action Learning and Wicked Problems, *Action Learning: Research and Practice*, 11 (3): 296–310.

116. Larsen, L., Harlan, S. and Bolin, B. (2004) Bonding and Bridging: Understanding the Relationship between Social Capital and Civic Action, *Journal of Planning Education and Research*, 24 (1): 64–77.

117. Seddon, J. (2016) New Public Management: Dystopian Interventions in Public Services, in Pell, C., Wilson, R. and Lowe, T. (Eds.) *Kittens Are Evil: Little Heresies in Public Policy*, Axminster: Triarchy Press, 11–17.

118. Bushe, G. (2017) *Whither Organisation Development? Three Short Articles on the Past and Future of OD*, Available at https://www.roffeypark.com/wp-content/uploads2/Whither-OD-Trilogy.pdf.

119. Scottish Government (2019) *The Scottish Approach to Service Design: How to Design Services for and with Users*, Edinburgh: Scottish Government.

120. Costello, A. (2018) *The Social Edge: The Power of Sympathy Groups for our Health, Wealth and Sustainable Future*, London: Thornwick.

121. Pritchard, S. (2010) Why Do Change Projects Fail? *Strategic HR Review*, 9 (2): 40–42.

122. Edmonstone, J. (2010) A New Approach to Project Managing Change, *British Journal of Healthcare Management*, 16 (5): 114–119.

123. von Bertalanffy, L. (1968) *General Systems Theory: Foundations, Development, Applications*, New York: Braziller.

124. Meadows, D. (2008) *Thinking in Systems: A Primer*, White River Junction, VA: Chelsea Green Publishing.

125. Huxham, C. and Vangen, S. (2005) *Managing to Collaborate: The Theory and Practice of Collaborative Advantage*, Abingdon: Routledge.

126. Pascale, R., Sternin, J. and Sternin, M. (2010) *The Power of Positive Deviance: How Unlikely Innovators Solve the World's Toughest Problems*, Boston, MA: Harvard Business School Publishing.

127. Bushe, G. (2013) Dialogic OD: A Theory of Practice, *OD Practitioner*, 45 (1): 11–17.

128. Guest, D. and King, Z. (2004) Power, Innovation and Problem-Solving: The Personnel Managers' Three Steps to Heaven? *Journal of Management Studies*, 41 (3): 401–423.

129. Minahan, M. (2016) OD: Sixty Years Down, and the Future to Go, *OD Practitioner*, 48 (1): 5–10.

130. Burrell, G. and Morgan, G. (1979) *Sociological Paradigms and Organisational Analysis*, London: Heinemann.

131. Dovey, K. and Rembach, M. (2015) Invisible Practices: Innovative Outcomes: Intrapreneurship Within the Academy, *Action Learning: Research and Practice*, 12 (3): 276–292.

132. Jackson, B. and Parry, K. (2008) *A Very Short, Fairly Interesting and Reasonably Cheap Book About Studying Leadership*, London: Sage Publications.

133. Vince, R. (2008) Learning-In-Action and Learning Inaction: Advancing the Theory and Practice of Critical Action Learning, *Action Learning: Research and Practice*, 5 (2): 93–104.

134. Vince, R. (2011) Learning in Action or Learning Inaction? Emotion and Politics in Action Learning, in Pedler, M. (Ed.) *Action Learning in Practice*, 4th edition, Farnham: Gower.

135. Gramsci, A., Hoare, Q. and Nowell-Smith, G. (2005) *Selections from the Prison Notebooks of Antonio Gramsci*, London: Lawrence and Wishart.

136. Edmonstone, J. (2011) Action Learning and Organisation Development: Overlapping Fields of Practice, *Action Learning: Research and Practice*, 8 (2): 93–102.

137. Wieland, G. and Leigh, H. (Ed.) (1971) *Changing Hospitals: A Report on the Hospital Internal Communications Project*, London: Tavistock Publications.

138. Weiland, G. (1981) *Improving Health Care Management: Organisation Development and Organisation Change*, Ann Arbor, MI, Health Administration Press.

139. Revans, R. (Ed.) (1972) *Hospitals: Communication, Choice and Change: The Hospital Internal Communications Project Seen From Within*, London, Tavistock Publications.

140. Kahnweiler, W. (2010) Organisation Development Success and Failure: A Case Analysis, *Organisation Development Journal*, 28 (2): 19.

141. Edmonstone, J., Lawless, A. and Pedler, M. (2019) Leadership Development, Wicked Problems and Action Learning: Provocations To A Debate, *Action Learning: Research and Practice*, 16 (1): 37–51.

142. Larsen, L., Cummins, J., Brown, H., Ajmal, T., Beers, H. and Lee, J. (2005) *Learning from Evaluation: Summary of Reports of Evaluations of Leadership Initiatives*, London: Office for Public Management/NHS Leadership Centre.

143. Kirkpatrick, D. and Kirkpatrick, J. (1998) *Evaluating Training Programs: The Four Levels*, 4th edition, San Francisco, CA: Berrett-Koehler.

144. Verhaeghe, P. (2014) *What About Me? The Struggle for Identity in a Market-Based Society*, London: Scribe Publications.

145. Easterby-Smith, M. (1994) *Evaluating Management Development, Training and Education*, Aldershot: Gower.

146. Pawson, R. and Tilley, N. (1997) *Realistic Evaluation*, London: Sage.

147. Thorpe, R., Gold, J., Anderson, L., Burgoyne, J., Wilkinson, D. and Malby, B. (Eds.) (2008) Collecting the Evidence Through Evaluation, in *Towards "Leaderful" Communities in the North of England*, 2nd edition, Cork: Oak Tree Press.

148. Burnes, B. and Cooke, B. (2012) The Past, Present and Future of Organisation Development: Taking the Long View, *Human Relations*, 65 (11): 1395–1429.

149. French, W. and Bell, C. (1973) *Organisation Development*, Englewood Cliffs, NJ: Prentice-Hall.

150. Cummings, T. (2005) Organisation Development and Change: Foundations and Applications, in Boonstra, J. (Ed.) *Dynamics of Organisational Change and Learning*, New York: John Wiley.

151. Cooke, B. (2007) The Kurt Lewin/Goodwin Watson FBI Files: A 60th Anniversary "There and Then" of the "Here and Now", *Human Relations*, 60 (3): 435–462.

152. Bridges, W. (1980) *Transitions: Making Sense of Life's Changes*, Boston, MA: Da Capo Lifelong Books.

153. Thompson, E. (1993) *Witness Against the Beast: William Blake and the Moral Law*, Cambridge: Cambridge University Press.

154. Browne, P., Cotton, C. and Golembiewski, R. (1977) Marginality and the OD Practitioner, *Journal of Applied Behavioural Science*, 13 (4): 493–506.

155. Dawkin, R. (1986) *The Blind Watchmaker: Why the Evidence of Evolution Reveals a Universe Without Design*, New York: Norton & Co.

156. Graeber, D. (2015) *The Utopia of Rules: On Technology, Stupidity and the Secret Joys of Bureaucracy*, New York: Melville House.

157. Ruskin, J. (2017) *The Ethics of the Dust*, Newton Stewart: Anodos Books.

158. Machado, A. (2007) *Fields of Castile*, Translated by S. Appelbaum, Chatham: Dover Publications.

An OD Practitioner Code of Practice

If the original humanistic and democratic values of Organisation Development (OD) remain as the desirable end state to be pursued, then the other ethical issue relates to the mode of conduct of OD practitioners themselves. These are likely to address such matters as confidentiality, the avoidance of client dependency and the need for the OD practitioner to be self-reflexive – continually reviewing their practice, often in collaboration with others. An example of such a "code of practice" for an external OD practitioner consultancy is offered here. Internal practitioners might well craft an equivalent version.

Description: XXX is an OD consultancy working in the public sector in all parts of the UK and internationally. It is dedicated to developing the capacity and capability of individuals and organisations to manage change successfully.

Approach: XXX emphasises:

- A client-friendly approach which recognises and respects the client's experience and seeks to add value.
- An eclectic approach, not tied to any single model or technique, and working in both facilitative and expert modes, as appropriate.
- Working alongside internal organisational resources, where that is applicable, in order to enhance their expertise by skill and knowledge transfer.
- Lessening of dependency on external help by equipping the client with the expertise and confidence to move on.

XXX believes that this guarantees a healthy working relationship and the best results for clients.

General: XXX will:

- Do its best to prioritise client needs and to deliver appropriate, efficacious and timely services.
- Work within, and comply with, all relevant law.
- Undertake diligently, impartially and honestly the work of any assignment and maintain at all times high professional standards and personal integrity in all work undertaken.
- Only accept those assignments which it believes it is qualified and able to carry out and will thus recognise the need to work from a base of relevant competence and experience. Should others be engaged by **XXX** to assist with the assignment, every endeavour will be made to ensure that their competence and experience are appropriate to undertake the work in question.
- Represent the competence and experience of **XXX** staff and associates objectively and avoid the use of inaccurate or deceptive language in describing persons or services.
- Give the continuing professional development of **XXX** staff and associates a high priority.
- Not practice any consultancy work during a period when the consultant's judgement is, or might be, impaired through any cause.
- Disclose to clients any personal or financial interest or other significant circumstances which might influence the work for that client in any way not stated in any proposal or initial agreement.
- Refrain from directly inviting any employee of a client to consider alternative employment.
- Strive, in those circumstances where an assignment involves collaborative working with other consultants, to develop a way of working which is sensitive to client need.

Work Processes: XXX will:

- Ensure that clients and all those participating in a work assignment know what will be involved and have their informed consent before the process commences.
- Take account of the rights, needs, pressures and problems of others and seek to avoid asking others to do things which offend their conscience.
- Ensure that it is clear to all **XXX** staff who are involved in an assignment:-

Who the **XXX** client is.

What the processes to be followed involve and what their implications are.
How the process will be delivered and by whom.
Where the review and potential exit points are.

Confidentiality: XXX will:

- Generally, maintain confidentiality and not abuse any position of power in which it may find itself.
- Consistently seek to work in an open manner, so that in any situation where a conflict of interest between an individual and their employing organisation may arise, the nature and direction of **XXX** loyalties have been explained to all parties.
- Keep confidential all information passed to it by the client (unless such information is already in the public domain).
- Respect confidential information concerning a client's business and not disclose, or permit the disclosure of, or use to the consultancy or the consultant's own advantage, any such information without the client's prior permission.
- Unless the client requests otherwise, **XXX** may mention to other potential clients the client's name and type of assignment carried out but without disclosing any confidential details.
- Description of the assignment in any publication will be by mutual agreement between **XXX** and the client.

Proposal: All work will be in accordance with initial agreements based upon a written proposal, as modified by any subsequent agreed variations, also in writing. All proposals are normally valid for thirty days from the date of issue, unless otherwise indicated.

Reports, Papers, etc:

- **XXX** accepts full responsibility to maintain effective communication with the client and to supply written reports and documentation when agreed.
- Production of a report or paper normally implies production of an "original". Production of further copies is then the responsibility of the client.
- All suggestion, recommendations and proposals are made in good faith and on the basis of the information which is available at the time. Their achievement will depend, among other things, on the effective cooperation of the client's staff.

Fees: Fees are charged for all time spent on client affairs, whether on the client premises or not. Fee structure is reviewed annually.

Expenses:

- Travelling, subsistence and other expenses necessarily incurred while engaged on client business, whether on client premises or elsewhere, will be charged at cost.
- Expenses will include car mileage at () per mile, second class rail travel and economy class air travel within the UK.
- Actual miles travelled will be calculated and charged, rather than any initial estimates contained in a proposal.
- If, during the course of an assignment, a need for any ancillary services not specified in the original proposal is identified, agreement to their use will be obtained before any expenditure is incurred.
- In such circumstances where a number of copies of a report or paper are produced, production costs of such material prepared for the client will be charged as an expense.
- Where a course, workshop, seminar, conference or other training event is involved, all administration, venue, residential and catering arrangements will normally be undertaken by the client, as will production of any audio-visual material, by agreement.

Invoicing:

- Fees and expenses will be invoiced at stages throughout the assignment on the basis of agreement between the client and **XXX**.
- Invoices are payable within thirty days of the invoice date.

Further Reading

Attwood, M., Pedler, M., Pritchard, S. and Wilkinson, D. (2003) *Leading Change: A Guide to Whole Systems Working,* Bristol: The Policy Press Covering public services, the book argues that whole systems approaches are required in order to lead towards new ways of working and also offers good practice guidance.

Ballatt, J. and Campling, P. (2012) *Intelligent Kindness: Reforming the Culture of Healthcare,* London: RCPsych Publications Taking a systems view of healthcare, this book reviews the NHS from a variety of perspectives – social psychology, ethology, group relations and psychoanalytic thinking. It develops the notion of "intelligent kindness" as an approach for policy-makers, managers, educators and clinical staff.

Buchanan, D., Fitzgerald, L. and Ketley, D. (Eds.) (2007) *The Sustainability and Spread of Organisational Change,* Abingdon: Routledge Based on material derived from the work of the then NHS Modernisation Agency, the book considers the context and experience of organisational change with special attention devoted to questions of sustainability and spread.

Bunting, M. (2020) *Labour of Love: The Crisis of Care,* London: Granta Books The centrality of caring within health and social care systems is the topic of this book, which examines how a range of factors have eroded the ability of employees to conduct compassionate relationships with patients/service users.

Burnes, B. and Cooke, B. (2012) The Past, Present and Future of Organisation Development: Taking the Long View, *Human Relations,* 65 (11): 1395–1429 The article reviews the long history of OD, chronicles and analyses major stages, disjunctures and controversies in a wider context. Arguing that OD remains the dominant approach to organisational change, it addresses a series of issues which need to be tackled.

Burrell, G. and Morgan, G. (1979) *Sociological Paradigms and Organisational Analysis,* London: Heinemann The book provides a "map" for social or behavioural science and the nature of society, based on four broad paradigms, enabling consideration of where OD might be positioned within that context.

Chokr, N. (2009) *Unlearning, or How Not To Be Governed?* Exeter: Societas Imprint Academic The author does not see education as about learning a trade or profession, but as a dynamic living thing in which the ability to unlearn is essential for developing a capable citizen, capable of freedom, autonomy and virtue.

Cole, M. (2020) *Radical Organisation Development,* **Abingdon: Routledge** The book highlights the gaping hole in OD practice – the role of power in the workplace. Drawing insights from critical theory, the limitations and negative impacts of OD practice are addressed, as is an alternative grassroots- based approach.

Cottam, H. (2018) *Radical Help: How We Can Remake the Relationships Between Us and Revolutionise the Welfare State,* **London: Virago** This book is concerned with social innovation and with remaking features of the welfare state. Based on a series of practical case studies, principles of "social design" for common good are elicited.

Dawson, P. and Andriopoulos, C. (2017) *Managing Change, Creativity and Innovation,* 3rd **edition, London: Sage** Intended as a core text for academic modules in organisational change, the book is a rich source of material on OD, learning, innovation and creativity.

Day, A. (2020) *Disruption, Change and Transformation in Organisations: A Human Relations Perspective,* **Abingdon: Routledge** The book explores the psychological and social dynamics of continuous, disruptive and discontinuous change, especially examining emotional strain. It contrasts the need for organisational adaptive capacity with the disorienting and unsettling nature of personal change.

Edmonstone, J. (2019) *Systems Leadership in Health and Social Care,* **Abingdon: Routledge** The book offers an alternative to a focus on leadership in healthcare alone and makes the case for systems leadership across local health and social care systems, including the means by which systems leaders may be developed.

Huxham, C. and Vangen, S. (2005) *Managing to Collaborate: The Theory and Practice of Collaborative Advantage,* **Abingdon: Routledge** While the notion of competitive advantage is a familiar one, this book offers the prospect of collaborative advantage through inter-organisational working in health and social care, drawing on practical examples and emerging theory.

Kernick, D. (Ed.) (2004) *Complexity and Healthcare Organisation: A View from the Street,* **Abingdon: Radcliffe Medical Press** This book describes the application of the complexity theory perspective in healthcare organisations in the UK.

Kuhl, S. (2019) *The Rainmaker Effect: Contradictions of the Learning Organisation,* **Hamburg: Organisational Dialogue Press** The learning organisation is a concept which many OD practitioners subscribe to, but this book suggests that those principles perceived as recipes for success fail to deliver on their promises, but do have other beneficial effects.

McMillan, E. (2008) *Complexity, Management and the Dynamics of Change,* **Abingdon: Routledge** Drawing from experience through the UK's Open University, the insights of complexity science and complex adaptive systems are embraced to deal with the challenges and uncertainties of organisational change.

Meadows, D. (2008) *Thinking in Systems: A Primer,* **White River Junction, VT: Chelsea Green Publishing** A classic exposition of systems thinking skills to a range of issues, from the personal to the global, offering a lexicon for use in and across organisations.

Peck, E. (Ed.) (2005) *Organisational Development in Healthcare: Approaches, Innovations, Achievements,* **Abingdon: Radcliffe Publishing** A comprehensive overview of healthcare OD theory and practice written by academics, managers, consultant and clinicians, most of which remains pertinent despite the passage of time.

Rigg, C. and Richards, S. (Eds.) 2006) *Action Learning, Leadership and Organisational Development in Public Services,* **Abingdon: Routledge** Covering a range of public service functions (healthcare, local government, police and probation services), the book focuses on developing organisational capacity in intra- and inter-organisational contexts.

Schon, D. (1973) *Beyond the Stable State: Public and Private Learning in a Changing Society,* **London: Pelican** A classic of its' kind, the book makes the original case for social systems (government, administration and business management) that can learn and adapt.

Seddon, J. (2019) *Beyond Command and Control,* **Oxford: Mayfield Press** The fallacies of command-and-control approaches to management are the subject of this book, which offers an alternative approach to the design of services and the reduction of costs.

Zuboff, S. (2019) *The Age of Surveillance Capitalism: The Fight for a Human Future at the Frontier of Power,* **London: Profile Books** The use of personal data by global knowledge-based technology giant organisations and the long-term implications for democracy and personal freedom – and hence for OD, are the subject of this book.

Index

Printed in the United States
by Baker & Taylor Publisher Services